Prolog + +

The Power of Object-Oriented and Logic Programming

CHRIS MOSS

Imperial College of Science, Technology and Medicine

ADDISON-WESLEY PUBLISHING COMPANY

Wokingham, England · Reading, Massachusetts · Menlo Park, California · New York
Don Mills, Ontario · Amsterdam · Bonn · Sydney · Singapore
Tokyo · Madrid · San Juan · Milan · Paris · Mexico City · Seoul · Taipei

© 1994 Addison-Wesley Publishers Ltd.
© 1994 Addison-Wesley Publishing Company Inc.

The programs in this book have been included for their instructional value.
They have been tested with care but are not guaranteed for any particular
purpose. The publisher does not offer any warranties or representations, nor
does it accept any liabilities with respect to the programs.

Many of the designations used by manufacturers and sellers to distinguish
their products are claimed as trademarks. Addison-Wesley has made every
attempt to supply trademark information about manufacturers and their products
mentioned in this book. A list of the trademark designations and their owners
appears on p. vi.

Cover designed by Hybert Design & Type, Maidenhead
and printed by The Riverside Printing Co. (Reading) Ltd.
Typeset by P & R Typesetters Ltd, Salisbury, Wilts, UK.
Printed in Great Britain at the University Press, Cambridge.

First printed 1994.

ISBN 0-201-56507-2

British Library Cataloguing in Publication Data
A catalogue record for this book is available from the British Library.

Library of Congress Cataloging in Publication Data applied for.

EAST GRID STAMP							
BB		SS		MM	2/95		
BA		SB		MW			
BT		SC		MC			
BR		SD		MD			
BY		SE		MO			
BC		SW		MY			
BG		SL					
BH		SV					
BS							
BN							

To Jane, who succeeded where I failed

Preface

Object-oriented programming and logic programming are two movements that have become very popular in computing in the last ten years. Object-oriented programming is usually associated with interactive graphics, reusable software and the programming languages Smalltalk and C++. Logic programming is seen as an outcome of Artificial Intelligence research for use in expert systems, appealing also to theoreticians and exemplified by the Prolog language.

Their roots go further back – to 1967, the publication of the Simula language, and 1973, the first implementation of Prolog. But the reasons for which these languages are valued today differ considerably from the expectations they aroused initially.

Simula introduced the notion of an object as an aid to performing simulations (from where the name came). When it was picked up by Alan Kay at Xerox Parc, and made the underpinning for the Smalltalk graphic environment, it became a means of describing the changing objects within a computer system. Since graphical objects have much similar behaviour, the use of inheritance quickly proved itself: it was easier to pick up an object which almost fitted the bill and modify it than to start again from scratch. This philosophy pervaded other areas and was taken up by increasing numbers of programmers and system designers.

Prolog has become the most widely used of the 'declarative' languages – languages which are not based on commands but on more neutral (declarative) statements from which many desired behaviours can be obtained. When it was originally conceived, the notion of symbolic 'search' as the basic paradigm in Artificial Intelligence was at its peak, and the concept of logic programming fitted naturally into this. But from the beginning it became a powerful tool for stating knowledge about the real world and it has developed into a powerful notation for encoding end-user applications.

Since the strengths of these two paradigms are so different – it is little easier to code a new application in C++ than in any other language, while the problems of reusability recur in Prolog – there is a great motivation for combining them within a single system. A great deal of effort has therefore been expended in the last ten years to see how they can fit together. The Prolog++ language from LPA is the most practical outcome of this work that is usable on present-day computers.

Prolog++ follows a pattern pioneered by languages such as Objective-C, and more recently Eiffel, in making objects an extra layer on top of the basic language. Prolog++ compiles into standard Prolog and therefore has the advantage of portability across compilers and of not disturbing the considerable expertise in the efficient compilation of Prolog. As a computer language, Prolog is unusual: it has a versatile unification process which subsumes other parameter passing mechanisms; it allows multiple solutions to any procedure – making code more versatile, helping especially when prototyping code; and it takes over entirely the space management of complex data structures – not only collecting garbage but deciding when it is necessary to allocate it too. Compilation techniques remove much of the potential inefficiencies of this process and make it comparable in efficiency to lower-level languages in the domains in which it excels.

The approach used to model changing objects in Prolog++ is conventional and it is one of the chief aims of this book to show what the assignment statement should be used for in a logic programming language, and where it is inappropriate. It is impossible, for example, to write a windowing system in a conventional sequential language without storing the intermediate state information about the window using something very like a conventional assignment statement. Despite a lot of research in the logic programming community on concurrent languages, none of these systems are yet competitive on conventional hardware such as a personal computer. Though we look at some of this work in the last chapter of the book, the use of Prolog++ does not depend on advanced hardware or system organization. Indeed, most of the examples in the book were tested on a Macintosh computer, using the excellent programming environment provided by LPA.

Audience

The book is aimed at several audiences: it can be used by practical programmers who have a background in object-oriented techniques, or in logic programming, or by those for whom both of these concepts are a mystery. No prior knowledge of either is assumed. It could also be used as a second- or third-year undergraduate or a graduate textbook. For this reason exercises are provided in the core chapters.

Outline of the book

The way in which the term 'object-oriented programming' is used varies considerably among different authors though it is possible to see a growing consensus on the main issues. The first chapter of the book looks at the background, development and basic principles of object-oriented programming. It also examines the rise of logic programming and what is behind the move to a declarative approach and tries to show how these two paradigms can be used together. Objects are seen as a way of organizing the programming process on the large scale, whereas logic provides a much clearer picture of the microstructure of the computation giving significant increases in programmer productivity.

Although Prolog++ is a language in its own right, many of the programming techniques used are those of Prolog, the language on which it is based, and many Prolog programs can be incorporated into a Prolog++ program without change. Chapter 2 provides a self-contained and relatively complete introduction to Prolog for readers who have little or no experience of it. These techniques are not included in the section on Prolog++ as they will be of little interest to those already well versed in Prolog. The language is introduced as a series of layers, each more powerful than the previous one: starting with the propositional calculus, it introduces predicates, compound terms and recursion, thus forming a complete picture of 'pure' Prolog. It then introduces negation and the cut, the use of metaprogramming techniques and finally the 'built-in' components of standard Prolog systems which have side-effects.

Chapters 3 and 4 introduce the basic elements of Prolog++, first as a purely declarative system and then addressing the dynamic aspects. Chapter 3 describes objects and attributes, the use of inheritance, including multiple, overriding and inclusive inheritance, the functional notation included in Prolog++ and the parts hierarchy for building more complex objects. The basic compilation techniques are described, showing how dynamic binding is implemented. Chapter 4 describes the use of mutable attributes, including default values, initialization and multivalued attributes. It shows how objects can help in error handling and the built-in features of Prolog++ for this purpose. The management of objects – creation, deletion and preservation over program invocation – is described, then the powerful mechanisms in Prolog++ for message broadcasting and the control structures available in Prolog++.

These chapters include a number of small examples, but to bring out the advantages of combining the object-oriented and logic programming paradigms it is necessary to look at some longer examples. This is done in Chapters 5 and 6. Chapter 5 applies the methods of object-oriented programming to graphical user interfaces and shows how it is possible to construct a hierarchy of objects which make it easy for the user to construct a practical interface including windows, dialogues and menus. Several tools to automate the process are described. Chapter 6 looks in more detail at the process of object-oriented design, using the approach known as the Object Modelling Technique. This is demonstrated by taking as an example the development of a library system including loans and bibliographic search.

Any description of object-oriented logic programming would be incomplete without some account of the other way of dealing with change in object-oriented programming that we have identified: concurrency. It is important both for theoretical reasons and because it will undoubtedly have much more prominence in the future. The final chapter contains a brief look at the new world of concurrent objects using the Step language, which is a layer on top of Strand-88. Another closely related area which is receiving a lot of attention is that of object-oriented databases. The chapter looks at the notion of persistence and how the two levels of representation in Prolog++ – term and variable level – provide a suitable engineering compromise for implementing persistent systems. The chapter surveys some of the other attempts at bringing together the two worlds of objects and logic, including languages such as ESP and LIFE.

Appendix A at the end of the book presents Prolog++ syntax and methods; Appendix B provides a German verb example; and Appendix C provides supplementary information on an example from an earlier chapter in the book.

A special offer

To help in appreciating Prolog++ there is a special offer available to purchasers of this book. A disk containing a complete copy of the Prolog++ system and the source code of all the examples in the book is available from Logic Programming Associates. This is available in two forms, for the IBM PC under Windows, and the Macintosh. Details are on a tearout reply card included in the book.

Acknowledgements

I would like to record my acknowledgement to colleagues and friends for considerable help without which I would never have finished this book. Firstly to Phil Vasey, the author of the Prolog++ language, who has been unfailingly patient in responding to my questions, comments, criticisms and suggestions. To colleagues at Imperial College, past and present, who have read and commented on various chapters, including Keith Clark, Andrew Davison, Ian Foster, Nihan Kesim, Frank McCabe. To Clive Spenser at LPA and Christian Schulte at DFKI. To Karen, who had to bear the brunt of my frustrations in a too-long gestation of the book and corrected numerous drafts, and Elizabeth and Barbara who kept me going at the later stages. Finally, to Addison-Wesley's editor Simon Plumtree who never ran out of patience.

· *Chris Moss,* April 1994

Contents

1

Object-oriented programming

1.1 Introduction

One of the success stories of computing in the 1980s was the emergence of the Macintosh computer with its windows, mouse and elegant styling. Its advent marked a radical change of emphasis in the user interface of computers, away from an almost exclusively verbal activity into a world of pictures and sounds. Instead of giving instructions to a computer by remembering names, as one does in a conventional system, for example

```
emacs myproject.c
```

one is confronted by a picture of a desktop from which one 'picks up' one's work, by pointing at it and opening it (Figure 1.1).

Underlying the Macintosh interface was a revolution in programming terms that was apparent only to a small circle of programmers. The programming system used to develop it was object-oriented. The Macintosh environment provided a springboard for developing applications which included a large repertoire of graphics routines built-in and a consistent user interface 'feel' that was only available to those who adjusted their programming style to this new orientation. Those who persisted with traditional programming techniques found the Macintosh a very difficult machine to come to terms with.

A simple but striking example of the effectiveness of the Macintosh environment is what happens when one chooses the 'Shut Down' command in the Macintosh's 'Finder' – its basic control program – to finish the day's work. One may have several programs operational at the time – say a word processor with an unsaved document, a spreadsheet in which you've made some changes and Hypercard, the Macintosh multimedia system which also

1

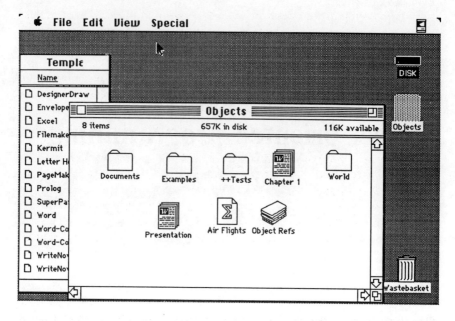

Figure 1.1   The Macintosh interface.

functions as a database. With most computers this is a recipe for disaster. One's day's work would be lost. The Macintosh system, however, takes it in its stride. Each program is given its regular message to 'quit' and the word processor, for example, will then politely ask you if you want to save the unsaved document. Hypercard will save any changes automatically and then quit. When all the housekeeping is done, the machine is turned off. Simple, but beyond the capabilities of many systems.

Many of the ideas expressed in what is now called the graphical user interface started in the early 1970s with the work of Alan Kay and his group at Xerox who developed the notion of the computer notebook, with windows and pointing devices. Their notebook used a language called Smalltalk, which gained many of its central ideas from a language called Simula developed in the 1960s in Norway by Ole-Johan Dahl and Kristen Nygaard. Kay spent some of his time exploring how children could use computers effectively and this was a formative influence in his approach:

'Children who have not yet lost much of their sense of wonder and fun have helped us to find an ethic about computing: Do not automate the work you are engaged in, only the materials. If you like to draw, do not automate drawing; rather, program your personal computer to give you a new set of paints. If you like to play music, do not build a "player piano"; instead program yourself a new kind of instrument.' (Kay, 1977)

The notion of a computer system as a tool that allows one to express new ideas easily is a central idea in object-oriented programming and contrasts strongly with some people's approach to Artificial Intelligence whereby it attempts to replace human creativity. The techniques that encourage the ideas of object-oriented programming have taken a long time to percolate and are far from complete even today. However, there is a growing recognition that large computer systems need to be structured in this way if they are going to meet the needs for which they are designed.

Progress in developing software has not matched the outstanding developments in computer hardware over the last two decades. The statistics are well known. The average speed of computer systems has doubled every five years. The amount of storage that can be accommodated on a chip has doubled every three years. The cost per bit has halved every two years. When Kay's *Scientific American* article was written in 1977, they had to use the massive resources of the Evans and Sutherland Corporation's graphics computers to produce the simulation. Now the same results are achieved on a computer that can be obtained for less than $1000.

Since software productivity has not grown at the same rate, the proportion of total cost spent on software has risen inexorably. Reliable statistics are harder to come by in this area but most people admit that much more money is spent on the software than the hardware. The worst offenders are clearly corporate computer users who will not tolerate off-the-shelf software for the simple reason their needs usually *are* different. Stories of badly conceived and over-ambitious projects which have led companies to bankruptcy are becoming more common.

The growth of a consumer market for software at the personal computer end means that the standard products – word processors, databases, spreadsheets – are more effectively used than ever before, and the quality is correspondingly higher. The need for mass production and distribution of software is obvious. Development and maintenance take up almost all the cost of software production and the larger the user base the better will the product be – the competitive market takes care of quality control. Buyers who complain about bugs in software don't know what the professionals had to put up with before!

It is interesting to note that all three of these standard product lines deal with essentially static products. Word processors are simply used to create and print a document, which is then filed or thrown away. Databases keep data over a longer period of time, but the changes made to the data are slower than they are in an algorithmic computer program. The spreadsheet presents a overall view of a set of (numerical) calculations. A calculation is normally considered in computing terms as a sequential process, but the spreadsheet makes it into a single internally consistent object.

Let's take a spreadsheet showing a simple invoice (Figure 1.2). Looking at the picture it is obvious that this mimics a familiar form which behaves as we would expect. Underneath each of the numbers are sets of formulae

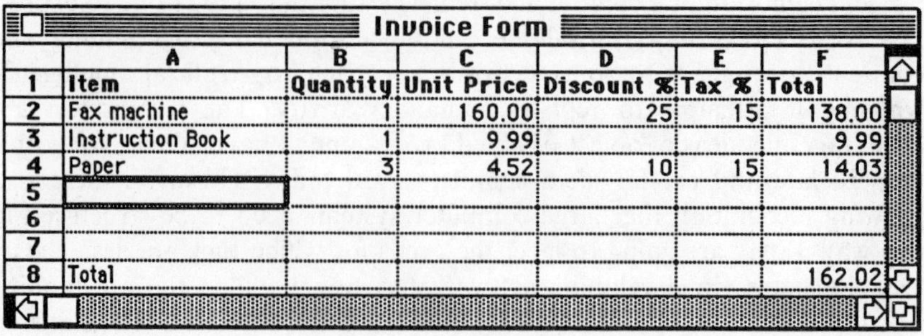

	A	B	C	D	E	F
1	Item	Quantity	Unit Price	Discount %	Tax %	Total
2	Fax machine	1	160.00	25	15	138.00
3	Instruction Book	1	9.99			9.99
4	Paper	3	4.52	10	15	14.03
5						
6						
7						
8	Total					162.02

Invoice Form

Figure 1.2   A simple spreadsheet.

which can be inspected if necessary and the whole is interlinked. If we make a change to any of the columns there will be a ripple of changes correcting the values using the underlying formulae. In its stable state, the spreadsheet is consistent. In computer terminology it is 'declarative'.

Yet spreadsheets did not originate from software engineering. They came from 'nowhere' – started by a product called VisiCalc from a small company named Software Arts (which incidentally is credited with saving the first computer line from Apple, the Apple II, much as it can be argued that the laser printer later saved the Macintosh). Spreadsheets succeeded because they combined the need for consistency with an almost infinite flexibility. They are indeed 'tools' which can used in a huge variety of circumstances, as Dan Bricklin, one of the authors, recalls:

'In those days, if you showed it to a programmer, he'd say, "Well, that's neat. Of course computers can do that – so what?" But if you showed it to a person who had to do financial work with real spreadsheets, he'd start shaking and say, "I spent all week doing that." Then he'd shove his charge cards in your face.' (Licklider, 1989)

The spreadsheet illustrates a general principle: in order to cope with complexity we have a need for consistency and comprehensibility in the components with which we draw the picture. Traditional programming languages prescribe a series of steps or 'operations' which must be composed together to give an overall picture. The functions of a spreadsheet (such as Sum or Average) correspond more with the way we think than these small steps and the consistency of the whole picture allows us to place each of the individual elements. The spreadsheet forms a single consistent relation. In programming terms this has been expressed by the growth of logic programming which is now emerging as a serious competitor for traditional languages in supplying 'application' computing.

But the main attraction of a spreadsheet compared with its paper equivalent is the ease with which we can change the contents and adapt them to new needs. For this purpose the spreadsheet is a straightforward tool which does not dictate the way in which we use it. We can change the cells in whatever order is convenient and use the power of the computer to restore the consistency of the result. In particular, we can reuse old spreadsheets for new purposes as they come along.

The problem of reuse is endemic in programming. Every programmer spends much of his or her time 'reinventing the wheel' because today's problem is never exactly the same as yesterday's. Despite the success of subroutine libraries in specialized areas such as numerical algorithms, approaches such as modular programming have failed to resolve the software crisis. Programming is essentially a *process*, starting with an idea and its realization, continuing through testing and refinement and, if the program is successful, to maintenance, development and interaction with changes in the outside world.

So although consistency is an important principle, we also need other principles to guide the construction of software. We need a larger and more flexible framework in which new ideas can benefit from old ideas without being bound by them. Programs evolve and change their function and a rigid understanding of the whole is impossible to maintain. There has to be as much delegation and shared responsibility in a program as there is in any successful organization.

These notions derive as much from the *organization* of the programming process as from the expressiveness of the *language* in which they are expressed. It is these that have gradually evolved into a set of principles known as 'object-oriented'. Although there is no universally accepted definition of this term, the broad outlines are becoming widely recognized and can form a basis for considering Object-Oriented Logic Programming (OOLP).

1.2 The evolution of object-oriented programming

Object-oriented programming started with the idea of the **class** definition of Simula which was developed in 1967. For over ten years there was no real development of this idea. The idea of a class is a conglomerate notion. At its simplest a class is a record definition, defining named components that can be referenced in a similar way to the record in Pascal or the struct in C, but a class can also include procedures in its definition, unlike records in more traditional languages.

The class in Simula was actually built on the foundation of the block in ALGOL-60, which defines the scope of identifiers in a program. But it managed to break out of the nesting constraints that this imposed in an ingenious way. Class definitions can be added to each other in Simula using the concept of 'prefix class'. This enables the programmer to build up definitions in a piecemeal fashion.

At its simplest, a prefix class provides a form of modularization. In Simula a typical class definition and use looks something like this:

```
class x;
    begin
... declarations for x
    end;
... anything else

x class y;
    begin
... all the declarations of x are available here
    end;
```

By putting the name of a class immediately before the begin one gains access to the declarations made in that class and the augmented class (y) can then be inherited in turn by other classes.

If the block x only contains procedures then it has the same effect as importing a module, but if it contains variable declarations then these also form part of the object. This enables us to abstract the declarations and procedures associated with a datatype and add them to any other definition.

For example, if we take the idea of a list, then operations such as insertion do not depend on the composition of the elements of the list. Yet the traditional means of building data structures by composition forces us to name the list components.

Thus a list in Pascal is specified by:

```
type list =
    record      head: Atype;
                next:  ^list;
    end;
```

where we must know in advance what is the type (Atype) of the element head. The striking thing in Simula is that a list can be specified without the contents! It *only* has a pointer to the next element (see Program 1.1).

In Program 1.1 a list declaration is shown with a sample function insert. The class intList inherits the properties of a list because the word list appears before class in its declaration. To create a new item and insert it in a list one might write:

```
new intlist(10).insert(I);
```

This example is not Simula style as normally an extra pointer would be used as a list head. This allows a nil list to be represented as an object.

The use of one class in defining another contains the kernel of the notion of *inheritance* of properties, which is one of the key notions of

Program 1.1   The class notation in Simula.

```
class list;
    begin ref(list) next;
        procedure insert(alist);
            ref(list) alist;
            begin
            if alist = / = none then
                next :- alist;
            insert :- this listitem;
            end;
    end;

list class intList(V); integer V;
    begin
        integer val; ...
        val :- V;
    end;
```

---

object-oriented programming. Inheritance allows us to reuse definitions in a number of different ways according to our present need.

A class defines a computational object including all its activity. It is *not* simply a record. In Simula one can define several instances of an object and they can all be computing simultaneously (as far as the computer hardware permits). This is the basis of the simulation components of Simula, and it imposes some execution overhead on Simula programs. No longer is the whole computation organized round a single 'stack' as in Pascal or C. Each process may need to have its own stack. This, and the relative inefficiency imposed by the generality of ALGOL-60 on which Simula was based, meant that Simula never gained as wide usage as the power of its concepts suggested.

Simula did not facilitate the *protection* of an object from outside interference. This aspect was largely pioneered by the developers of Smalltalk in the late 1970s. Here the jargon changes. In Smalltalk one does not 'call a procedure'; one 'sends a message to an object'. But is this just in-talk or is it something really different?

What is different is not necessarily the mechanism but the perspective. Sending a message is much the same as calling a procedure in terms of the subroutine call-and-return mechanism (though identifying which procedure is intended may be different). But an object is opaque. One cannot, as a programmer, examine its internal structure. If an object changes its state then it may respond to a message differently. The caller has to accept that. It is therefore much more like sending a message to another person and expecting a reply than calling a subroutine over which one has total control.

Smalltalk was unique in being constructed around objects from the ground up. Even the simplest number is conceived as an object to which one sends a message. Hence the benefits of the change of perspective are realized even for basic arithmetic. An example of this is with error handling, traditionally one of the bugbears of programming languages. When an error occurs in Smalltalk the response is simply to send an error message back to the object which made the request.

Message passing clearly involves some overhead, in identifying the appropriate objects in the presence of inheritance and bundling up the arguments as parameters: in other words, the full mechanism of procedure invocation and some more. To achieve acceptable performance practical compilers do not invoke this mechanism just to add two small numbers! Some optimization is essential but this can be incorporated without compromising the basic philosophy.

Smalltalk also incorporated a graphics environment with the original graphical user interface ('GUI'), to help achieve Kay's goal of making the computer a tool which is easy to use. This incorporated a visual program editing system that was intimately bound up with the language definition and was the foundation later built on so successfully by the creators of the Macintosh.

The biggest strength of Smalltalk, however, is the set of class definitions which is the backbone of its programming environment. Its object protocol showed how to organize a complex environment which could be extended naturally to suit new needs. It is organized around a strict hierarchy of classes, which are all subclasses of a class called 'object'. The names of some representative sections of this protocol are shown in Figure 1.3. These give a better idea of the language than its somewhat unusual syntax.

The objects in the first column in the figure deal with basic objects that a programming language has to deal with, including numbers, Booleans and the basic components of the graphics system. Collection includes all the different ways of grouping objects together, a much richer set than is available in many languages The third column deals mainly with computational processes, including such composite notions as streams and the basic BitBlt class for manipulating graphics images.

The set of classes is represented as a single tree, reflecting the single, as opposed to multiple, inheritance available in Smalltalk-80. This sometimes leads to some strange groupings (why is ReadWriteStream under WriteStream but not ReadStream, for instance) but on the whole it works rather well. Collections are intrinsically groupings of objects, but there is only duplication where necessary. Thus a string is an ArrayedCollection of Character, and needs its own class because there are some characteristics peculiar to it: the method of comparing two strings, for example.

Smalltalk posed a challenge to the programming language community. Clearly its ideas had to be taken on board, but did this mean throwing away all the existing languages and their compilers? Much has been learned about programming languages in the last 30 years and Smalltalk incorporated some, but not all of what had been learned.

Magnitude	Collection	Link
Character	SequenceableCollection	Process
Date	LinkedList	Stream
Time	Semaphore	PositionableStream
Number	ArrayedCollection	ReadStream
Float	Array	WriteStream
Fraction	Bitmap	ReadWriteStream
Integer	DisplayBitmap	ExternalStream
LargeNegativeInteger	Runarray	FileStream
LargePositiveInteger	String	Random
SmallInteger	Symbol	BitBlt
LookupKey	Text	CharacterScanner
Association	ByteArray	Pen
UndefinedObject	Interval	ProcessorScheduler
Boolean	OrderedCollection	Delay
False	SortedCollection	SharedQueue
True	Bag	Behavior
Point	MappedCollection	ClassDescription
Rectangle	Set	Class
DisplayObject	Dictionary	MetaClass
DisplayMedium	IdentifyDictionary	
Form		
Cursor		
DisplayScreen		
InfiniteForm		
OpaqueForm		
Path		
Arc		
Circle		
Curve		
Line		
LinearFit		
Spline		

Figure 1.3 The subclasses of object in Smalltalk.

Two alternative responses to the challenge of object-oriented programming were not slow in coming. One came from the programming group at Apple Computers who decided to use Pascal as the basis for their Lisa and Macintosh range and hired Niklaus Wirth, the creator of Pascal, to design a new version – Object Pascal. The other came from a company called Productivity Products International, which pioneered a language called Objective-C, which compiled directly into the C language. This has now been incorporated into the NeXt range of computers as its primary programming language.

Finally AT&T came out with a product called C++ which augmented its very successful proprietorship of the C language with an object-oriented version. The primary selling point of C++ is that the speed of programs which are only using the simpler object-oriented features is 100% of that of C. Almost all the added features are resolved at compile-time. It follows Smalltalk less closely in that programs do not need to be organized textually around objects: a class is simply given by a datatype definition and its associated procedures can be defined elsewhere in the program.

Opinions vary as to the relative merits of these three languages, but certainly objects have reached the mainstream of computing. They demonstrate that the main benefit of using objects is as an organizational tool for large and continuing programming projects. It is not so much that the languages are easier to program at the beginning, but that it is easier to manage a complex environment. The set of class definitions in Smalltalk has been modified and extended for different environments. Programming in a graphical or windows environment, which currently takes much of the programming effort for a new application, is much simplified because the default behaviour comes 'for free' without explicit provision in each new application.

One characteristic of many of these newer languages is that existing programs in the base language can be incorporated into a new object-based product. One obviously does not expect the benefits of object-orientedness to apply retroactively to the existing code. But a smooth transitional path is essential for any large organization which wants to preserve its investment. This is not a new phenomenon. Many large companies still need to use program code that was originally written in obsolete programming languages for entirely different machines, even when it is necessary to simulate the old machine on the current hardware. They learned the lesson painfully that investment in a programming language is a long-term commitment and having switched to machine-independent high-level programming languages such as C they don't now want to lose all that investment by starting once again.

Many of the aims of object-oriented programming are also found in Ada, the language designed for embedded military systems. Its modularity and generic functions give some of the advantages of object-oriented systems, but many of the critical ideas of inheritance are absent so that it is common to call it 'object-based' rather than object-oriented (see for example, Wegner, 1987).

One other language is worth mentioning – Eiffel. This language, designed by Bertrand Meyer of Interactive Software Engineering, is the first to apply traditional software engineering principles to object-oriented languages. It allows the incorporation of logical assertions in a Pascal-like object-oriented language which permits many checks to be carried out at the debugging stage and the formal requirements of the modules of a program to be expressed.

Some anecdotal evidence is emerging that the piggyback approach is the most successful approach in practice and it is easy to see why. The basic strata of languages are critical to their reliability and efficiency. The development of a language such as C has taken a long time and a lot of implementation expertise is locked up in its compilers. To invent an entirely new language means re-engineering all of this substratum as well as developing the new object layer and inevitably entails a cost. (This might indeed be seen as part of the object-oriented philosophy!) So the initial

versions of languages such as Smalltalk and Eiffel had disadvantages, m₁
concerned with efficiency and the unexpected interaction of ideas, tha₁
more well-understood languages can avoid.

Other languages such as LISP have long experimented with object
ideas in products such as Loops, Flavors and ObjectLISP. Now the
standardization committee for LISP has adopted an object system for
Common LISP known as CLOS. The style of programming in CLOS is rather
different to most object-oriented languages: it works from the idea of a generic
function. A function such as 'add' might have many different meanings
dependent on the types of its arguments. So there is no single 'object' which
is identifiable from the source text.

Finally in this brief survey of the object-oriented scene, it is important
to mention object-oriented databases (OODB, see Atkinson *et al.*, 1990).
These originally arose from the need to combine databases with higher
performance than was possible with the relational approach in areas such
as computer-aided design and geographical databases. With the emergence
of products such as Gemstone and Orion, the traditional approaches to
databases suddenly found they had strong competition. Currently most
OODB systems are based on the imperative object-oriented languages such
as C++, but, as we shall see, Prolog is rapidly becoming a favoured language
for implementing object-oriented databases as its underlying concepts match
well with a database approach.

1.3   What is object-oriented programming?

Object-oriented programming is not a single idea. Over the years four basic
notions have emerged which are relatively independent of each other, but
that combine to form a unified picture of object-oriented programming. These
notions are generally called **encapsulation, class, inheritance,** and **identity** in
the object-oriented literature. This section will attempt to clarify these notions.

Modularity has always been one of the chief goals of software
engineering. If one can chop up a large project into a set of modules, each
of which is relatively independent of the others, then clearly different
programmers can cooperate more effectively, the correctness of the individual
modules can more easily be checked and hopefully some of the modules can
be reused in other projects.

This dream has always been hard to achieve in practice. It is often
hard to decide how best to subdivide an individual project. Do we simply
try to minimize the communication paths between the modules by putting
bits of code together that communicate with each other? When people tried
to use a 'top-down' functional design methodology the results were often
modules which interacted in many and subtle ways.

Gradually practitioners came to realize that the unifying element in
a module should be the data object, not function. What should go in a
module is all the pieces of code that affect the meaning of that type of data

and are dependent on it. It is then possible to seal it off from the outside world and allow only specified operations on it.

Thus was born the idea of encapsulating what has come to be called an *abstract data type*. The idea of abstraction is similar to encapsulation in that as far as the outside world is concerned only a limited portion of the possible behaviour of an object is visible – other behaviour, which is incidental to the purpose of the module, is hidden from sight.

The emphasis on data rather than procedures is already half way to objects and corresponds to the principles taught by many of the leading exponents of software design methods (Yourdon, Jackson, Orr and so on). It also corresponds to the mathematical notion of a *group*, consisting of a type and the operations that can be performed on it. In the context of object-oriented programming this is one aspect of what has become known as a *class* – a template for creating objects with a built-in description of their behaviour.

The main purpose of encapsulation is to be a tool for organization and comprehension. The idea is not so much to build fire walls around a piece of code, which might serve to protect proprietary interests in the contents, but rather to identify a stable group of ideas which may usefully live together. The aim of *abstraction* is to hide the inessential or implementation details in order to foster a sensible contractual relationship between implementer and user of the datatype. If all the details of an implementation are available, the users may not be able to tell which are incidental and which are essential to the design. They will inevitably tend to use any aspects of the design that are available to them to cope with the problem in hand and this frequently goes beyond what the designer had in mind.

The contribution of Smalltalk to this process has been to encourage a programming style in which changes are localized to the object which owns them. In Smalltalk, an object's local variables, called *instance variables*, are not immediately accessible to change from outside. Even though the object might provide methods which make them available for reading or writing, there is a shift in emphasis from Simula, where objects were basically records which could be changed in the normal way through pointers by any code which had access to the object.

By itself, encapsulation is not enough. The reason is that in the real world one rarely uses *exactly* the same set of ideas again. There are always exceptions, or augmentations that are necessary, and the basic idea of encapsulation does not allow for this.

Language has a standard way of coping with this situation. The oldest method of defining words, propounded by Aristotle, was the method of genera and differentiae. In other words one says what an object is like and how it differs from similar objects. A zebra is horse with stripes. A tiger is a big, fierce, striped cat. Even when new words are not used, old words can acquire extra metaphorical meanings to apply to new situations.

It has taken a long time for this insight to develop in programming. The original notion of inheritance in Simula introduced the idea of a class.

This had two distinct aspects. The first extends the idea of building an object as a data structure by allowing one to add more components to an existing object. Thus a bird shares many of the common characteristics of vertebrates, such as a backbone and central brain, but also has wings and feathers. In this way features common to related classes of objects could be described once only rather than many times.

The second notion in a class is that a local implementation of a routine could override a more global one. This actually arose from the block structure of Algol and although this aspect of block structure has been rejected in later languages, such as C, because of the inefficiencies it introduces, the use of this notion in inheritance is one of its few indispensable applications. Alternative implementation mechanisms have now been developed which in many cases do not cause run-time penalties.

Unlike a traditional programming language where the name of a procedure uniquely identifies one piece of code, a procedure implemented within a subclass might be defined in several possible locations, so that the choice is only made at run-time. So a different terminology has arisen. Instead of calling a procedure one sends a *message* to an object which is handled by a *method*. The provision of *dynamic binding* of messages to methods is one of the crucial ingredients of an object-oriented language.

Because the class notion was so mixed with the implementation it took a long time to recognize the features that gave it its power, and also to recognize the inevitable accompanying limitations. The primary limitation of the original class notation was that a class object was almost inextricably linked to a computer object built up piece by piece. Because space can only be allocated to an object in one dimension, the idea of an object inheriting from two independent sources simultaneously could not be realized. Yet as we shall see, multiple inheritance – inheriting properties from several different objects simultaneously – is one of the more powerful tools for building systems. But even today, many object-oriented languages, such as Smalltalk-80 and Objective-C, do not support this notion.

The fourth important aspect of objects is usually referred to by the heading object identity. It captures the idea that the states of objects can *change* independently of each other but the objects can still remain recognizably the same. It is such a commonplace of normal programming experience that an object is represented by a variable (or set of variables) that can change over time that one scarcely thinks of it as anything remarkable. But the identity of an object is one of the oldest philosophical conundrums. The water in a river changes all the time, and its course changes year by year, yet we don't hesitate to refer to the river as one object. We now know that all the atoms in our bodies will be replaced in the course of a few years, yet this fact does not cause us identity problems (though we may well acquire those elsewhere).

The rise of a declarative approach to programming has resurrected the logical notion that an object is simply the sum of its attributes. By representing the attributes we have in some way captured the essence of the object. Thus, to take a simple bureaucratic example, if two individuals have the same name and were born on the same day, then they are, of course, the same individual. Aren't they?

In logic, we are careful to choose our attributes so that we can distinguish all the objects we are dealing with. But that isn't sufficient in a dynamic situation. It's not simply that we can't always choose an exhaustive or mutually exclusive set of attributes to describe an individual. The value of many of the attributes that we do select may change and, over a longer period, the object may even acquire a different set of attributes (think of the metamorphosis of a caterpillar into a butterfly). If the attributes change, do we then have a new object?

The normal answer, which is accepted in the object-oriented world, is no. The object remains the same despite the fact that it has changed. Its *identity* has remained the same. To take a computer example, if we are representing a windowful of information on a screen, then its position, size and its contents may all change, but it can remain the same window. An influential account of objects puts it like this:

> 'An object has a set of "operations" and a "state" that remembers the effect of operations. Objects may be contrasted with functions, which have no memory. Function values are completely determined by their arguments, being precisely the same for each invocation. In contrast, the value returned by an operation on an object may depend on its state as well as its arguments. An object may learn from experience, its reaction to an operation being determined by its operational history.' (Wegner, 1987)

The role of state in programming languages has always been controversial. Many subtle bugs in computer systems can be traced to misunderstandings about a change to a global variable made by a call to a subroutine. Using global variables is therefore routinely discouraged in computer-science teaching. But many academics have gone further by proposing the total abolition of the assignment statement. They point out that the potential of a variable to change its value places computer languages on an entirely different basis to mathematics. If the system were declarative, such that a single value could be substituted for a variable anywhere that it appears, then all the powerful techniques of logic and mathematics could be harnessed to guarantee that programs worked correctly. The growth of logic programming is one response to this challenge.

So are object-oriented programming and logic programming fundamentally incompatible? Before answering this question, we need to look rather more carefully at the emergence of declarative languages. This will enable us to distinguish the different ways in which state is used in programming and we will see that some uses of change of state are reasonable and others can be avoided.

1.4 The declarative challenge

Object-orientedness has taken a long time to emerge on the programming scene as a dominant force and it is not hard to see the reason. It is a philosophy aimed at the organization of large and extensible systems, at a time when most academic computing has been preoccupied in solving the small-scale problems associated with computation. This has scarcely been completed and it is unfortunate that most approaches to object-orientedness have learned very little from these researches (a notable exception is Eiffel).

The small-scale problems of computing are features such as the assignment statement and the termination of a computation. They are problems because they make it very difficult to apply traditional mathematical and logical techniques to computer programs. Take the simple assignment statement:

$$f = f + x$$

It is clearly not a mathematical equality (unless x happens to have the value 0). So it is normally written ':=' instead of '=' for this reason. What does it signify? It signifies that the value of f is increased by the value of x. If its value before was f_0 and the value of x was x_0 then its value afterwards is $f_0 + x_0$. The use of subscripts is important because it distinguishes the values from the locations which contain the values.

If we apply this to a well known and simple algorithm, we will see the difference it makes. The nth Fibonacci number is the sum of the $n - 1$th and the $n - 2$th, while the zeroth Fibonacci is 0 and the first is 1. The task is to come up with a program for the nth Fibonacci number.

Anyone with a little programming experience might soon come up with the following program:

```
t0:=0; t1=1; i:=n−1;
while i>0 do
        f:=t1+t0;
        t0:=t1;
        t1:=f;
        i:=i−1;
        end while;
```

This program is optimal (in one sense) in computing the Fibonacci F of a number N where $N \geqslant 2$. Of course, de Moivre's formula for the Fibonacci function is more efficient in the limit. That is, $F_n = (1/2^n\sqrt{5})((1+\sqrt{5})^n - (1 - \sqrt{5})^n)$. Yet it is not at all obvious from the program text that this is what it achieves. This is because the working variables, f, $t0$, $t1$ and i, hold different values at different times during the computation. To understand the program, one has to go through all the assignment statements, see what effect they have, then take an inductive 'leap' to reassure oneself that it happens for all possible values and that the program will terminate correctly.

Expressing the problem in a functional language such as Miranda or Hope provides the most readable computing solution to the problem:

```
fib(0) = 0
fib(1) = 1
fib(n + 2) = fib(n + 1) + fib(n)
```

These are simply equations – pure mathematics – where the right-hand side gives the value of the left-hand side. Since n is assumed to be a natural (non-negative) number, the third equation only applies to arguments of 2 or more. The equations will compute the solution.

Considered as a program, this is far less efficient than the imperative version (which *commands* the computer to perform the calculation). The most important reason for the inefficiency is that most of the work in computing F_{n+1} is repeated when calculating F_n and this effect multiplies exponentially. A minor reason is that the program necessarily involves recursion, which takes more time and space than an iterative program. It is more useful to consider this functional version as a *specification* of the Fibonacci function.

How does one make certain that the functional or mathematical form is the same as the program? The most obvious answer is by testing, and this represents the most common practice. Yet it is a fallible one. As Dijkstra has said, 'testing can show the presence of bugs, but not their absence'. In simple cases one can be reasonably sure of testing all the different cases, but as the complexity of software increases, so the impossibility of considering all the interactions between different parts quickly becomes apparent.

There are evolutionary and revolutionary methods proposed to meet this problem. Eiffel uses the evolutionary approach: propositional logic assertions may be added to the program text that can then be employed in proving characteristics of programs. The revolutionary methods are functional and logic programming, both of which throw away the traditional assignment statement altogether.

Functional programming makes the mathematics easier but it does not add a great deal to a language. Indeed, one can program 'in a functional style' in most computer languages by avoiding the undisciplined use of assignments. The exceptions are in languages such as BASIC and COBOL which do not (in most versions) have adequate procedure definition capabilities. Some of the more powerful features, such as higher order functions and closures, are also not supported in languages such as Pascal or C. Functional programmers would claim that these features transform programming, but not everyone shares this view.

But it is difficult to express specifications for many programs in a functional style. As a simple example, take the definition of sorting. This might be simply stated as:

> rearrange the items to be sorted so that they are in a nondescending order

Here we have not said anything about data representation, whether the items are, for instance, an array, a list or a file. We have not given in any sense an 'algorithm'.

To break down this specification we need to distinguish 'rearranging' and 'order'. We can refine the specification into two steps as follows:

> choose a permutation of the items
> check that it is in nondescending order

At this point we still do not have something which is a function. There are many possible permutations, and only some of them will satisfy the second criterion. Also, if there are repeated items, there will be more than one permutation which satisfies both criteria. Yet it is hard to express the problem more concisely without introducing some part of a solution, which finds the 'right' permutation.

It is this type of situation that has made logic programming attractive to many people. Unlike most computer languages, a language such as Prolog can handle this situation easily. The specification above becomes a non-deterministic program. It can be stated in pseudological terms as an implication which is nearly a Prolog program:

> Items X are sorted to items Y if
>   Y is a permutation of X and
>   Y is in order

In conventional Prolog syntax this would be represented as follows:

```
sort (X, Y) :−
    perm(X, Y),
    ordered(Y)
```

There are many possible permutations Y, yet it is permissible to write this as a program and possible to execute it (by providing definitions of permutation and ordering), though it will obviously not be efficient. The nickname for this method of sorting is 'slowsort'! The speed does not matter: what is important is its clarity as a specification.

It is this ability to write down something very close to a specification and execute it as a program that makes logic programming attractive. At the same time, the exact form of logic used by Prolog can be compiled into an efficiently executing program which achieves the same order of efficiency as ordinary imperative programming languages, and indeed can even gain on it in the complex application areas which are its forte, including electronic design, planning, genetics, expert systems and natural language processing.

In the fifteen or so years since the first efficient Prolog compiler was developed there has been an extraordinary growth in the use of this language worldwide. There are over fifty Prolog systems currently being distributed on machines ranging from personal computers to high-speed parallel processing machines. For the recent conference on the Practical Application of Prolog (Bowen and Moss, 1992) there were over 120 submissions from 24 countries of which 44 were presented. The domains ranged from pig farming to airport scheduling and from electronic design to object-oriented database construction. The vast majority of these were fielded applications in use for their intended domain.

What people are discovering above all is that Prolog is a cost-effective tool for application programming. Prototypes and finished products can be finished sooner and with smaller amount of effort than with traditional languages. The productivity of the design and development effort is being improved by an order of magnitude over traditional techniques. Maintenance and adaptation is also easier because the programs are expressed more directly in terms of the application and so changes in requirements can be quickly handled.

This does not usually mean a total abandonment of other approaches – indeed the close interweaving of Prolog code with code in other languages is often crucial to the success and profitability of the product. But since the major suppliers now offer this ability as standard, the best tool can be used for each part of a project, whether it be assembler for an inner loop, C for system interaction or a database package for interfacing with a large database.

What makes functional and logic programs different is that their effects do not depend on 'state'. They are, in a sense, 'stateless' and this is part of what is called 'declarative'. Their values don't depend on the changeable values of variables such as F and i in the Fibonacci program, which change from moment to moment. In functional programming once an assignment is made it is fixed and invariable. In logic programming one has the extra flexibility that if it is discovered that the assignment is incorrect then the program can 'backtrack' and try a different value. This doesn't change the declarativeness, but it does make the programming system more versatile.

It is therefore not surprising that in logic programming circles a great deal of effort has been expended on the task of 'reconciling' logic and change in objects. Any re-introduction of the assignment statement inevitably compromises the declarative nature of these systems and is therefore viewed with great suspicion. While this has given rise to some interesting developments, particularly concerning concurrent, or parallel, systems, it has so far been somewhat disappointing when considered from the perspective of traditional sequential computers.

The declarative nature of these systems presents us with the fundamental challenge in combining object-oriented programming with logic programming. The notions of encapsulation and inheritance, which were the first two characteristics of object-oriented programming that we identified, are quite compatible with the declarative approach and the means of doing this will be demonstrated in due course. But the third characteristic of object-oriented programming, identity, involves the use of 'state'. Classical logic was developed to describe static, stateless, situations. How can the two be combined?

1.5 Handling change

When we examine the use of changing state in programming we can divide the uses into three categories:

(1)   Cases where change is so intrinsic to the problem that there is no escaping it;

(2)   Cases where the declarative approach provides an alternative approach so that 'imperative' programming techniques are no longer necessary;

(3)   Borderline cases in which the issue is programming style and which may therefore introduce some controversy.

Let us examine these cases in more detail.

(1) The context which is carrying object-oriented programming forward – indeed some would say that it is its primary application – is the graphical user interface (GUI). Constructing a GUI is a complex business, involving programming the standard operations for windows, pointers, menus, dialogues and so on. The design of the GUI is not arbitrary: it is derived from a great deal of ergonomic research and experimentation into the use of short-term memory and the cues which are necessary to perform the common operations. It is scarcely surprising therefore that GUIs from different manufacturers look surprisingly similar (a fact which has led to lawsuits alleging the poaching of the 'look and feel' of an interface).

The operation of a GUI consists of a series of changes which are arbitrary and unpredictable from the program's point of view. The user may wish to open, rearrange, resize windows and change the contents of the windows. It is the program's function to accept possible changes and work within the criteria laid down. In effect there is *concurrency* between the program and the user.

This is an application for which the conventional notion of a 'program variable' is entirely suitable and is hard to improve on. The variables describe the current *state* of the system: which windows are open, their size, where the cursor is and so on. The operations of the program start from these values, compute new ones and store these new values back in the variables.

It is perfectly *possible* to program these operations in a declarative manner – indeed we will demonstrate this later in the book using a concurrent logic programming language. But there are several problems using conventional Prolog in practical situations. One is that Prolog wants to finish each operation before it starts another, but windows operations are inherently concurrent. Another, which blocks some possible solutions to the first problem, is that windows operations need to be very efficient. The response to a mouseclick is commonly handled through an interrupt routine using code that is still often coded in assembler for efficiency.

In practice, parts of a window system are implemented at different levels using different techniques: the bottom level is usually handled at a system level, and the *state representation* is only accessible to the programmer by specific calls to system routines. In this situation the programmer does not even have the option of programming declaratively. Much of the state information is outside of the declarative part of the program. What one needs to do is to use the system level and modify it where necessary.

In object-oriented terms one normally wishes to *inherit* the low-level behaviour of the windowing system and *override* those parts which are specific to a particular application. Hence a conventional approach using state variables which are updated by different parts of the programming system is unavoidable at some level. Because of this, the Prolog++ language provides state variables so that the same techniques may be used within the language.

(2) There are many cases in which program variables are commonly used in the imperative paradigm where they need not be. The most obvious is where change is local to a procedure invocation. It is handled routinely in the declarative programming paradigm by the use of extra parameters to procedures, usually called 'accumulators'. As an example, let us take the example introduced earlier, the Fibonacci function.

The Fibonacci specification takes exponentional time to execute because at each level two similar processes are spawned. It is not necessary to incur this penalty just because one is writing in a declarative language. The imperative algorithm can be easily expressed in a declarative language as well, and this eliminates most of the inefficiencies. All we need to do is to use an auxiliary function definition in which the auxiliary variables are represented by parameters called 'accumulators'.

In Hope or Miranda, for example, this would be expressed by the following equations:

```
fib(0) = 0
fib(1) = 1
fib(N + 2) = fib1(N, 0, 1)

fib1(0, F0, F1) = F0 + F1
fib1(N + 1, F0, F1) = fib1(N, F1, F0 + F1)
```

In fib1, the first parameter counts down to the value and the second and third parameters are used to accumulate the Fibonacci numbers as we move upward to the required value. The second equation of fib1 still appears to require a recursion, but it is a special case of recursion: a *last-call* or *tail* recursion. Any reasonable declarative programming system will spot this characteristic and optimize it to the equivalent of the while loop.

This program is more complex than the specification but can be relatively easily shown to be equivalent to the simple version by a process known as 'program transformation' which has been applied both to functional and logic programs. The rest of the task of making this as efficient as Fortran or C is just 'compiler technology'.

Accumulators are the equivalent in declarative languages of local assignments. Because of the way in which Prolog systems are compiled, they can be just as efficient – indeed, if a parameter remains unchanged from one procedure invocation to the next, it often happens that no code at all needs to be generated by the compiler, in the 'Warren Abstract Machine' (WAM) model used for Prolog compilation. Many beginners in Prolog discover that it has the equivalent of an assignment statement (the *assert* and *retract* statements), use them, and discover their programs are hopelessly inefficient. Changing the code to use accumulators often solves the problem completely.

This use of state and state change is nothing to do with object-oriented programming and should not be confused with it.

(3) There is a subtle influence on programming style arising from the practice of the incremental changing of an object. This is difficult to define, but it is often important in the development of software engineering techniques for programming.

It may be illustrated by the notion of the *cursor*, which is normally associated with text on computer screens but is of much general usefulness. For example, consider the task of processing a list of items (courtesy Meyer, 1988, Chapter 9). One may wish to specify a variety of operations on lists, such as adding or deleting an item, splitting the list into two parts, or getting the next item after a specified one. In all of these cases one can partition the tasks into two separate activities:

- first locate the position in the list,
- then make the required change.

If we have five methods for locating the position and five changes that can be made, we would generate 25 separate routines if these were all coded individually. Clearly the two stages should be separate operations. So the intermediate picture will look something like the following:

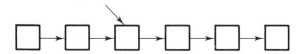

The question, if we are wanting to encourage encapsulation of the list operations, is: where do we hold the pointer to the intermediate list item? The traditional answer of both structured and declarative programming schools is that the find operation would return a pointer to the user, which would then be passed back to the module for the second operation. Yet this solution contradicts one of the basic aims of encapsulation, which is that internal details of the representation should not be accessible by the user.

The solution is to add the idea of a 'current position', or cursor, to the concept of the list. The *locate* operation sets the cursor, the *change* operation uses it. There is no need for the value of the cursor to be known by the user, as long as the abnormal events, such as the cursor moving outside the list, are taken care of in a sensible way. Instead, one adds operations to the list-manipulating routines to support the notion of the cursor. This has the added advantage that the number of parameters of the routines are reduced, so the user interface is also simplified in this way.

Thus the notion of the current *state* of an object draws together both the timeless and unchanging aspects of the object and its temporal and changing aspects. Because the state can only be changed from inside, the task of ensuring that changes are made correctly is much simplified. At the same time, the biggest impediment to concurrency – the global variable – is entirely eliminated.

This example is interesting since the use of a cursor does not change the list or affect the way in which one performs the list manipulations internally. One can do this by imperative or declarative means. (In Prolog one would probably use the concept of a difference list – see Chapter 2.) Yet it provides a systematic way of reducing the complexity of the interface for the user of these routines.

Thus it is important to distinguish major changes of state, that should not be ignored or eliminated, from the multiplicity of small changes that add unnecessary complexity to the programming process. One of the strengths of the object-oriented approach is that it makes such a distinction possible, but choosing when to employ the declarative means and when to encapsulate state is an art that can only be acquired by practice. Throughout the rest of this book we will attempt to demonstrate this aspect.

To summarize, we can say that change in object-oriented systems is essentially concerned with the macro level rather than the fine grain of change. This macro level is harder to eliminate from a practical system: at root it derives from the fact that programs interact with the real world, which changes in ways that cannot be formalized. The main benefit of the declarative approach derives from eliminating many small assignments and the side effects which make programs so hard to understand.

Whereas the declarative approach helps us with change on the small scale, we need to look elsewhere for help at the larger scale. At the present time, the object-oriented approach seems to offer the best strategy for coping with this problem. The effects of change are localized in object-oriented systems by keeping changes within object definitions. The most pernicious form of assignment is assignment to 'global variables', which some object-oriented systems, such as Smalltalk (and Prolog++), prohibit entirely. By making this restriction, every variable is 'owned' by an object, which can ensure that any changes are sensible. This eliminates at a stroke a large category of common programming errors.

The steps that we have been outlining correspond to developments in the world of systems analysis and design as summarized most clearly by Rumbaugh *et al.* (1991). In their Object Modelling Technique, they extend the earlier methods of functional specification of a problem (modelled using data flow diagrams) by dynamic modelling of objects, based on Harel's (1987) state transition diagrams. The relationship between these they describe as follows:

> 'Noninteractive programs, such as compilers, have a trivial dynamic model; their purpose is to compute a function. The functional model is the main model for such programs, although the object model is important for any problem with nontrivial data structures. Many interactive programs also have a significant functional model. By contrast, databases often have a trivial functional model, since their purpose is to store and organize data, not to transform it.' (Rumbaugh *et al.*, 1991, p. 123)

Much of the work in the logic programming field to date has been at the levels of functional models and data description (and we should not confuse this use of the word *functional* with the use of the word in functional programming). Compilers are some of the more significant Prolog programs, demonstrating the power of the new paradigm in addressing significant computing problems. But they are representatives of a relatively well-understood class, in computer-science terms. Time or state-dependent computations still present problems, though significant attempts are being made to address them (for example, Fiadeiro and Maibaum, 1990, also Kowalski and Sergot, 1986).

Although the analysis of time dependencies has much in common with earlier attempts to understand the mathematics of imperative programs, it is important to understand the difference in motivation. What people are now trying to do is to model the inevitable and irreducible time dependencies that occur in the real world, rather than the artifical dependencies introduced by a particular, von Neumann, style of computation. A reversion to earlier imperative styles of programming in the implementation of the functional component of an object-oriented system does not help in the overall goal of making the programming process more productive.

In the two different approaches to the design of object-oriented languages that have developed – making objects the centre of the language or grafting object-orientedness on the top of an existing language – the primary benefit is in objects as an organizing or design tool. We will have more to say about this important topic in Chapter 6. In this respect, adding object-oriented features to Prolog is no different to any other language. A language can be designed which compiles into standard Prolog and takes advantage of all the implementation experience associated with the language. Prolog has shown itself to be ideal for stating and solving small problems, but it is lacking when it comes to larger systems.

Using this approach brings many of the benefits of the object-oriented approach with sequential computers. However there is an alternative approach, the process interpretation of change, that fits in with a concurrent model of computation. This requires parallel or distributed computers to show any real benefits, but it does have some promise for the future.

It is no coincidence that Simula, the original object-oriented language, was originally designed to carry out simulations of concurrent processes. In a simulation a set of objects are posited which capture some aspect of the world that one wants to model. For example when studying the effect of different queuing strategies in a bank the objects might be the customers, the queues and the tellers. The behaviour of the individual objects when confronted with changes in the rest of the world is described; then the whole model is set to move forward in time, each object changing simultaneously. For practical reasons one generally uses *discrete* steps rather than *continuous* movement, and uses scheduling or time-slicing techniques on a sequential computer instead of real concurrency.

Simula was the first block-structured language to support this type of concurrency. Part way through a computation a process could suspend and pass control to another process, which might, in turn, execute only part of its code before passing control back to the original process. Inevitably, this tends to be inefficient on a sequential computer.

Concurrent execution is one of the most active areas in logic programming today, and languages derived from this paradigm, such as Strand-88, are even being used to 'parallelize' existing programs written in Fortran or C. The meaning of a logic program depends very little on ordering so there is plenty of scope for executing programs in parallel. Methods of message passing have been devised which allow synchronization of interconnected processes with the necessary flexibility to gain almost linear speed-ups using tens of processors in experimental situations.

The ideas of concurrency have been most consistently worked out by Carl Hewitt from the MIT AI laboratory in his Actor model (Hewitt, 1977). This views computation as a totally distributed network of processes which communicate by sending messages to each other. This model was taken up by Shapiro and Takeuchi (1983) in the earliest attempt to express object-oriented ideas in a logic programming context. They developed an interesting approach to storing simultaneous changes in objects in a declarative manner. This allows effective abstraction and safe message passing on a parallel machine, though the ideas are naturally not so useful on single processor systems.

A message-passing system does not make a complete object-oriented system by itself, though it meets two of our three criteria (encapsulation and identity). The other aspect – inheritance – is usually replaced by a subtly different concept: delegation. If a message is sent to an object, it may react by sending the message on to another object. Apart from efficiency problems, this has some different effects, and has not in general proved so popular.

The process view of objects therefore deserves consideration as an alternative paradigm for objects, and this will be explored later in the book in a chapter which considers two such languages, called Parlog++, and Step which operate on the concurrent logic programming languages Parlog and Strand-88 respectively.

1.6 Prolog and objects

It would be pleasing to consider the object layer as simply an encompassing layer for Prolog – a type of module system. The organization of a large Prolog program around predicates is not convincing, any more than organizing large imperative or functional programs around procedures and functions has proved an adequate approach. But, because the strength of object-oriented programming lies in the combination of the three aspects outlined earlier in this chapter – encapsulation, inheritance and identity – an OOLP language needs to balance these aspects carefully.

Most commercial Prolog systems have a form of module system because it is essential for constructing large programs, but modules without objects are somewhat artificial and therefore involve arbitrary choices. The author has unhappy memories of many meetings in the BSI and ISO standardization process devoted to finding an agreed approach – attempts which were doomed to fail. Interestingly, it was precisely in the area of dynamic programs (the Prolog features of *call* and *assert*) that the differences in approach became apparent. Dynamically changing modules proved impossible to agree about and the reason essentially was that a module was not seen as an object. Once one takes on board the notion of object, the whole approach to modules changes: there is something concrete to describe and to change.

But modules do have a static function as well – that of dividing up the name space of a program to avoid naming conflicts between groups of programmers. The concept of inheritance also has important applications in knowledge representation areas which have nothing to do with identity problems. So it is important in an OOLP language to be able to show the declarative strengths of object-oriented techniques before exploring the applications where change and concurrency are important. Prolog++ allows this, and this is the approach we will use in this book.

Inheritance is a relatively easy addition to the Prolog framework, because it is essentially 'deductive' and thus fits in neatly to the logical framework, though there are many choices to be made when it comes to the details. Multiple inheritance comes easily in the context of Prolog which it expects to find several solutions for any problem, but proposals differ in providing *inclusive* or *overriding* inheritance. There are also subtle points concerned with the definition of *self* that affect the usability of the language considerably. These considerations will be dealt with in due course.

But coping with change in order to conserve the identity of objects is, as we have seen, both essential and problematic.

There are several possible approaches:

(1)   Ignore change. This has been explored by Zaniolo (1984) and Aït-Kaci and Nasr (1986).

(2)   Use the equivalent of the assignment statement to implement change. This is the approach favoured by most commercial implementations.

(3)   Use concurrency (or coroutining) to implement change. This has been explored by Shapiro and Takeuchi (1983) and Davison (1987).

Since in this book we see objects as primarily an organizational tool, we will take the second approach, as it is the only approach that is practical on today's computers. We include a section on concurrent systems because these are already beginning to make inroads, mainly in the 'personal supercomputer' market. A fourth approach, based on reasoning about change (see Sergot and Kesim, 1991) may give benefits in the longer term, but as yet is nowhere near providing useful implementations.

An additional dimension of choice is the implementation strategy. Some proposals define a new language, and others build on existing implementations. With the exception of Login (see below), the advantages of a new implementation have not been evident. So it appears that it is possible to build an object system on the back of an existing Prolog system.

With these constraints in mind, we have chosen to concentrate on one language in this book, rather than talk in the abstract. The language we have used is one called Prolog++, available currently with LPA Prolog products on the IBM PC and Apple Macintosh, though it will shortly be ported to several Unix-based platforms.

Prolog++ is an example of the hybrid approach to object-oriented programming, like Objective-C. It has its own notation, but compiles directly into Prolog. Because of the way Prolog compilers are built, it is relatively easy to add extra layers on top of an existing system. Many Prolog systems already support different forms of syntax for specialized purposes, such as expert and hypertext systems, so there is plenty of experience in providing these front ends within the Prolog community.

Prolog++ is not the first object-oriented system based on Prolog. Papers appeared on the subject as early as 1983. The ICOT Research Center in Tokyo, the centre for Fifth Generation computer systems, had a product called ESP (Extended Self-contained Prolog) available in 1987 based on object-oriented ideas and implemented on LISP workstations. A Unix version (CESP) was distributed in 1989. A number of theoretical proposals were made, of which the most interesting was Aït-Kaci's Login system (Aït-Kaci and Nasr, 1986). This, in a sense, turns the whole of logic 'upside-down', basing the language representation on data rather than on the predicate, and providing an appropriate form of unification. More recently he has pioneered another language called Life, which integrates several programming styles. The number of object-oriented extensions to Prolog that are available seems to be growing rapidly. Examples are Lap running on Quintus, Spiral, developed by CRIL in France, Emicat, which runs on Delphia and IBM Prolog, and Object-CS Prolog from Hungary.

In contrast to some of these, Prolog++ succeeds in balancing the differing strengths of the two paradigms (OO and LP) successfully. It is possible to regard the absence of the assignment statement in Prolog as a simple deficiency which needs to be corrected, and this has been suggested by some other products. This is to miss most of the point of logic programming! At the other end of the spectrum attempts to merge the two paradigms in a totally 'pure' fashion without incorporating assignment has not succeeded in producing systems that significantly add to the usefulness of Prolog.

SUMMARY

- The main benefits of object-oriented programming occur in the construction of software systems – as an organizational tool, and in encouraging consistency and reusability.

- The key aspects of object-oriented programming are encapsulation, inheritance and object identity. These are demonstrated in the construction of classes and the use of concurrency.

- The strengths of logic programming lie in constructing programs which are close to specifications, so that the programming process from prototype to finished product can be handled efficiently and economically.

- The addition of encapsulation and inheritance to logic programs strengthens this paradigm significantly. The main design choice in combining the two approaches concerns the handling of change, to maintain the identity of objects. Approaches using assignment and coroutining are possible.

- Prolog++ is an example of the hybrid design of object-oriented programming languages: a portable layer on top of a Prolog system giving the benefits of the object-oriented approach.

2
A Prolog primer

2.1 Introduction

The aim of this chapter is to provide a background knowledge of Prolog for those who have either not come across it or only looked at the basic principles – it should get you 'up to speed' in order to follow the rest of the book. Anyone who has experience in Prolog should be able to skip this chapter, and simply use it for reference as the need arises.

Although the notation of Prolog is different from that of Prolog++, every clause of Prolog++ is valid Prolog and has an interpretation in Prolog. The principles of programming in Prolog++ include those of Prolog, and this is what sets both languages apart from other object-oriented languages. Because they are essentially *symbolic* and *declarative*, it is often possible to achieve a working program in a fraction of the time and size that is necessary with other imperative programming languages. But the whole approach to writing Prolog is substantially different from writing in C, BASIC or Smalltalk, and programmers often make the mistake of assuming that you do things in much the same way in Prolog: for some types of code this is true, but it is essential to appreciate the differences. No analogs to unification or multiple solutions exist in the vast majority of programming languages, and thinking about backtracking is entirely novel.

The aim of this chapter is to give an informal understanding of practical Prolog programming. No previous acquaintance with the ideas is assumed. It develops the theoretical basis for the language progressively. Each section presents a new layer which is absent from the previous layer. We start with propositional logic and extend this to database languages; then data structures and full unification are treated, including lists, arithmetic terms and the implementation of automatic storage allocation and garbage collection. Only after this are recursion and iteration introduced, followed by various control features which add negation and greater efficiency to the language. The concept of metaprogramming is briefly introduced, together with the various language primitives which support it. Finally programs with side-effects, such as input/output and database modification, are covered.

In 1993 a draft international standard for Prolog was finally published (ISO, 1993). This chapter follows, as far as possible, the ISO draft, except in certain areas such as I/O where the standard diverges significantly from the normal 'Edinburgh' dialect.

2.2   Facts and rules

The most common forms of sentence in English, or any other ordinary language, are commands, questions and statements. Young children's sentences are almost entirely commands, or expressions of feeling. 'Mama' is not an existential statement about a discovered relationship to the world, but an immediate request, usually for attention. The next stage of development is to ask questions but it is not for several years that they discover that they can make informative (or indicative) sentences about the world.

Programming languages appear to be going through the same stages. The principle type of sentence in most languages is a command: add two numbers, display the result on a screen, accept input from the user and so on. Early languages did not have many declarations (one form of indicative statement) and no questions. But sentences in the indicative mood are more versatile than commands. They can be made to answer questions or check conditions or express relationships as well as to construct definitions. Indeed, they are also used in human conversation to express commands and questions as well (for example, 'you are going to work?').

Initially, we will look at simple statements, or propositions. A **proposition** is something that is either true or false but has no other value. Propositions can be used to build three types of sentence (or clause) in Prolog: facts, rules and questions. **Facts** are positive assertions or propositions; **rules** contain a positive assertion but impose some conditions; **questions** can be regarded as purely negative or conditional propositions.

The way of writing these three types of sentences is as follows:

```
Fact:         proposition.
Rules:        proposition :- proposition, proposition, .... .
Questions:    :- proposition, proposition, .... .
```

The symbol ':-' may be read as 'if'. Facts and questions are simply special cases of rules in which the condition and assertion parts respectively are empty. You will see that although Prolog has a syntax rather like English, including commas and full-stops, it does take some liberties. Every sentence ends with the same full stop, so that questions start with ':-'.

In fact, the syntax for questions varies somewhat between Prolog systems. Some systems now use dialogue boxes rather than the syntax above and others use different modes for statements and questions. A useful distinction is between the use of ':-' and '?-' to introduce questions. The first simply evaluates the question, or directive, whereas the second also gives a reply – either 'yes' or 'no' for propositional questions. We will use the '?-' for questions that expect an answer in the examples to be presented in this book, as it is simple for presentation and unambiguous.

Propositions are written in a similar way to the identifiers in most programming languages, normally starting with a lower case letter, but possibly including digits and the underscore character (_).

Let us consider an extremely simple set of rules. These can be used for deciding what to do in the morning. There are three possible actions: go to work, go out, or stay in bed. What we need in order to decide what to do are some rules and some facts. Here are the rules, expressed in Prolog syntax:

Rules

```
goOut :- sunny, dayOff, well.
goOut :- bored.
goToWork :- weekday, well.
stayInBed :- raining, dayOff.
stayInBed :- sick.
dayOff :- saturday.
dayOff :- sunday.
weekday :- monday. weekday :- tuesday. weekday :- wednesday.
weekday :- thursday. weekday :- friday.
```

We can render these rules in English very simply:

Go out if it's sunny and a day off and I'm well.
Go out if I'm bored.
Go to work if it's a weekday and I'm well.
Stay in bed if it's raining and it's a day off.
Stay in bed if I'm sick.
Saturday is a day off.
Sunday is a day off.
Monday is a weekday, and so on.

Rules thus contain a conclusion and one or more conditions, which must all be true if the conclusion is valid. There can be several rules with the same conclusion. This gives us alternatives without the need for any 'or' statement in the language.

One abbreviation in notation can be noted. If there are alternative conditions for the same conclusion it is permissible to join them up using the separator ';', read as 'or'. Thus we could write the rules for weekdays as:

```
weekday :- monday ; tuesday ; wednesday
    ; thursday ; friday.
```

This notation adds nothing to what we can express. The two sets of statements are identical as far as their truth value is concerned. It is simply a notational convenience. However we are *not* allowed to put any separator on the left hand side of the ':-'. That would extend the meaning of what can be said.

To derive any conclusions from these rules we need some facts. Here is one possible set:

Facts A

```
sunday.
sunny.
well.
```

To find out what to do we have to ask questions which have a yes/no answer, as in the old British radio game known as *Twenty Questions* in which the aim of the game was to guess the identity of an arbitrary object in only 20 yes/no questions. The answer to the first obvious set of questions (animal, vegetable, mineral or abstract) was given in advance. So here are the questions, as they might be posed to Prolog, with the answers one would get:

```
?- goOut.
yes

?- goToWork.
no

?- stayInBed.
no
```

Note that many Prolog systems have a special trap which is invoked when a predicate is undefined. When executing propositional programs such as those in this section, this trap is inappropriate as it is ultimately the presence or absence of a propositional fact that controls the program execution. Check the manual for your system to find out how to turn this check off. For instance, on some systems a call unknown(_,fail) will turn a trap to the debugger into a normal failure.

The answers depend on the facts, as one might expect. A different set of facts produces different answers. Here's another set:

Facts B

```
monday.
well.
bored.
```

And here are the questions:

```
?- goOut.
yes

?- goToWork.
yes

?- stayInBed.
no
```

There is thus nothing exclusive in these options. If we give the necessary facts, any or all of the questions can give the answer 'yes'. Nor is there anything magical about the replies. Try telling your boss that the computer told you to go out rather than go to work, and she or he will doubtless correct your belief in the infallibility of mechanical reasoning! Both the rules and the facts must be correct before the conclusion is correct.

So how does Prolog arrive at a yes or no answer? There are two different but equivalent ways of answering that question. The first is called the *declarative* (or model-theoretic) way and the second the *procedural*. The declarative method depends simply on the correctness of the deductions. The procedural method involves a mechanical procedure, finding those deductions.

Let us take the first set of facts, facts A, and trace the logic of the answer declaratively. A question is true if all of its propositions are true. So to answer the question:

```
?- goOut.
```

we simply have to check whether goOut is true. To show that, we have to see whether it can be shown by a rule or a condition.

The conclusion of a rule is true if all its conditions are true. So the rule

```
goOut :- sunny, dayOff, well.
```

implies goOut if all its conditions are true. So we must check all of the three.

Sunny is declared as a fact, so we know it is true. So is well. So that leaves us with showing dayOff. There is a rule:

    dayOff :- sunday.

so if we can demonstrate that sunday is true then we can prove dayOff is true. But sunday is also a fact, so it is true.

In this way we have proved all the conditions for goOut so we know it is true. This finishes the *declarative* or model theoretic proof.

Now let us go back and answer the same question *procedurally* or mechanically. This is the way that a Prolog machine will set about answering it.

We start with the question:

    ?- goOut.

and the Prolog system has two possible rules to try (there are no facts for this proposition). So it will try them, one after another, in the order given. To solve a rule it replaces the conclusion by the conditions, and tries to solve these in turn. So one is left with a new set of questions (which we write with :- as it does not expect explicit answers):

    :- sunny, dayOff, well.

To solve several questions, Prolog attempts to solve each of them in turn starting with the first, which is sunny.

Sunny corresponds to a fact that we have written down. A fact can be considered as a special case of a rule. It is one which has no conditions. So if the conclusion matches there's nothing else to do. Prolog simply progresses to the next proposition:

    :- dayOff, well.

This time, the proposition dayOff matches a rule. So applying the same principle as before, its replaces the conclusion by the goals and gets the rule list:

    :- saturday, well.

Note that the system hasn't forgotten the other condition (well) that is still awaiting an answer.

It tries to execute the query saturday and there is no matching fact or rule. So the goal *fails*. But all is not lost. At this point it will *backtrack* and try to find another way of solving the goal. The system reconsiders the query:

    :- dayOff, well.

There is another way of solving dayOff by using the second clause:

    dayOff :- sunday.

If this is used, it gets a new set of queries:

    :- sunday, well.

Now it can progress. Sunday matches a fact and reduces to nothing, leaving the query:

    :- well.

This in turn matches with a fact and leaves the empty goal, which can be represented by:

    :-□

Since there are no more queries to answer, the process terminates successfully and the Prolog machine prints out 'yes'.

For completeness, let us briefly consider what happens when the process fails. Let us take the query goToWork with the first set of facts. The first step succeeds by matching the goal with the head of the clause:

    goToWork :- weekday, well.

leaving the query to be answered as:

    :- weekday, well.

There are five possible ways to answer the query weekday corresponding to the five clauses in the program. The first yields the new query:

    :- monday, well.

but this fails and causes backtracking to the next clause. This in turn fails (it isn't Tuesday) and so do the rest. Since there is no way of solving weekday, this causes a failure in the next clause up, the clause for goToWork. But there is no other clause for goToWork so this too fails.

Because the top level goal has failed, Prolog prints out the answer no and terminates.

This is (almost) all there is to the basic control mechanism of Prolog! Although we haven't yet looked at the treatment of variables, which gives Prolog much of its power, we can see the basic search mechanism which attempts to find an answer – if there is one – by systematically evaluating all the possibilities. This mechanism isn't efficient enough by itself to implement a good chess machine, for example, but it does enable very rapid prototyping in situations where the space to be searched is relatively small.

Whilst the order of search is predetermined, the programmer can adjust both the order of the clauses and the order of the conditions within a goal to ensure reasonable performance. The search strategy is 'goal directed' in that it starts with the proposition or goal to be proved and works backward to known facts.

The order in which the subgoals are presented makes no difference at all to the set of answers found, nor does the ordering of the clauses. This accords with the normal meaning of 'and': a and b should mean the same thing as b and a. While this is true in the propositional (and datalog) case, it is not, unfortunately, maintained in full Prolog, because a query may terminate with one clause ordering and fail to terminate with another.

The model method that was used first is important for two reasons. One is that it can be used to give a sound theoretical (semantic) basis for the language; something that few computer languages have. The other is that it gives the programmer an intuitive reading of the meaning of the program. In so doing one can easily ignore all the blind alleys that a machine must trudge down and concentrate on the part of the program that applies in a particular case. This is the biggest difference between a mathematical and a mechanical understanding. Since the truth of each clause depends solely on the truth of its conditions, the truth of the answer to a complex query can be subdivided repeatedly into the truths of its component parts.

We can present this very concisely as a *proof* of the answer. Here is one way of presenting it using indentation to show the conditions for each conclusion and noting which arguments are facts:

```
goOut :-
    sunny               fact
    dayOff :-
        sunday          fact
    well                fact
```

Each line ends with either the symbol :- or the word fact. Sunny is a fact, and this is indicated at the right. The proof of dayOff is just the line indented underneath it. It doesn't depend on any other part of the program. The proof of goOut depends on the three lines with a single indentation below it: the proofs of sunny, dayOff and well. If we are confident of these we can be confident of the conclusion. We can also represent this graphically as a *proof tree* as shown in Figure 2.1.

The complete set of possibilities can also be represented as a tree. In this case we must distinguish alternatives (or-nodes) from conditions which must hold simultaneously (and-nodes). This is conventionally done by adding an arc to the and-nodes. The result, or *search tree*, is called an *and-or* graph, and the and-or graph for goOut is shown in Figure 2.2.

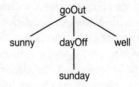

Figure 2.1   Proof tree for goOut.

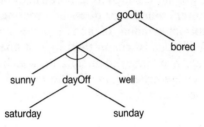

Figure 2.2   And-or graph (search tree) for goOut.

Graphs such as these can be very useful for visualizing what is going on in a Prolog program.

Summary

- Symbols are written starting with a lower case letter and can include digits, upper or lower case letters and the underscore character.

- Propositions can be symbols (as well as other terms to be discussed later).

- The sentences, or clauses, of a program are composed of propositions and connectives, terminated by a period character (which must be followed by a space or new line). A rule consists of a proposition optionally followed by :- and one or more propositions, separated by commas (,). A question begins with :- and contains one or more propositions separated by commas.

2.3   Predicates and variables

So far we have considered very simple propositions which take no arguments, include no variables and yield programs which only give yes/no replies. Although many computer scientists often use only a slightly more complex logic for much of their theoretical work, this logic is scarcely adequate as the basis of a programming language. In this section we will expand the propositions of the previous section to include **predicates** – propositions which include explicit parameters, or arguments.

Predicates are written in Prolog much like functions in most other programming languages: name of predicate, open brackets, arguments separated by commas, close brackets, for example loves(antony, cleopatra). One point to notice is that there should not be a space between the predicate name and the opening bracket (this slightly annoying restriction is because of the way operators can be defined). Although, strictly speaking, predicates have a single argument and relations have more than one, we will refer to both as predicates.

We can consider the facts to be a database. So let us take a traditional database which shows the structure of a company, with employees, managers, rooms and telephones. The schema for each of the database is written first as an end-of-line comment, which is indicated by the '%' character. **Comments** are written to the right of the '%' symbol. Prolog also supports non-nested multiline comments which start with '/*' and end with '*/'.

```
%dept(name, manager)
dept(sales, 'C.J.').
dept(design, jill).
dept(accounts, fred).

%employee(name, dept, salary)
employee(bert, accounts, 17000).
employee(jean, sales, 20000).
employee(fred, accounts, 16000).

%room(person, roomNumber)
room(fred, 523)
room(jean, 133).
room(bert, 522).

%telephoneIn(room, telephoneNumber)
telephoneIn(523, 1033).
telephoneIn(133, 2034).
telephoneIn(522, 6616).
telephoneIn(523, 2022).
```

Most of the arguments are symbols as described in the previous section, written for convenience as lower case words. But notice the sequence 'C.J.'. Any sequence of characters (except a new line) may be enclosed in single quotes to form a symbol, or **atom** as it is usually called in Prolog. To include a quote in the atom, double it. Numbers may be used, written as in most computer languages.

A straightforward question to this database, such as

Is Jill the manager of the design department?

then becomes simply

```
?- dept(design, jill).
yes
```

Not only the names of predicates but also the arguments must match the facts. This doesn't give us any more power than before. But we can now get answers back from the database by putting variables in the question, which make it correspond to who or what questions. **Variables** are indicated in Prolog by starting a name with a capital letter or an underscore (_) and the names we choose are entirely arbitrary so long as different variables have different names. For example,

Who is the manager of the design department?

```
?- dept(design, Who).
Who = jill
```

If there are variables in the question, the Prolog system answers the ?- query by printing out the values of all of them. But variables are not assigned in the same way as most programming languages. Instead they are **bound** or **instantiated** to a single value by **unification** when a variable in the query matches a constant in the database. If an attempt is subsequently made to bind it to a different value, then that part of the computation will fail.

This can be illustrated by a slightly more complex query. Let us pose the query:

What is Jean's telephone number?

We can do this by observing that we have to find which room Jean is in and then to find which telephone is in that room. So we connect the two queries with a comma and a common variable:

```
?- room(jean, Room), telephoneIn(Room, Phone).
Room = 133, Phone = 2034
```

Prolog prints the value of both variables which are consistent with the queries. Neither variable started off with a value, but Room was given a value, or instantiated, by the only fact in the room relation which matched jean in the first argument. At this point the query to the second relation became in effect:

```
:- telephoneIn(133, Phone).
```

Although the first argument was a variable it could not be reassigned by this second query. So while the original query looks as if it has two output values, when called it has one input and one output. Prolog works in the same way in both cases: the arguments are unified. In this case it is the same as a test for equality.

For this query only one possible set of values satisfies the conditions. But the same query for Fred will yield a different answer.

```
?- room(fred, Room), telephoneIn(Room, Phone).
Room = 523, Phone = 1033;
Room = 523, Phone = 2022;
no
```

We show here the results from a simple interface to Prolog, in which the user interacts with the system when using a 'glass teletype' interface (which cannot overwrite the screen). When the first value is printed out, the system waits until the user either types ';' which asks for an alternative answer (using the 'or' symbol introduced in the previous section) or another character such as *return* which signifies 'enough'. Since room 523 has two recorded phones, two sets of values are printed out, followed by no which signifies that there are no more possibilities.

Queries such as these can easily be encapsulated in rules such as those below. These give what in database terminology are called *views* of the database. The names of predicates and variables have been chosen so that the intended meaning should be obvious.

```
phone(Person, Phone) :-
    room(Person, Room),
    telephoneIn(Room, Phone).

manages(Manager, Employee) :-
    employee(Employee, Dept, _),
    dept(Dept, Manager).

sameDepartment(PersonA, PersonB) :-
    employee(PersonA, Dept, _),
    employee(PersonB, Dept, _).

salary(Person, Salary) :-
    employee(Person, _, Salary).
```

One interesting difference between these relations and functions in most languages is that it does not make any difference which of the arguments are bound to values when making a query. The following queries both work:

Who is on phone 1033?

```
?- phone(Who, 1033).
Who= fred;
no
```

Which people are in the same department?

```
?- sameDepartment(A, B).
A=bert, B=bert;
A=bert, B=fred;
A=jean, B=jean;
A=fred, B=bert;
A=fred, B=bert;
no
```

This last answer yields some answers we probably weren't expecting. Of course Bert works in the same department as Bert, but we would not expect to use this procedure to ascertain that fact. But Prolog is a simple language which performs all inferences when asked. If we want to exclude similar answers, then we must put in some extra conditions. It would be easy to specify in the predicate that Person A and Person B should not be the same (we will show the syntax for this in the next section), but it is not so obvious how to exclude the pair of answers A=bert, B=fred and A=fred, B=bert, because one might legitimately ask any of the questions

```
?- sameDepartment(fred, X).
?- sameDepartment(bert, X).
?- sameDepartment(fred, bert).
?- sameDepartment(bert, fred).
```

and expect to get an answer. The 'trick' of only returning answers which obey some lexicographic ordering, for example, would prune two of those queries.

One other feature of Prolog used in these examples that is not entirely obvious is the use of the variable '_'. This is known as an 'anonymous variable' and has the property that each time it is used even within one clause it signifies a different variable. So in the program for sameDepartment it is *not* required that the two people have the same salary! Apart from being easier to type, it is useful for checking programs. Any variable *except* the anonymous variable that does not appear at least twice in a clause may well be mistyped. Many Prolog systems have automatic warning messages based on this idea.

Unlike many other formalisms, Prolog does *not* require that variables are declared before use. There are several reasons for this. The use of each variable is limited to one clause and variable declarations would be onerous. Type declarations for variables are not necessary – if type checking is required it is enough to specify the types of predicates from which the typechecker can deduce the types of individual variables.

Finally, unlike the full first-order predicate calculus, only one type of quantifier (the universal quantifier $\forall$) is needed. The existential quantifier ($\exists$) is made unnecessary by the practice of Skolemization using functors (see Section 2.4). However a variable that *only* appears in the body of the clause is effectively governed by an existential quantifier. The definition of sameDepartment above could be paraphrased:

> Any two people are in the same department if there exists a department such that both of them are members of it.

The explanation, for those who are familiar with the predicate calculus, is that the body of a clause is negated, so that a universal quantifier for the whole clause when negated becomes an existential quantifier for the body. Despite this, Prolog will still succeed twice if there are, say, two departments of which the people are members.

Note: the queries in the program above are very similar to those available in most database query languages, such as SQL. The type of Prolog which is limited to these queries has been called *Datalog*. It has several properties that make it easy to analyse: It has only constants and variables (no structural terms) and in addition no recursive procedures (although full Datalog does allow these).

Summary

- Predicates consist of an atom followed optionally by arguments in brackets separated by commas.
- Arguments of predicates can include: atoms (including quoted atoms), numbers and variables.
- Variables are written starting with a capital letter or underscore.
- A request for more answers to a query is indicated by a semi-colon.
- Anonymous variables are indicated by '_' and when used several times in the same clause they stand for different variables.

2.4 Compound terms

What sets unification apart is not its ability to match simple terms in both input and output modes but the fact that this can be extended to complex terms which include standard data structures. These are normally referred to as **compound terms**. They give rise to forms of pattern matching and partial construction of terms which enable many programs to be expressed very succinctly.

Let us take a data structure which is so common that it is built into most database systems as a special entity: dates. A date is normally specified by a triple: year, month, day (in an order which varies between Europe and the USA). This can be represented as a term with a similar syntax to a predicate, such as date(1992,12,31), but this is not a function which returns a result, but a **data constructor** or record, with three fields. (As we shall see, functional terms can be manipulated and compared in the same way as any other term. Putting the year first ensures that dates sort properly.) In Prolog date is normally known as a **functor** of **arity** 3.

We can then use such terms directly in making definitions.

```
joined(fred, date(1973, 2, 18)).
promoted(fred, manager, date(1987, 3, 17)).
```

These express the facts that Fred joined the company on 18 February 1973 and was promoted to be a manager on 17 March 1987. These terms can then be passed around as single entities and manipulated. For example, we could define a set of procedures to access the components of a date:

```
year(date(Year,_,_), Year).
month(date(_,Month,_), Month).
day(date(_,_,Day), Day).
```

These can then be used to ask questions without needing to know the internal format of a date:

What year did Fred join the company?

```
?- joined(fred, Date), year(Date, Year).
Date = date(1973,2,18), Year = 1973
```

As well as breaking apart a term that is already constructed, these procedures can be used to construct a term that does not yet exist. For example:

```
?- day(D, 1), month(D, 1), year(D, 1992).
D = date(1992,1,1)
```

The date returned is the only possible date compatible with the three constraints that have been placed on it. It is worth tracing the progress of this query to see how the value of D is assigned successively:

call	*variable value*
day(D, 1)	D = date(_1, _2,1)
month(D,1)	D = date(_1, 1, 1)
year(D,1992)	D = date(1992, 1, 1)

The variables _1 and _2 are used to signify variables allocated by the Prolog machine. Variables of this form are frequently printed out: the number has no direct significance, except that different numbers signify different variables. As an easy way of ensuring this criterion, large numbers related to the actual storage location within the machine are often used but rarely is the original symbolic name of the variable incorporated as this may not be unique.

One can also unify two terms which are each partially instantiated. For example:

```
?- date(X, 2, 13) = date(1992, 2, Y).
X = 1992, Y = 13
```

This query uses the **equality** predicate '=', which simply attempts to unify its two arguments. In this case it succeeds by binding each of the variables. But if any item is incompatible, the unification will fail:

```
?- date(X, 2, 13) = date(1992, 8, Y).
no
?- date(X, 2, 13) = 13205.
no
```

2.4.1 Prolog unification

This behaviour can easily be generalized. Two terms A and B will unify if one of the following conditions is satisfied:

(1)   Either A or B is an (unbound) variable, and the variable is then bound to the other term;

(2)   Both A and B are atomic terms and A = B;

(3)   Both A and B are compound terms having the same functor and arity, and the arguments of A and B each unify by these conditions.

There is one problematic case in this definition. Because the terms can be compound, it is possible that a variable A can be embedded in a term B with which it is being unified. The simplest case is the following:

```
?- X = f(X).
```

The resulting situation may be pictured as a graph (as shown in Figure 2.3) where the pointers are invisible to the programmer. If the system tries to print out the result the effect will be never-ending:

```
X = f(f(f(f(f(f(f(f(f(f(f(f(f(f(f(f(f(f(f(f(f(f(f(f(f(f(f(f(f(f(f(f( ...
```

Figure 2.3 ?-X = f(X).

Because of this, an extra condition is required in case (1) so that it reads:

(1)   Either A or B is an (unbound) variable which does not occur in the other, and the variable is then bound to the other term.

This is conventionally called the *occur check* and is required to avoid infinite circular terms. Unfortunately this check is expensive to implement as it is necessary to look through the whole of the other term at each step of the unification that tries to bind a variable. Several alternative implementation possibilities are available. The simplest, and commonest, is to ignore the problem. It is the programmer's responsibility to avoid such situations. This is not as cavalier as it sounds. The outcome is relatively easy to avoid in most programming situations and most Prologs supply an extra predicate called 'unify' to handle the few situations where the occur check is vital.

An alternative is to allow for the possibility of circular terms. If one is detected the question arises of how to handle the resulting situation sensibly. An additional requirement for this strategy is to have some way of printing out the circular term. This turns out to be simple. All one needs is a special function symbol (for instance #) which takes a single argument which is an integer. This is then read as 'this value is bound to a value *n* levels above the present level'.

So instead of attempting to print out an infinite term, the system would simply print the following:

    X = f(# (1))

To see why the integer is required consider the following somewhat artificial, but possible, unification:

    ?- f(g(A), B, A, B) = f(X, h(X), Y, Y).
    A = h(g(# (2))), B = h(g(# (2))), X = g(h(# (2))), Y = h(g(# (2)))

This may be pictured diagrammatically as shown by Figure 2.4.

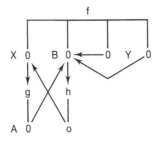

Figure 2.4   ?-f(g(A), B, A, B) = f(X, h(X), Y, Y).

Each of the loops in the bindings goes through two levels: the number indicates how many levels to 'jump out'.

Although the cost of handling circular terms correctly has been reduced to an overhead of only about 5%, even in compiled Prologs, most implementations of Prolog do not yet support circular terms. The usually cited reason is that it is nice to be able to process terms which are trees, without worrying whether they do in fact contain cycles.

[Note: the queries above are good tests of the robustness of a Prolog system. If it does not handle circular terms correctly one of three things can happen: it can get into a tight loop from which it can only be rescued (if at all) by pressing an interrupt key; it can run out of temporary storage space and thereby fail the entire computation; or it can result in a system crash!]

2.4.2   Lists

Compound terms in Prolog have two specific notations which need to be considered. The first is the list and the second is the arithmetic term.

Lists have so many uses in a symbolic language that a special syntax has been given to it. A simple list may be written in Prolog as

[apples, bananas, cherries]

but it conceals a more basic structure. A list can be considered as a pair: a head and a tail. The head is an item of the list, which may be of any type (including a list). The tail is itself a list, of the same type. A list must end somewhere and this end is the empty list, which is written [].

So, as well as a sequence enclosed in square brackets and separated by commas, we also need a pair, which is normally written in Prolog as:

[Head | Tail]

By this analysis, the first list we gave can also be written as:

[apples | [bananas | [cherries | []]]]

The profusion of closing brackets is in itself sufficient explanation as to why we use a special notation. However even this representation is not the same as the general definition of compound term that was given earlier. In fact, a list in Prolog can be written without any special syntax, as a binary term whose functor is '.'. The reason for this choice is historical: it corresponds to the 'dotted pairs' used in S-expressions in LISP. So the same list could also be written as:

.(apples, .(bananas, .(cherries, [])))

We therefore have three different ways of saying the same thing! This is solely a function of the 'reader' of a Prolog machine. The three forms are converted into the same internal representation and cannot be distinguished internally. We can even unify them:

?-[apples,bananas,cherries] = .(apples,.(bananas,.(cherries,[]))).
yes

A list with a single item is written as, for example, [apples]. The notation with square brackets and a bar also allows 'open lists' – lists which end in an unbound variable:

?- [apples,bananas | X] = .(apples,.(bananas,X)).
yes

We will see a number of uses of these open lists later. The section on recursion and iteration demonstrates a number of typical uses of lists.

2.4.3   Arithmetic terms

The second special syntax for compound terms is 'infix' and 'prefix' notation. 'Postfix' terms may also be defined, but there are none predefined. This is used by the system for arithmetic expressions. Thus the term:

$-A*B+2*C$

can also be written as a standard term in the form:

$+(-(*(A, B)), *(2, C))$

The normal rules of operator precedence apply, so that * binds more tightly than + or −. But an arithmetic expression is still a compound term; it does *not* stand for the value to which it is equivalent (except that negative numbers are recognized: − 5 is not the same as − applied to 5, that is, −(5)). If we assume that it is, our program will fail:

```
?- 2*3 = 6.
no
```

However, Prolog *does* provide a means of evaluating arithmetic expressions at the outermost, or predicate level. The essential predicate is called 'is' and is itself written in 'infix' form, with the arithmetic expression on the right hand side:

```
?- X is 2*3.
X = 6
```

As a convenience, a number of other predicates are provided which can take arithmetic expressions on either the left or the right hand side:

<	less than
= <	less than or equal (or ⩽)
>	greater than
> =	greater than or equal (or ⩾)
= : =	arithmetically equal
=\=	arithmetically unequal

The following operators may be used in an arithmetic expression:

+ − */	the normal operators (/ always yields a float)
// mod	integer division and remainder
/\ \/	bitwise 'and', 'or' and (unary) complement
≪ ≫	left and right shift

In addition, the common arithmetic functions are available, such as: abs, sign, int, sqrt, ln, sin, cos, tan (using radians).

We will illustrate these operations by showing the basic routines for calculating the number of days between any two calendar dates. This is done by the arithmetic method known as Zeller's congruence, which uses a direct calculation from the date. To cope with leap years, it assumes the year starts in March, as it did in Roman days. The routine returns what is known in astronomical circles as the Julian Day. It presupposes the use of 32-bit integer arithmetic – a smaller constant could easily be substituted with a smaller range of allowable dates. It could equally well be expressed using floating point arithmetic, though this is not available in some versions of Prolog.

```
days(From, To, Days) :-
    day(From, Day1),
    day(To, Day2),
    Days is Day2 − Day1.
```

```
%Julian days from Gregorian date − only valid after 1752
day(date(Year,Month,Day), Days) :-
    JF is (12−Month)//10, % JF is 1 in Jan & Feb only
    Y is Year−JF,
    Days is (306*(12*JF + Month) − 614)//10 + Day + 365*Y
        + Y//4 − Y//100 + Y//400 + 1721089.
```

The routine days simply calculates the day number for each of the dates by using the routine day and returns the difference. The routine day shows the value of computing intermediate results, such as JF and Y, that are used in several places. The style is reminiscent of assignments in an imperative language such as Pascal though it must be remembered that the same variable cannot be reassigned to a different value.

The day routine performs no checks on the dates for validity. Possible code is shown in the predicate checkDate, which both checks and returns the date in internal format (Program 2.1). This code illustrates several aspects of programming in Prolog. The exceptional case of the leap day, February 29, is dealt with in a separate clause so that it can be ignored in the general case. Years in the range 0–99 are given a 19 prefix. The call to checkDate might use any of the forms:

```
?- checkDate(92, Month, 28, feb, Date)
    Month = 2, Date = date(1992,2,28)
?- checkDate(1992, 2, 28, MonthName, Date)
    Monthname = feb, Date = date(1992,2,28)
?- checkDate(Y,M,D,MN, date(1992,2,28))
    Y = 1992, M = 2, D = 28, MN = feb
?- checkDate(1992, 2, 28, feb, date(1992,2,28))
    yes
```

where the variables shown are unbound at the time of the call. Because the first thing checkMonth does is to call month, the unbound variable which is either Month or MonthName will immediately be given a value. At the same time these are checked for validity. The call will fail if what is given is out of range.

The third form of query requires an extra check integer on the year parameter in the second clause of checkYear. Though this can be considered as an arithmetic predicate we are using it for a slightly different reason, which will be introduced in a later section. Integer has the property that it will fail

Program 2.1 Code for the predicate checkDate.

```
checkDate(29,2,Year, feb, date(Y,Month,Day)) :-
    checkYear(Year, Y),
    leap(Y).
checkDate(Year, Month, Day, Name, date(Y,Month,Day)) :-
    month(Month,Name,Days),
    Day = <Days,
    checkYear(Year, Y).

checkYear(Y, Y) :-
    integer (Year),
    Y> = 100.
checkYear(Year, Y) :-
    integer(Year),
    Year> =0, Year<100,
    Y is 1900+Year.

month(1, jan, 31). month(2, feb, 28).
month(3, mar, 31). month (4, apr, 30).
month(5, may, 31). month(6, jun, 30).
month(7, jul, 31). month(8, aug, 31).
month(9, sep, 30). month(10, oct, 31).
month(11, nov, 30). month(12, dec, 31).

leap(Year) :- Year mod 4 =:= 0, Year mod 10 =\= 0.
leap(Year) :- Year mod 400 =:= 0.
```

if its parameter is unbound (or not an integer). If it was not included, the comparison Year> =0 could produce an error message, if Year does not have a value at this point. In the first clause this does not matter as the two parameters would already have been unified at this point.

Note the use of '=:=' and '=\=' in the definition of *leap*. These evaluate their arguments as arithmetic expressions and compare them for equality. They are thus different to the '=' and '\=' pair which test unification (and also to the '==' and '\==' pair which test identity – see below). One can write comparisons with a fixed number as, for instance, 0 is Year mod 400, where the result of the expression on the right is unified with the constant on the left, but the style of the expressions shown is better.

The sensible place to use a validity check for dates is in the conversion of an external date into internal form. As a final exercise we give the routine 'dateForm' below. This demonstrates the use of arithmetic operators as data constructors. It will take dates written as 25/12/92, 25/dec/1992 and 92-12-25 and convert them all to date(1992,12,25). In these expressions the '/' and '-' are simply data constructors and have no connection with the division or subtraction operators.

To handle both American and European styles of writing dates, there is another parameter, which should be bound to us, euro. If it is *not* bound it would allow a genuine ambiguity in dates such as 2/1/93, and that is not the purpose of nondeterminism in Prolog, though one might use it sensibly at a higher level.

```
%dateForm(External_form, Country, Internal_form)
dateForm(Day/MonthName/Year, euro, Date):-        %European
    checkMonth(Year, Month, Day, MonthName, Date).
dateForm(MonthName/Day/Year, us, Date) :-         %U.S.
    checkMonth(Year, Month, Day, MonthName, Date).
dateForm(Day/Month/Year, euro, Date) :-
    checkMonth(Year, Month, Day, _, Date).
dateForm(Day/Month/Year, us, Date) :-
    checkMonth(Year, Month, Day, _, Date).
dateForm(Year-Month-Day, _, Date) :-
    checkMonth(Year, Month, Day, _, Date).
```

2.4.4   Space allocation and garbage collection

Because of unification, the Prolog programmer often does not know whether a particular pattern is analysing an existing term or creating a new one. Therefore the responsibility for the allocation and deallocation of space is cast back on the designers of the Prolog system, whether they like it or not.

It is in fact an opportunity for the designer. Because the user never manipulates a pointer explicitly a discipline can be established for the use of pointers on which the compiler can depend. The very few fundamental data types in the language mean that a tagged architecture can be employed very efficiently which gives all the information necessary for both unification and garbage collection – the deletion of objects to which reference can no longer be made.

Prolog implementations are based round a series of stacks which correspond to the likely lifetime of the object. For example, information relating to the evaluation of a procedure will have a shorter life than the data structures that those procedures create. Therefore much of the allocated space can be discarded without the time-consuming necessity of examining every location to determine whether another cell is pointing at it. This does not completely obviate the need for a garbage collector, which most Prolog systems make available either automatically or on user request, but it substantially reduces the overhead caused when the garbage collector is run.

Prolog is thus uniquely powerful in an area which causes a great deal of discussion in object-oriented circles, where consideration is usually limited to the desirability and costs of automatic garbage collection and does not consider automatic space *allocation*. Unfortunately, this does not mean that it is more efficient in its use of space than special purpose data structures designed by a programmer. Prolog is certainly *more* hungry for space than most programming languages (with the probable exception of LISP). But it does relieve the programmer of one of the more time-consuming and error-prone preoccupations of programming. As memory prices continue to fall, the temporary use of memory is becoming less crucial.

Summary

- A compound term has a functor with arguments, written in the same way as a predicate, acting as a data constructor.
- Unification applies to atomic and compound terms recursively.
- Prolog unification does not normally include the occur check.
- Lists, written [a,b,c], and arithmetic expressions such as $-A+2*B$ are simply convenient notations for compound terms.
- Arithmetic expressions are evaluated by the is predicate and certain others such as '$>$'.
- Space allocation and deallocation is handled automatically by the Prolog system.

2.5   Recursion and iteration

So far none of the programs considered can ever fail to terminate. They may succeed or fail, or, as with the arithmetic predicates, produce an error message and terminate early. But they cannot fail to produce a result and head into an indeterminate loop from which they may or may not emerge. Any computationally complete language has this somewhat maddening property. In this section we examine the way in which Prolog programs express repetitive actions.

In most programming languages, repetition is introduced in terms of an activity that continues until some condition occurs which stops it. If we want to sum a series of numbers, we start with the first, add the next and continue till we have reached the last.

In a declarative language, repetition is seen primarily as breaking down a task into simpler subtasks. This is easiest to appreciate with repetitive data structures, such as the list. Consider the task of summing the elements of a list such as [4, 7, 15]. This may be pictured as the data structure in Figure 2.5.

The task of summing the list marked *a* is more complicated than summing the list marked *b* while summing the list *c* is almost trivial. Thus one can in general sum a list by adding the first number to the number which is the sum of the rest of the list. In Prolog this would be represented as a binary predicate: for example, sumList(List, Sum), and the rule for this is composed by a mixture of pattern matching and delegation. If the first element

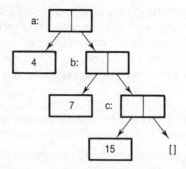

Figure 2.5   Data structure for the list [4, 7, 15].

is X and the sum of the rest of the list is S, then the sum of the whole list is X + S.

```
sumList([X | Xs], Sum) :-
    sumList(Xs, S),
    Sum is X + S.
```

Here the pattern [X|Xs] is used both to split the list and to assign the variables X and Xs. The addition is placed after the delegated call to sumList to conform with the left-to-right evaluation order of Prolog, so that S is bound before the arithmetic is performed.

This clause applies to all the lists in the diagram except the last. How do we deal with a simple list? Two representations are possible – a one element or a zero element list – both of which can be stated as simple facts:

```
sumList([X], X).
sumList([], 0).
```

We don't need both and the second is rather more general than the first, though less efficient, as it will return a sensible result even if the original argument to sumList is the empty list. It is therefore usually preferred. The combination of the first and third clauses give us a complete *recursive* definition of sumList.

Such recursive definitions are the only method of defining iteration in Prolog and they always have a similar pattern: one or more *base cases* which are either facts or rules which call other predicates, and one or more *recursive cases* where the body of the rule contains a call to the predicate being defined (or possibly a second predicate which in turn calls the first).

```
base case:          sumList([], 0).
recursive case:     sumList([X | Xs], Sum) :-
                        sumList(Xs, S),
                        Sum is X + S.
```

If we execute this predicate and print out the proof as an indented tree it is easy to see the pattern as it is built up:

```
sumList([4,7,15], 26) :-
sumList([7,15],22) :-
    sumList([15],15) :-
        sumList([],0)        fact
        15 is 15 + 0         built-in
        22 is 7 + 15         built-in
    26 is 4 + 22             built-in
```

Every time a predicate is invoked in this way it uses a different set of variables so there is no confusion between the different levels: each is a separate computation.

Many recursive definitions are composed in a similar way by taking specific cases of the data structure. The composition of new structures can be combined with the analysis of existing structures. For example, joining together two lists to form one long list is a very basic routine for list processing which can be expressed in this way. The base case occurs when one of the lists is the nil list and the result is simply the other list. The recursive case builds a new list from the first element of the first list and the result of joining the rest of this list to the other. The routine is as follows:

```
%append(List1, List2, List3)
%      List3 is the concatenation of List1 and List2
append([], A, A).
append([A | B], C, [A | D]) :- append(B,C,D).
```

And the proof of a typical invocation of this routine:

```
append([a,b,c],[1,2,3],[a,b,c,1,2,3]) :-
append([b,c],[1,2,3],[b,c,1,2,3]) :-
    append([c],[1,2,3],[c,1,2,3]) :-
        append([], [1,2,3], [1,2,3])      fact
```

Because the analysis of the existing pattern and the building up of the new one use exactly the same operations it is impossible to deduce from the proof what was the original query. It is tempting to assume that it was:

```
?-append([a,b,c],[1,2,3], X).
```

but in fact it could have been any of the following queries, or even some others:

```
?-append([a,b,c], X, [a,b,c,1,2,3]).          1
?-append(X, [1,2,3], [a,b,c,1,2,3]).          2
?-append([X,Y,Z], A, [a,b,c,1,2,3]).          3
?-append(X, [1,2 | Y], [a,b,c,1,2,3]).        4
?-append(X, Y, [a,b,c,1,2,3]).                5
```

In other words, the same append routine can be used to join two lists together, remove the first (1) or last (2) part of a list, find the first three items (3), search a list for a given sequence (4) or break apart a list in all possible ways (5). And all for the price of one definition!

With the last method of use illustrated (5), the indicated solution is only one of many possible solutions. Here are all of them, in the order they would be generated:

```
append([], [a,b,c,1,2,3], [a,b,c,1,2,3])
append([a], [b,c,1,2,3], [a,b,c,1,2,3])
append([a,b], [c,1,2,3], [a,b,c,1,2,3])
append([a,b,c], [1,2,3], [a,b,c,1,2,3])
append([a,b,c,1], [2,3], [a,b,c,1,2,3])
append([a,b,c,1,2], [3], [a,b,c,1,2,3])
append([a,b,c,1,2,3], [], [a,b,c,1,2,3])
```

All of these queries are 'well-behaved' in the sense that the query terminates properly when all solutions have been explored. But it is unfortunately possible to make queries that do not terminate. For example:

```
?-append(X, [1,2,3], Y).
```

and here are the first few solutions:

```
append([], [1,2,3], [1,2,3])
append([_1], [1,2,3], [_1,1,2,3])
append([_1,_2], [1,2,3], [_1,_2,1,2,3])
append([_1,_2,_3], [1,2,3], [_1,_2,_3,1,2,3])
append([_1,_2,_3,_4], [1,2,3], [_1,_2,_3,_4,1,2,3])
    ...
```

Each of these solutions is effectively a template which incorporates all the possible lists of a given length which end in [1,2,3]. But there are still an infinite number of possibilities. Eventually the Prolog machine will run out of space and stop, and this might even happen before one's patience is exhausted.

If we analyse these patterns it can be seen that for a successful termination, either the first or the last argument of append must be sufficiently bound. The state of the second argument serves only as a check in the case of the third argument being bound.

A convenient notation has arisen to describe these 'modes' as they are called. If an argument must be bound a '+' is put at the argument position. If it should be unbound then '−' is used, and if it can be either, then '?' is written. So the required modes for append to terminate satisfactorily may be specified as append(+,?,?) or append(?,?,+). These may also be combined with the names of types as in append(+list,?list,?list). '−' is rarely used except to specify modes to compilers that can take advantage of such annotations to produce optimal code.

Despite the power of recursion, many programmers instinctively avoid its use because of its inevitable inefficiency in building new storage space on the stack for each iteration. So some might ask why there is no iterative notation in Prolog to permit extra efficiency. The surprising answer to this question is that it isn't necessary! In situations where the code is *actually* iterative, a good Prolog compiler will generate iterative code that does not build a new stack frame for each step around the loop but reuses the same registers. This is known as tail recursion.

Append is the classic example of this. Its main 'loop', the clause:

```
append([A | B], C, [A | D]) :- append(B,C,D).
```

has the vital property that the recursive call is the last call in the body of the procedure – in fact it is the only call. When it is executed, the other variables will no longer be required and an interpreter or a compiler can optimize their behaviour significantly. Some systems will only optimize if, in addition, it is the last clause of the predicate.

In example (5) of append, where it is used nondeterministically, some of this gain is offset by the need to store a 'choice point' internally. But this does not usually lead to the explosive use of storage which is suggested by recursion since much of the local storage can be reused.

It is sometimes necessary to rephrase a program to take advantage of tail recursion. A typical example is the program 'sumList' used earlier. This is *not* tail recursive because the addition takes place after the recursive call so it is necessary to build a stack internally to hold the intermediate values which were illustrated in the proof tree.

What is required is to have not just one parameter for the answer but two. The extra parameter accumulates the partial answer as the recursion is done (and so is normally called an *accumulator*) and at the end it is unified with the real answer parameter. An extra 'encapsulation' call is required to start it off with an initial value. The code is as shown:

```
sumList(List, Length) :-
    sumList1(List, 0, Length).

sumList1([], L, L).
sumList1([A | B], Partial, Answer) :-
    Accumulate is Partial + A,
    sumList1(B, Accumulate, Answer).
```

It is worth noting that although this is an optimization, it still has a 'declarative' reading.

```
sumList1(A,B,C) is true if the length of list A plus the
    number B equals C
```

If the proof of this computation is listed one can easily see the difference from the recursive version as the recursive call is always last:

```
sumList([4,7,15], 26) :-
        sumList1([4,7,15],0,26) :-
            4 is 0 + 4,                           built-in
        sumList1([7,15],4, 26) :-
            11 is 4 + 7,                          built-in
            sumList1([15],11,26) :-
                26 is 11 + 15,                    built-in
                sumList1([],26,26)                fact
```

It is sometimes suggested that these optimization techniques are against the spirit of logic programming. Certainly it will be be easier when compilers have advanced to the point that they are performed automatically, because they do obscure the point of the program. But each programming paradigm has its special techniques and Prolog is no exception. It's better to learn these properly than find that the tool is useless because, for example, a vital program always runs out of space.

Summary

- The ability of a procedure to call itself is the basis of all iterative programs in Prolog.

- Recursive definitions often will only terminate satisfactorily for specific *modes* of use, which may be represented by '+', '−' and '?'.

- Efficient recursive programs have the recursive call as the last call in the clause.

2.6   Negation and the cut

There is one type of logical construct that is inexpressible in the language that we have so far presented, which is the language of pure Horn clauses. If we want to make something depend on the negation of another condition we simply cannot do it.

Let us take a simple example. Suppose we are dealing with people and wish to refer to their gender. Then we want to ensure that a person is designated either as male or female. If we simply record the facts as:

```
male(bert).      person(bert).
female(jill).    person(jill)
male(fred).      person(fred).
```

then we run the risk of recording someone as both male and female. This might lead to some curious deductions! What we want to do is to make the statement: a person is either male or female but not both. This might be expressed in the full 'clausal form' of logic as:

```
male(X) ; female(X) :- person(X).
:- male(X), female(X).
```

The first statement says that any person is either male or female (the ';' is the Prolog version of 'or'); the second may be read as a denial that there is anyone who is both male and female. Neither of these statements are valid positive Horn clauses (though they are valid first-order clauses).

One possibility is to use them as checks on our programs to ensure that any person was recorded as male or female, with no one recorded as both. But as program statements they are potentially explosive (and even nonterminating) operations and are therefore not allowed for a programming language such as Prolog.

An alternative approach is to record only one gender and deduce the other as a default if the gender is not stated. In this case, consistency is always maintained: a person will be one or the other, but not both.

This can easily be incorporated in our proof procedure: if we fail to prove something then we assert that it is not true, or in other words that it is false. This involves the assumption that we have stated all there is to know about the issue in question.

This implementation of negation is incorporated into most Prolog systems by a predicate called '\+' – which can be read as 'not provable'. (\ for not, + for provable). (Many systems know the same predicate by the name 'not'. The distinction between \+ and *not* will be discussed below.) It is declared as a prefix operator so there is no need to surround its arguments with brackets.

We can therefore restate the gender information above by one fact and one rule:

```
female(jill).

male(X) :- person(X), \+ female(X).
```

Here are some sample queries with this database:

```
?- male(bert).
yes
?-male(jill).
no
?-male(joe).
no
?-male(X).
X = bert;
X = fred;
no
```

The last query shows why it is important to include the proposition person(X) in the clause for male. If it wasn't there, the clause would have an entirely different effect when the parameter is not bound to a value on entry: it would fail and mislead us into thinking that there were no known males. To follow this, we need to follow the computation step by step assuming person(X) is absent, that is, we have the clause:

```
male(X) :- \+ female(Y).
```

Let us draw this out as a nested query:

```
male(X)
    \+ female(X)
        female(X)      % succeed with X=jill
            fail \+    % because female(X) succeeded
    fail male(X)
```

Conversely, if there were no recorded female the result would be true for any X. The meaning of this use of the clause is thus 'X is male if there is no known female'.

The proposition person(X) in the original version acts as a *generator* for candidates to the negated proposition and this constraint is exactly the same as that used in database systems which allow negative constraints. There must be a generator for each variable used in a negative clause to ensure that it is bound in the call.

A proper negation in Prolog must therefore check that no variables are instantiated by the computation that is within the negated part. With this condition *negation as failure* has been added to the theory of Horn clauses as a theoretically sound notion, yielding a theory which is referred to technically as SLDNF – Linear resolution with Selection function for Definite clauses, augmented by the Negation as Failure rule. This can be incorporated into Prolog (as for example in NU-Prolog) by suspending the strict left-to-right evaluation order if an unbound variable is found in a negated goal, but this is not yet widely practised.

The \+ predicate does not incorporate this check – that is historically why it is *not* called 'not' – so the programmer must be careful not to use it in invalid ways.

The main reason for this omission is that negation is built on top of an earlier and more machine-oriented feature, the **cut** – normally written as '!' – which was introduced to avoid unwanted backtracking. Unlike negation, which has a well-defined declarative meaning, the cut can only be understood in terms of the Prolog proof procedure. To consider its effect let us consider a toy database, which contains a single cut in the first clause:

```
lucky(Y) :- generous(X), !, likes(X,Y).
lucky(X) :- content(X).
```

```
generous(adrian). generous(bill).

likes(bill,adrian).
likes(adrian,cheryl). likes(adrian,david).

content(edwin). content(frank).

happy(X) :- lucky(X).
happy(X) :- generous(X).
```

In the *absence* of the cut symbol we would get the following set of answers to the open query lucky(P):

```
?- lucky(P).
P = cheryl;
P = david;
P = adrian;
P = edwin;
P = frank;
no
```

The cut commits the system to any choices made since the *parent* of the clause in which the cut appears was invoked, in this case lucky. So it has two effects: the other clause for lucky is not examined, and any subsequent solutions of goals earlier in the clause are also discarded. The solutions edwin and frank disappear because of the first; the solution adrian (who is liked by bill who is generous) because of the second. So if we query the stated program, we will simply get the response:

```
?- lucky(P).
P = cheryl;
P = david;
no
```

It is important to note which parts of the computation are discarded and which are retained. The part *after* the cut can still return multiple solutions (david was not lost), and any higher level computations are unaffected. For instance, happy which calls lucky can still derive solutions from *its* second clause:

```
?- happy(X).
P = cheryl;
P = david;
P = adrian;
P = bill;
no
```

It may appear from these examples that all the cut can do is to reduce the number of possible solutions. This is not the case. Consider the following definition of male:

```
male(X) :- female(X), !, fail.
male(X).
```

Fail is a proposition which has no definition and therefore is bound to fail (but it does not cause any 'unknown predicate' traps). So if there is a definition of female that matches, the query fails but the second clause is not tried; if there is not, the cut will never be reached and the second clause takes over, always succeeding. So the execution of the second clause is conditional on the failure of the test before the cut. The combination of cut and a failing predicate inverts the whole logic of the program and introduces the possibility of negation. This is precisely the 'not provable' behaviour of the \+ operator.

Cut is a powerful operator which is in many ways the analogue of the 'goto' in conventional languages: to give an account of its behaviour one has to trace through the action of the program. So 'Cut considered harmful' is a commonplace warning of logic programming in the same manner as Dijkstra's famous 'Goto considered harmful'. It is very easy to obscure the meaning of a Prolog program by abuse of the cut.

The remedy is also reminiscent of the remedies for the goto: wrap it up in other control constructs (for example, if-then-else and while) which have a more controlled meaning, even though their implementation is pragmatic. Avoid its direct use wherever possible. One of these constructs we have already seen – negation. We will briefly consider two more: conditionals and single solutions.

We often need to find only a **single solution** to a problem which may have many. This may be either because we only need to know that a solution exists (the existential quantifier of logic) or that any one solution is as good as any other. The operator 'one' written before a predicate achieves this purpose:

```
?- one male(X).
X = bert;
no
```

The effect is the same as placing the call in a clause by itself with a cut after it, but is often different from placing the cut in the same clause as the call (because this may cut more things) and is far preferable to placing a cut in every clause of the original predicate. This is called 'once' in some Edinburgh versions of Prolog, but does not appear in other recent versions (such as Quintus). The name 'one' is that used by MacProlog. It can be simulated in Quintus using –> (see below).

The single solution operator cannot be expressed in either Horn clauses or simply by use of negation, but it has not yet received the theoretical treatment given to negation as failure.

A **conditional** is written:

```
test  ->  then_branch ; else_branch
```

and the binding power of each branch is lower than that of the comma, so if it is introduced within a clause it must be bracketed using (). Here is a simple example:

```
retire(X, Age) :- female(X)  ->  Age = 65 ; Age = 70.
```

In this case the effect is identical to the following two clauses:

```
retire(X, 65) :- one female(X)
retire(X, 70) :- \+ female(X).
```

which expresses the same information using negation, but has the disadvantage that it is necessary to write and evaluate male(X) twice, or

```
retire(X, Age) :- female(X), !, Age = 65.
retire(X, 70).
```

which uses the cut directly. Note that in all cases at most one solution of female will be found, even if X is unbound at entry.

There is the possibility of a subtle bug in the version using the cut which explains why we have used the equality predicate in the first clause. It is tempting to write this version as follows:

```
retire(X, 65) :- female(X), !.      %incorrect
retire(X, 70).
```

but consider what happens when we pose the query

```
?- retire(jill, 70).
```

assuming that jill is defined as female. The first clause fails to unify and the second clause succeeds! Take care with the cut! The equivalent of this bug appears as an example in several Prolog textbooks.

Conditionals can be written without the 'else' part, or cascaded to give a number of options. In the first case, one needs to consider what happens if the test fails. The answer can only be sensibly given by considering the second. Suppose we have a series of tests:

```
test1 -> body1
; test2 -> body2
; test3 -> body3
```

Then the right hand side is evaluated only for the *first* left hand side match. If no left hand side matches, the whole construct fails. Thus a single $->$ simply has the effect of limiting to one the number of solutions of the test. In other words

```
goal1, (goal2 -> goal3)
```

has exactly the same effect as

```
goal1, one goal2, goal3
```

(Note that we have to be careful in this case about bracketing. If the brackets were left out then multiple solutions of goal1 would also be eliminated.)

For this reason, $->$ is often called a 'soft cut', because it has half the effect of a cut. It has the advantage of being an effect strictly local to the clause and it removes the theoretical requirement for one or once.

The tendency to extra use of the equality symbol is a definite drawback to the conditional. Consider the two almost equivalent definitions:

```
f(a,b).
f(b,c).
f(c,a).
```

and

```
f(X,Y) :-
        X = a -> Y = b
      ; X = b -> Y = c
      ; X = c -> Y = a.
```

The first is a lot clearer, and can be used in both 'directions' (for example, to compute f(b,X) and f(X,b)) whereas the second is limited to one use. On the whole, programs with separate clauses are often the neatest, despite the repetitions contained in them. The clauses are then separate and independent of each other and this encourages error-free programming.

The proper use of the four primitives – negation, cut, one-solution and conditional – is a delicate question of style for which it is hard to give definitive rules. Examples in the rest of the book will attempt to give illustrations.

Summary

- Negated goals may be used in Prolog programs by preceding the goal with the \+ symbol.

- An unbound variable in a negated goal introduces the effect of an existential quantifier, and should generally be avoided.

- The *cut* predicate (written '!') allows a clause to ignore both remaining clauses for the predicate and alternative solutions for goals already evaluated within that clause.

- One-solution and conditional constructs can often be used in place of the cut to write programs not expressible in pure Horn clauses.

2.7   Metaprograms

A 'meta'-something is a 'something' that refers to an entity of the same sort as itself. Thus a metaprogram is a program that refers to a program. Because Prolog is a symbolic language, this is conceptually very easy and many of the most powerful programs are conceived this way. This section will only outline the basic tools available for metaprogramming and give a few simple examples.

'"Jack" is a four letter word' – this is not a statement about Jack, but rather about the word that names Jack. Careful usage avoids paradox by using quotation marks to separate out the target words. But it is not always easy to detect – even in a computer language – what is language and what is metalanguage. Are type predicates logical or metalogical for example?

Before we can explain the 'how' of metaprogramming, we need to introduce a number of the predefined predicates that occur in most Prolog systems. We will distinguish a number of different predicates:

(1)   Term inspection – giving information
(2)   Term manipulation – changing terms
(3)   Database inspection and Metacall

2.7.1   Term inspection

Since Prolog is a typeless language, one needs a number of predefined predicates to be able to distinguish between the different predefined types. In fact, this number is very small, since there are no arrays, character or string types and all records are built up from compound terms. Table 2.1 shows the essential list.

Some of these term inspection predicates shown in Table 2.1 – mainly those after the first group – are definitely metalogical: the most obvious is var. Var refers not to the value of a term but to its current state. Thus the predicate assign below will succeed if and only if its argument is initially a

Table 2.1   Term inspection predicates.

atom(X)	X is currently a symbolic term of arity 0
atomic(X)	X is currently an atom or a number
compound(X)	X is currently a term of arity greater than 0
integer(X)	X is currently an integer
float(X)	X is currently a floating point number
number(X)	X is currently a number (integer or float)
var(X)	X is currently a variable
nonvar(X)	X is not currently a variable – bound to some term
X = = Y	X is an identical term to Y (variables match)
X\ = = Y	X is not identical to Y
X@ < Y, X@ = < Y, X@ > = Y,	X is before Y in the standard ordering (and so on)
X@ > Y	

variable, but the final test atom (which is mutually exclusive of var) will then also succeed.

      assign(Var) :- var(Var), Var = foo, atom(Var).

Table 2.2 provides some sample results of these to clarify doubtful cases. In all of these, the argument will normally be a variable bound to the value indicated. An unbound variable is signified by X.

The main purpose of the term ordering predicates is to provide a unique ordering for any two terms in a Prolog program. The '= =' predicate would better be called '@ =' because it belongs with the other term ordering predicates. They are needed for many practical purposes, such as sorting, in order to delete duplicates in a set. So the arguments can be atoms, numbers or arbitrary terms which may include unbound variables. The actual ordering is not significant, though it is sensible. Thus the major ordering is for the type (integers and floats are different), and the minor ordering varies with the type. For numbers it is arithmetic; for atoms lexicographic; for terms it is first for the primary functor (including arity) then (recursively) for the arguments. For variables the order is entirely machine dependent. The only requirement is that the ordering of particular variables does not change during the course of execution.

So the '= =' or *identity* predicate applied to two variables tests that they are bound to the same location, even if they are different variables. In other words if one is subsequently instantiated the other will be too. But it *never* binds any variables itself; this is what makes it different to '=' which often does instantiate its arguments. The same terms tested subsequently might produce a different ordering if the instantiation has changed. If you know LISP, then '= =' is more liberal than 'eq' and much the same as 'equal', because variables bound together will print the same.

Table 2.2　Sample results of inspection predicates.

True	True	False
atom(foo)	integer(−3)	atom(3)
atom(=)	float(42.3e−14)	atom(f(a))
atom('(')	number(4)	atom(X)
atom([|])	var(X)	compound([])
atomic(3)	nonvar(a)	number(X)
compound(a(1,2))	nonvar(a(X,Y))	nonvar(X)
compound([1,2])	atom('X')	float(X)
compound('abc')	ab@<abc	float(e)
X==X	4@<3.2	a(1,X)==a(1,2)
a(X,b(Y))==a(X,b(Y))	33@<a	abc@>cde
X\==Y	a(1,2)@<a(1,3)	
a(b, c(D))\==a(b,c(E))	a(2)@<a(1,2)	

2.7.2　Term manipulation

The routines in Table 2.3 provide the basic facilities for analysing or composing arbitrary terms in Prolog. Unlike var they don't change the theoretical capabilities of the language, because for any particular program one could provide a set of assertions that performed the same operation (though this isn't true when we consider side-effects such as input). But they do provide very powerful facilities for manipulating symbolic terms.

All of these routines can be used in two ways. For example, functor can be used on an existing term, or to create one:

```
functor(a(b), X, Y).
X=a, Y=1
?- functor(T, a, 2).
T=a(_1, _2)
```

The term that results is a skeleton which is the most general term compatible with the description. Table 2.4 clarifies some of the less obvious examples. Note: Entries in italics are true in some Prologs such as MacProlog, which has a somewhat extended view of what is a term.

Table 2.3　Term manipulation predicates.

functor(T,F,N)	T is a term with functor F and arity N
arg(N,T,A)	The Nth argument of term T is A
T=..L	L is a list of the functor and arguments of term T
name(A,L)	L is a list of the character codes of the atom A

Table 2.4 Sample results of term manipulation predicates.

True	True	False
functor(f(1,2), f, 2)	arg(2,a(2,3),3)	functor(X,1,0)
functor([1]), ., 2)	arg(1, [2,3], 2)	functor(X,a(Y),1)
functor(a, a, 0)	arg(2, [2,3], [3])	functor(X, a, Y)
functor([], [], 0)	name(abc, 'abc')	
a(1,b(2)) = ..[a,1,b(2)]	name(abc,[97,98,99])	arg(1, a, X)
foo = ..[foo]	name(12,[49,50])	

The arg and functor routines can be used to simulate arrays as long as the algorithms used adhere to a 'once-only assignment' rule. Table 2.5 shows the approximate equivalents between the use of arrays in Pascal and Prolog.

As an illustration that such algorithms can be used, Program 2.2 is the classic benchmark 'Eratosthenes Sieve' used as a test of BASIC systems by the magazine *Byte*. It computes the number of prime numbers in the first N odd numbers starting with 3 by setting all the primes to have the value p and all the composite numbers to c. A simple execution gives the result:

```
?- sieve(10, A, B)
A = 7, B = sieve(p, p, p, c, p, p, c, p, p, c)
```

This algorithm works surprisingly well because it never requires the content of the array to be changed once it is fixed. Using arrays for other activities, such as sorting, is not appropriate in Prolog. In these cases, other data structures, such as lists, are usually more appropriate.

There is no string or character type in Edinburgh Prologs but there is a notation for **strings**, using double quotes, which is treated internally as a list of small integers. Thus "abc" is treated identically to the list of integers [97,98,99], where the numbers correspond normally to the ASCII representation of the character. So 'abc' is an atom and "abc" is a list.

Conversions between one representation and the other can be performed by using the **name** predicate. It can be used in either direction – to break an atom or a number into its components, or to construct a new

Table 2.5 Approximate equivalents between the use of arrays in Pascal and Prolog.

Pascal	Prolog
a: array[1..100] of integer	functor(T, a, 100)
a[4]	arg(4, T, X)
a[4]: = 5	arg(4, T, 5)

Program 2.2   Sieve.

```
%sieve(N, T, A) generates an array term A of length N of
% odd numbers starting at 3 which includes a total of
% T prime numbers
sieve(N, Total, Array) :-
    functor(Array,sieve,N),       %creates an array
    prune( 1, N, 3, Array, 0, Total).


%prune(A,B,C,D,E,F) marks the A'th element as prime and
% steps by C up to B in array D producing a total of
% F primes, using the current total of E
prune(N,Max,Step,Array,Total,Total):-
    N>Max, !.
prune(N,Max,Step,Array,Tot,Total):-
    arg(N,Array,p), !,                % we have a prime
    Next is N+1,
    Nextmul is Step+N,
    mark(Nextmul,Max,Step,Array),     %set multiples to 0
    Newstep is Step+2,
    Newtot is Tot+1,
    prune(Next,Max,Newstep,Array,Newtot,Total).
prune(N,Max,Step,Array,Tot,Total):-
    Next is N+1,
    Newstep is Step+2,
    prune(Next,Max,Newstep,Array,Tot,Total).


%mark(A,B,C,D) marks as composite every C'th element in
% array D until B starting at A
mark(N,Max,Step,Array) :-
    N>Max, !.
mark(N,Max,Step,Array) :-
    arg(N,Array,c), %set to c for composite if not yet
    Next is N+Step,
    mark(Next,Max,Step,Array).
```

atom or number. Thus the following queries all work:

```
?- name('a b', X).
X=[97,32,98]
?- name(X, [97,98,99]).
X=abc
?- name(12, X).
X=[49,50]
?- name(X, [49,48]).
X=10
```

The last query may be somewhat of a surprise. If name can make sense of a list of character equivalents as a number, then it produces a number, otherwise it produces an atom. The fact that one cannot depend on name to produce an atom makes it rather tricky to use, though it is very convenient in some applications.

2.7.3   Database inspection and metacall

The set of clauses which makes the program may be regarded as a database. Apart from the theoretical distinction between predicates and terms there is a practical distinction. Predicates are normally stored in the database in a compiled form, so that the symbolic form may be unrecoverable. But the value of recovering the symbolic form was demonstrated in early implementations of Prolog which were interpreters. So most Prolog systems support the predefined predicate clause at least for some compilation methods, if not all. There is often some performance penalty, but the benefits, for instance when debugging, will offset this.

The converse operation is taking a term and evaluating this as a predicate. In most Prolog systems this can be expressed simply by placing a variable (which must be bound at runtime) in place of a predicate in the clause, but we will follow the normal implementation practice of using a predefined predicate call which takes a single term as argument (Table 2.6).

A program clause p :- q,r corresponds to a term whose primary functor is :-, and the conjunction q,r has , as its primary functor. This creates some difficulty for the syntax of Prolog which also uses , to separate arguments to a function. To distinguish the two it is necessary to use an extra set of brackets when one of the operators ,, :-, ; and –> is used as a term. The clause could therefore be written :-(p, (q,r)) or :-(p, ','(q,r)). In the last form, the quotes around the comma are also necessary to avoid ambiguities in the syntax.

A call to clause must instantiate the first parameter. It cannot be used to search the entire database. If what is recovered is a fact, then the second parameter is bound to the atom true. For example,

```
?- clause(sumList(A,B), C).
A=[], B=0, C=true;
A=[_1 | _2], B=_3, C=(sumList(_2,_4), _3 is _1+_4);
no
```

With these primitives it is possible to write a simple meta-interpreter for Prolog. The point of writing meta-interpreters is to be able to do more

Table 2.6   Database inspection and metacall predicates.

clause(H, B)	A clause in the database has head H and body B
call(A)	The term A is executed as a predicate
findall(T, G, L)	L is the list of all terms T formed by all possible executions of the goal G

than the basic Prolog machine. We will illustrate this by generating a proof of a computation of the type already illustrated in this chapter.

The simplest possible interpreter is shown below. It takes two arguments: the first is the goal to be proved; the second is the proof of that goal. It comes down to three clauses corresponding to the possible cases:

```
provo(truc, true).
prove((A,B),(Pa,Pb)) :- prove(A,Pa), prove(B,Pb).
prove(A,(A:-Pb)) :- clause(A,B), prove(B,Pb).
```

This has two disadvantages. First, it will not run correctly on many Prolog systems! This is because it will attempt to apply clause to true and to ',' /2 which will yield an error message on many systems. Second, it will not run with programs which include calls to predefined predicates, including itself. To provide such an interpreter requires another predicate called system which succeeds for every term corresponding to a valid predefined predicate (most systems provide this with some name or other). At this point we can omit the clause for true since it is itself a system goal, and the meta-interpreter stays at three clauses:

```
prove((A,B),(Pa,Pb)) :- prove(A,Pa), prove(B,Pb).
prove(A, system(A)) :- system(A), A\=(_,_), call(A).
prove(A,(A:-Pb)) :- clause(A,B), prove(B,Pb).
```

Note: The \= predicate means 'not equals' and may simply be defined by: X\=X :- !, fail.

It should be noted that this does *not* allow any of the extra control structures discussed above (;, ->, ! and so on). In particular, it will produce incorrect answers if the cut is used. To write a meta-interpreter which handles the cut correctly is much more tricky.

An example execution follows, where the only tidying done on the output is to indent it. A program to do this will be presented in Section 2.8.

```
?- prove(sumList([4, 7, 15], X), Y)
X=26, Y=sumList([4, 7, 15], 26):-
   (sumList([7, 15], 22):-
    (sumList([15], 15):-
     (sumList([], 0):-system(true)),
     system(15 is 15+0)),
    system(22 is 7+15)),
   system(26 is 4+22)
```

The final metapredicate, findall, allows us to generate a list of all the solutions of an arbitrary goal, using a template to generate the form of items in the list. As an example, consider the employee database used earlier:

```
?- findall(X, employee(X, accounts), List).
List = [bert, fred].
```

In this case the first parameter is used in the query employee(X, accounts) which is repeatedly evaluated to find all the employees in the accounts department. The solutions are listed in the order they are found, including possible repetitions. (There is also a predicate which returns a proper set, called setof which has similar arguments. But it has several more subtle features that will not be explored here.)

The first argument can be any expression, so that the list can be composed of complex terms. For example, even if we hadn't defined the phone view of the database, we could generate a phone book with the query:

```
?- findall(P = F, (room(P, R), telephoneIn(R, F)), List).
List = [fred = 1033, fred = 2022, jean = 2034, bert = 6616].
```

In this case, = is simply used as a constructor for the term, and the query is constructed out of two queries using , as an operator standing for the *and*. The inner set of brackets are necessary to avoid this comma being taken for an argument separator.

Summary

- Many of the built-in primitives of Prolog are in fact metapredicates, because they talk about the program and its current state. Metapredicates allow terms to be inspected and dissected into their components and to be created from more primitive components.

- The call predicate, together with clause, allows for genuine metaprograms in Prolog, including the definition of Prolog interpreters.

2.8   Side-effects

One of the aims of declarative programming languages is to eliminate programs with side-effects. This means programs which change the state of the world in some way so that executing the same instruction again might have a different effect. While it is an excellent mathematical aim, there is one area where this philosophy falls down absolutely. As has often been said, the whole point of executing a program is to produce some output. Input is optional – some programs don't need any other than the program – but output of some form is essential. The output may be displayed on a screen, stored on the disk or it may only be deduced from the length of time the program takes to run, but the result of a program must be tangible.

Prolog takes a realistic view of the task of programming. In order to provide a practical programming language, one needs input and output and one needs to be able to change the state of the program. The changes that are made are global in effect, and that is worse than making local changes. But until we have something like an object-oriented language, there is no way we can resolve the issue.

2.8.1 Input/output

We only deal here with the simplest input/output (i/o), from a single input and to a single output channel. Unfortunately, as in most programming languages, i/o is by no means standardized in Prolog and facilities for manipulating files vary from system to system (Table 2.7).

The pair get0 and put operate on characters which are small integers as discussed in the previous section. (There is also a procedure get which will skip any nonprinting characters and return the first printing character. In the ISO draft (1993) get0 is called get_code.) Much more powerful are read and write which operate on complete Prolog terms, including all the operators. One thus has the complete Prolog 'reader' available, which considerably simplifies i/o programming.

As an example of printing, consider 'pretty printing' the proof generated by the program in the previous section. The main part is a simple case analysis of the possible patterns that appear in the proof.

```
printProof(X) :- printP(X,0), nl, nl.

printP(system(true), _) :- write(' fact').
printP(system(A),D) :- nl,tab(D),
    write(A),
    write(' system').
printP((A:-B), D) :- nl, tab(D),
    write(A), write(' :-'),
    D1 is D+3,
    printP(B,D1).
printP((A,B),D) :-
    printP(A,D),
    printP(B,D).
printP(A, D) :- nl, tab(D),
    write(A).
```

Table 2.7 Input/output predicates.

get0(C)	read next character from current input
nl	write a new line to the current output
put(C)	write character to current output
read(C)	read a term from the current input
tab(N)	write N spaces to the current output
write(C)	write a term to the current output

An example of the use of the printProof procedure on the proof produced earlier is reproduced below:

```
:-prove(sumList([4, 7, 15], X), Y),printProof(Y)
sumList([4, 7, 15], 26) :-
   sumList([7, 15], 22) :-
      sumList([15], 15) :-
         sumList([], 0) :- fact
            15 is 15+0 system
         22 is 7+15 system
      26 is 4+22 system
```

Write is a very powerful primitive, as it will print any Prolog term, including arithmetic operators and variables, and print the results in the proper expression format. Corresponding to it is the read primitive, which will read any valid Prolog term and convert it into internal form. This raises a practical problem: what is the end of a term? The answer is the same as for clauses: a period followed by a nonprinting character. In fact, the read predicate can read in any Prolog clause.

As a simple yet powerful example, consider the following definition of a calculator which will evaluate any arithmetic expression available in Prolog.

```
calculate :-
      write('Input an expression:'),
      read(Expression),
      call(Val is Expression),
      write(' -> '),
      write(Val),
      nl,
      calculate.

?- calculate.
Input an expression: 3.1+1.2.
->4.3
Input an expression: sqrt(3*3+4*4).
->5
```

It is thus easy to provide the effect of a LISP-like expression evaluator.

There are two non-obvious details of this program: the use of the call primitive before the evaluation of the is predicate. Some Prolog compilers will not allow a variable in an expression to the right of is to be bound to an expression. The use of call forces the whole term to be re-evaluated. Although this isn't necessary in many systems its presence doesn't cause problems.

The other detail is that there is no base-case to the program! The program never terminates. In fact, it will continue until it is interrupted in some other way – such as the use of an interrupt key. We could, of course, define a special term (such as quit) which would signal the termination of the program and handle this specially. But it is a characteristic of some i/o programs that they are intrinsically nonterminating. Instead of having a declarative 'meaning' they achieve their effect by means of side-effects – the data that is input and output.

One of the dangers of Prolog programming is to embed input/output statements deep within otherwise declarative programs. Not only does this make them far less flexible to use, but it makes debugging a lot harder. With declarative programs there are a number of powerful techniques which can locate and correct errors. Though these can be extended to programs with side-effects, they are not so convenient to use as they may require repeated evaluation of parts of a program.

Generally, it is better to try to keep i/o and algorithms separate: to allow programs with side-effects to call programs which are 'pure', but not vice-versa. This means that the most complex parts of the program can be tested and validated without a complex sequence of i/o operations. These themes will be taken up in later chapters.

2.8.2   Database manipulation

A more fundamental characteristic of Prolog is the ability to be able to change its own program, or database. The basic facilities are two predicates called assert and retract which add and delete clauses from the database respectively (Table 2.8).

As a simple example of the use of these facilities, let us suppose that we wish to print out the solutions of a problem omitting any duplicates that may occur. If the solutions are generated by backtracking, then keeping a list of the items so far printed in the database is the easiest way to keep track of them. We will keep the solutions as the argument of a predicate called pU and use the predicate printUnique to write out the value to the output. The first clause of printUnique simply checks the database using the clause primitive and if it finds the value it prevents the second clause being invoked by using a cut. The second clause prints out the value and asserts it at the front of the database. A second predicate clearUnique is provided

Table 2.8   Database manipulation predicates.

assert(C)	Add a clause to the database
asserta(C)	Add a clause to the database as the first clause
assertz(C)	Add a clause to the database as the last clause
retract(C)	Erase the first clause whose head matches C
abolish(N,A)	Remove the procedure with name N and arity A

to allow reuse of the predicate by 'forgetting' what was known.

```
printUnique(Value) :-
   clause(pU(Value),true), !.
printUnique(Value) :-
   write(Value), nl,
   asserta(pU(Value)).

clearUnique :-
   abolish(pU, 1).
```

Here is a sample database and a query that will cause all unique values to be printed.

```
a(adrian). a(bert). a(adrian). a(bert). a(cheryl). a(dave). a(dave).
?- a(X), printUnique(X), fail.
adrian
bert
cheryl
no
```

This query demonstrates a programming style that inevitably creeps in when side effects such as printing are permitted. The purpose of the call to 'fail' at the end is simply to force backtracking and thereby cause all the possible solutions of *a* to be generated. This query has no declarative reading at all – it is inevitably false.

This is another candidate for providing a more 'logical' equivalent and many systems provide a predicate called forall which will do the same thing better. It is a metapredicate which succeeds if all the instances generated by the goal which is the first argument succeed in the goal which is the second argument. For instance:

```
?- forall(a(X), printUnique(X)).
```

achieves the same effect as the previous illogical query. A simple definition for this predicate is:

```
forall(X,Y) :- \+ (call(X), \+ call(Y))
```

This example can be generalized to incorporate programs which generate the set of all solutions to a problem. The interested reader should consult a Prolog textbook for details.

These are such basic tools that there is a tendency to abuse them. For instance, they can be used to simulate global variables with values asserted and retracted when they should simply be passed as arguments to a procedure. Fortunately, Prolog has a built-in bias against this: assert and retract are relatively expensive operations and programs written this way are usually far less efficient than 'properly' written programs. The valid uses of assert tend to be those which accumulate intermediate results which are true. In other words, the database is used as a 'memo pad' or 'lemma list' to avoid repeating computations that have already been achieved. However, it takes the object-oriented paradigm to provide a better setting for side-effects, so we will not expand further on this aspect in the current chapter.

SUMMARY

This chapter has built up a full picture of Prolog in layers:

- Propositional logic, which demonstrates the basic declarative and procedural proof methods of Prolog, including multiple solutions and backtracking.
- The use of variables and their use in providing answers to queries.
- The use of compound terms, including function or record structures, lists and arithmetic expressions. Parameter matching from goal to head involves the notion of unification and this allows automatic space allocation of compound terms and requires garbage collection when it is no longer needed.
- Procedures can call themselves, and this provides the mechanism for iteration in Prolog. Many recursive programs can be executed in fixed space because of last-call optimization.
- Negation is only provided in the body of Prolog clauses and is interpreted as detecting the failure to prove a goal. It is implemented by means of a rather more general device called the cut, which can also be used to implement other control primitives.
- Metaprogramming is a powerful technique for writing programs which manipulate programs. A number of primitive predicates are provided in Prolog for this.
- The final layer of Prolog consists of built-in predicates which have side-effects. These are of two types: those that perform input/output and those which manipulate the Prolog database.

3

Declarative Prolog++ programming

3.1 Introduction

This chapter introduces the notion of 'pure' or 'declarative' object-oriented programming in Prolog++. This type of programming is particularly appropriate in knowledge-representation situations where one is describing static situations. The notions of attributes and values are introduced; various aspects of inheritance are distinguished; the functional notation; aggregate objects and parts. While this does not exhaust the versatility of object-oriented programming, it shows the value of the ideas of encapsulation and inheritance in organizing any large logic program. By organizing a program around its objects, many of the problems found in Prolog can be overcome. These problems are typically associated with providing unique names for objects and with extending previously written programs. The techniques outlined in this chapter are particularly useful in knowledge representation.

3.2 Objects and attributes

Programs in Prolog++ are constructed by describing a series of objects and their interactions. This can give rise to a very different programming style than when using Prolog, where the relation is the basic organizing tool.

   We will use a classic logic example – family relationships – to introduce the formalism and show how using objects leads to a natural formulation of the necessary information.

   Suppose we want to express the facts about a family tree and use this to deduce the various relationships within the family. The only family tree

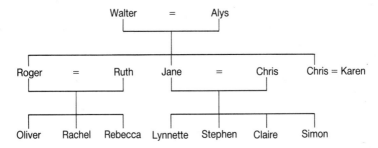

Figure 3.1   A typical family tree.

most people are interested in is their own and there is no one family, famous or mythical, of interest to everyone. Do people really want to think about Adam and Eve or Queen Elizabeth II? Therefore I will use some facts from my family as an illustration and encourage you, my reader, immediately to make up your own in the same style.

Figure 3.1 is a simple representation of a small part of my family tree, showing my immediate family and their descendants. Each of the people in this tree may be described separately. Here are a few facts about my sister, in the form of a complete object declaration in Prolog++. Similar declarations could be made for all the other members of the family.

```
class jane.
      name('Jane Hindley').
      nee('Jane Moss').
      sex(female).
      height(167).
      birth(1942).
      death(1993).
      father(walter).
      mother(alys).
      brother(chris).
      brother(roger).
      husband(chrisH).
      child(lynnette).
      child(steven).
      child(claire).
      child(simon).
end jane.
```

Descriptions of objects in Prolog++ are braced by the **class** and **end** pair, each of which must be followed by the name of the object, which is always an atom and must be unique to the system. Don't be put off by the word 'class' were. It can refer simply to one object, and this is all that we mean by it at this stage. Later we will use the ability of a class to act as a template for many objects.

Following the opening are the descriptions of a number of attributes of the object, as simple Prolog assertions, terminated by a full stop, or period. Each attribute has the form of a Prolog atom, while the value, the argument, may be a general Prolog term. The simplest form of atom is a word beginning with a lower case letter, but any sequence of characters enclosed in single quotes may also be used (as in 'Jane Hindley'). The attributes all express facts about the object being defined and so do not need to include the name of the object.

In conventional object-oriented languages, there is a clear distinction between an **attribute**, which is a field in the type definition of an object, and a **method**, which is a procedure local to the objects definition. Yet in logical terms the word attribute merely means a characteristic of an object, similar to the notion of a predicate (it is not an accident that the French word *attribut* translates both the English words *predicate* and *attribute*). It does not distinguish whether that value is permanent or temporary.

An important contribution made by logic programming to computer science was to reduce the difference between the notions of procedure and data.

'Data in logic programs can be represented by means of terms or relations. The use of terms as data structures gives Horn clause programs many of the characteristics of a list-processing language like LISP. ... The use of relations in logic programs, on the other hand, is like the representation of data by relations in database formalisms. Relations are also like tables and arrays in conventional programming languages.' (Kowalski, 1979, p. 107)

A consequence of this view is that one does not wish to distinguish between a value which is stored explicitly and one which is calculated or deduced. But there is a further distinction. In Prolog++, unlike logic, there is a notion of change. This means that, in addition, it is necessary to distinguish attributes that can change from those that are static.

From the outside, these distinctions shouldn't matter. Whether something is stored as a permanent fact, is calculated on demand or is stored in such a way that it is changed easily, is an implementation decision that should not affect the way it is addressed.

Prolog++ has both *methods* and *attributes*. A method is static, an attribute dynamic. What we have so far described are actually methods, and while we will also introduce attributes later in this chapter, we will postpone the discussion of changing objects to the next chapter.

The value of an attribute, or method, may be obtained by sending a **message** to the object using the infix operator ' <— '. The message is the name of the attribute, and it takes a single parameter, which is bound to the value of the attribute.

Thus to find Jane's height we could say:

```
jane <- height(A)
```

As a result, A would be bound to 167.

One might well ask what the difference is between a *message* and a *procedure call*. There are two main differences. One is syntactic, the other is organizational.

From a syntactic point of view, the object is primary, rather than the procedure. A number of different objects might define the same procedure, so we need to send the message to correct procedure within the object. But at this level, there is little difference between the object-oriented approach and any system with modules in which one might say, for instance,

```
module: procedure(parameters)
```

The real difference is organizational. It is within the programmer's head. Object-oriented programming actively encourages an approach in which different objects use the same method names, where appropriate. Thus the use of the message terminology is appropriate. The object (or to be more precise, the programmer implementing the object) decides what is the meaning of the message and is therefore in charge. A conventional procedure is in charge of all its parameters, though some object-oriented systems (such as CLOS – Common LISP Object System) maintain the procedural syntax, with the object (or objects) as parameter.

On present machines a message is implemented by a procedure call. We may observe that '<-' is available as a predefined Prolog++ predicate that takes the object as its first argument and the message as its second. It can therefore be invoked from ordinary Prolog programs. Within a Prolog++ program the interpretation of '<-' from within Prolog++ is slightly different, though it still uses a procedure call. However, in a distributed system other message-passing mechanisms might be used.

Unlike most object-oriented languages there is no need for this operation to return a 'value'. Variables in the call are used both to pass and return values, by unification. Thus we could equally well pose the query

```
jane <- height(167)
```

which would succeed with no resultant variable bindings, or

```
jane <- height(182)
```

which would simply fail, with no error message, because it is the incorrect value.

Nor is there any need for an attribute to be unique. The query

jane <− brother(X)

yields two answers:

X = roger
X = chris

These objects provide all the factual data about one individual and could be repeated for all the individuals in the family. Yet there is clearly repetition as well as incompleteness. For example, each of the siblings roger, jane and chris will include the information about their parents and each of their other siblings, while their more distant relatives – nephews, grandparents and so on – are not known.

3.2.1   Facts, rules and inheritance

It is clearly a desirable aim to provide the minimum amount of factual knowledge for the individual and to deduce the rest by a number of general rules that apply to everyone. This is obviously the case for nephew and grandparents. But it also applies to direct relationships too. In the case of father, it is only necessary to record the father for the eldest in any family. For any other member of the family one can deduce it by passing the message up the line to the eldest sibling. Similarly, only the eldest child need be recorded for a couple. How is this to be expressed in Prolog++?

In Prolog, facts are simply special cases of rules. It is common to mix facts and rules indiscriminately. For instance, we might combine the special fact:

father(roger, walter). %the father of roger is walter

with the general rule:

father(A,B) :- olderSibling(A,C), father(C,B).

This particular solution will work but there is clearly something awry. The general knowledge about how to find a father should be separated from specific facts. Imagine we are maintaining a large family database. We may add or delete specific facts at any time. Should the general rule be at the beginning or the end? How do we ensure it stays in the desired place?

In Prolog the problem shows itself in another guise. It is very easy to land up with an infinite recursion which yields a nonterminating program. A more sensible solution in this language is to have two different names: one for rules and the other for facts. If we indicate the facts by appending the characters '_f', then the rules might look something like this:

```
father(A,B) :- father_f(A,B).
father(A,B) :- olderSibling(A,C), father(C,B).
```

Unfortunately, every possible predicate which might contain a fact must be treated in this way. And in a realistic family database, this means every relationship. We might well know, and wish to record, that John's sister-in-law is called Rachel, but have forgotten the name of his wife. So this rather indirect relationship would need to be recorded as a fact.

A solution to this problem comes very easily by the use of inheritance. In Prolog++ an object can inherit any of the attributes of another object. It is therefore possible to put the *individual facts* into one object and the *general rules* into a separate object. Each object which describes an individual person inherits the set of general rules which describe the indirect relationships. Let us call this new object person. As an initial design we may expect it to have a number of definitions such as mother, father and so on:

```
class person.
    mother(A) :- ...
    father(A) :- ...
    brother(A) :- ...
    sister(A) :- ...
end person.
```

so that if we send a message such as 'father' to an individual for whom this information is not recorded, then it will be passed to the person object to be solved.

We may note in passing that words like 'mother' and 'father' are more natural attributes than predicates. In the Prolog definition above, it is always difficult to predict whether people will write code for 'the father of x is y' or 'x is the father of y'. With inheritance it is obvious who is father and who is child.

The 'inheritance' path we will use for this problem is in no way connected to the natural 'inheritance' path of the problem domain. All we have is a flat inheritance pattern in which each object inherits from the same one. Graphically this may be represented as shown in Figure 3.2.

Let us decide what factual information must be recorded about each individual in order to deduce other relationships. This can be done in a

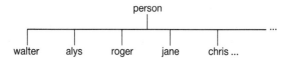

Figure 3.2 A flat 'inheritance' pattern.

number of different ways. Here is one scheme:

> Record the parents only for the oldest of a set of siblings (brothers and sisters). For each of the set of siblings record their younger *and* older siblings. For parents, record only their oldest child (we omit the question of half-brothers and sisters, for simplicity). Deduce all other relationship information.

There is clearly a certain amount of redundancy in this scheme. If we have recorded the older sibling, then we can invert this relationship to retrieve the younger sibling. The same applies to parents and children. There are efficiency considerations for introducing this redundancy which will be discussed later, but we can note that it is not strictly necessary: we could work from the minimal information in Prolog++. We will demonstrate alternative ways later.

It is now possible to restate the description of Jane with this in mind. The father and mother attributes have gone, as have brother and sister. In their place is a single attribute sibling from which all of these can be deduced. A declaration inherits has appeared, which links this object to another object called person.

```
class jane.
      inherits person.
      name('Jane Hindley').
      nee('Jane Moss').
      sex(female).
      height(167).
      birth(1942).
      death (1993).
      olderSibling(roger).
      youngerSibling(chris).
      husband(chrisH).
      child(lynnette).
end jane.
```

The inherits declaration is very like a normal attribute but it has a special interpretation within the Prolog++ system and is declared as a prefix operator so that the brackets around its argument are unnecessary. The argument of inherits names one or more objects from which this object inherits properties. For example, given the query:

```
jane <- father(X)
```

the Prolog++ system finds there is no definition of father in the object jane and will then try to find a definition in one of the objects named by inherits.
      Let us turn to the definition of the person object. If father is not recorded as a fact (which only happens for the eldest child) then the rule is

to pass the message to the next older sibling. This can simply be written as follows:

```
father(B) :-
    olderSibling(C),
    C <- father(B).
```

Both the head of the rule and the call olderSibling have an implicit parameter which is the object concerned, in this case jane. This applies even though the declaration appears textually in a separate object called person. In Prolog this would be written:

```
father(A,B) :-
    olderSibling(A,C),
    father(C,B).
```

Here both the head of the clause and the first goal have an additional argument corresponding to the object itself. The second goal is almost identical, except that in Prolog++, the first parameter becomes the object to which we send the message.

This missing parameter is one of the keys to object-oriented programming and is normally called **self**. It always refers to the *original* object to which a message is sent, regardless of the amount of inheritance involved. In Prolog++ it is quite acceptable to write the parameter explicitly, so that the above method appears as:

```
father(B) :-
    self <- olderSibling(C),
    C <- father(B).
```

although it is not necessary. Any procedure call in the body of an object is assumed to be a message to self by default, although as we shall see, if there is no method of that name defined, Prolog++ will attempt to interpret it as a call to Prolog.

To see how the inheritance works let us take the example of determining Jane's father, given that the relevant parts of the object definition of roger are:

```
class roger.
    inherits person.
    father(walter).
    ...
end roger.
```

In order to show proofs in Prolog++ it is necessary to extend the notation given in Chapter 2. For example, here is a proof of the goal:

```
jane <- father(X)
```

indented to show the structure of the proof:

```
jane  <— father(X)
++person <— father(X)  ++ jane
    olderSibling(C)
    ++jane <— olderSibling(C)
        (C=roger)
    roger  <— father(X)
        (X=walter)
```

This tree is extended in several ways from the proofs given in the previous chapter:

(1)   Some extra deductions must be shown corresponding to the inheritance. These we will call 'metalevel deduction steps' for reasons that will be discussed later. They are prefixed by ++ instead of being indented. This is partly to reduce the amount of indenting and partly to stress that these goals simply replace the goal from which they are derived and do not add new goals – as we shall see later, they can often be executed at compile-time.

(2)   The original receiver of the message is indicated after the inherited step, following the second ++. This identifies the 'extra parameter', or self, which is always passed with an inherited message. Note that explicit messages – such as roger <— father(X) – do not have this parameter.

The first metalevel deduction step passes the original message through to the person object, remembering the name jane. This matches with the definition of father and generates two subgoals. The first, olderSibling(C), is interpreted as a message to the original object, jane, and it succeeds, binding C to roger. The second subgoal now becomes a message to be sent to roger. This also succeeds, binding X to walter.

It is easy to see where the value for the self symbol comes from within the original object: it is simply the name of the object to which the message is sent. But how does it keep the same value within an inherited object? The answer is that Prolog++ passes this value to the inheriting object as part of the inheritance protocol. Effectively, every attribute has an extra parameter, the self parameter.

> self is a Prolog constant, not a variable. It can be used anywhere in a Prolog++ program, but it has a potentially different interpretation wherever it is used. It thus departs from the traditional 'Herbrand' interpretation of constants in Prolog, in which a symbol stands for itself. It can best be considered as a parameterless function. This is the first of several such departures in the syntax of Prolog++, which help to make the resultant code much more readable than Prolog.

The power given by the availability of the self variable is normally referred to as *dynamic binding* in object-oriented programming. The value of the self variable can be different in two recursive calls to the same predicate. For example, if we asked who is the father of chris, the proof tree would be as follows:

```
chris <- father(X)
++person <- father(X) ++ chris
    olderSibling(C)
    ++chris <- olderSibling(C)
        (C=jane)
    jane <- father(X)
    ++person <- father(X) ++ jane
        olderSibling(C)
        ++jane <- olderSibling(C)
            (C=roger)
        roger <- father(X)
            (X=walter)
```

In the first case, self is chris and in the next, jane. Without this power, it isn't easy to abstract predicates out of the objects that refer to them.

Inheritance in Prolog++ is like that in Smalltalk in that a local definition *overrides* an inherited definition. So in the above example, the definition of father in person is never tried for the object roger because there is a local definition. It doesn't matter whether this local definition succeeds or fails: in Prolog, failure is as important a type of behaviour as success. But one lesson that has been learned from experience with logic programming is that there is a qualitative difference between the normal failure of a predicate and the absence of any definition. Most Prolog systems have an option of treating the absence of a definition as a run-time error instead of a quiet failure, and programmers quickly learn to leave this option on.

So the search for an inherited definition, which is performed 'behind the scenes' in Prolog++, stops when a definition of the correct arity is found. If the person object inherited another object which contained a definition of father this would never be referenced from person. This corresponds exactly with the normal notion of a default. If there is a local definition, use that; as a default, check for a definition higher in the search tree.

In some situations, an overriding definition is not adequate. We will see later how to provide other forms of inheritance.

So far, all the characteristics of an object have had a single parameter. To show that there is no restriction on the number and usage of parameters let us consider the problem of finding all the brothers and sisters (or siblings) of a given individual.

For each individual, we have their older sibling and younger sibling recorded, if there are any. Hence to generate all the sisters, for example, we need to move along both these chains and then reject those who are male.

A sensible approach is to generate all the siblings from oldest to youngest. Hence it is sensible to parameterize the 'older' and 'younger' aspect and use two recursive loops for sibling. Here are the definitions:

```
sibling(older, A) :-
    olderSibling(B),
    (B <- sibling(older,A)
    ; A=B).
sibling(younger, A) :-
    youngerSibling(B),
    (A = B.
    ; B <- sibling(younger, A)).
```

Having done this it is easy to define sister and brother relations, by leaving it open whether we want older or younger:

```
sister(A) :-
    sibling(_, A),
    A <- sex(female).

brother(A) :-
    sibling(_, A),
    A <- sex(male).
```

If these definitions are added to the object person and we pose the query

```
jane <- brother(X)
```

we will then get the following results:

```
X = roger
X = chris
```

The manner in which the sibling clauses has been written ensures this ordering. The base case is A=B, which is contained within a disjunction (;). We have used the known ordering of Prolog to ensure the solutions are produced in the desired order. In the case of older siblings, the recursive call B <- sibling(older,A) occurs before the base case, so we continue searching till the end of the chain. For younger siblings it is the other way round; we return the first result immediately and only later come to the recursive case.

3.3   Class inheritance

Inheritance in classes is a form of progressive specialization. At the top level we put attributes which are the most general. We may then define subclasses

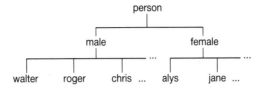

Figure 3.3   A new hierarchy introducing 'male' and 'female' objects.

which either introduce new attributes which are not appropriate to the other, or give different definitions for the same attributes.

In our family we could introduce two new objects, 'male' and 'female' to store all the attributes that are common to males and females respectively but not to persons. This will give us a new hierarchy, shown in Figure 3.3, and it is now possible to reduce the amount of information in each of the inheriting objects and provide some extra utility for each of them which is appropriate to the gender:

```
class female.
    inherits person.
    sex(female).
    female.
    retirementAge(60).
    spouse(X) :-
        husband(X).
end female.
```

Instead of having a record sex(female) for every female in the database, this is now stored once only, and there is no extra information required. Everything that was derivable about jane is still derivable, and it would not even be necessary to recompile the object person if this change was made in a dynamic system.

There are a couple of characteristics of the female object that are worthy of note. One is the multiple uses of the word itself. It is used as the name of the object, as the value of the attribute sex and also as a Boolean, or parameterless, attribute itself. Thus the call jane $\leftarrow$ female will succeed, just as will jane $\leftarrow$ sex(female). The advantage of the latter form is that it can also be used to return a value from a query where it is unknown, but the former is more convenient in some situations.

The second is the definition of spouse. Here is a word which has a different connotation for males and females. Often relationships are easier to express using it: for instance one definition of a sister-in-law is the sister of one's spouse. Whether one uses 'wife' or 'spouse' in the individual entry doesn't change the fact that both are needed at various times. By providing the definition within the object female (and a corresponding definition in the object male), the correct definition is supplied without any searching or testing.

One of the most striking uses of specialization is in what is called 'late binding'. In this case a general rule is written at a high level which is realized in different ways lower down the specialization tree. A good example of this is the way in which verbs are conjugated in many of the European languages. Although there is a common structure of person, tense, mood and voice, this can be realized in different ways.

As an example, let us take German: most verbs fall into one of three categories, normally called weak, strong and irregular. Weak verbs mainly change their endings; strong verbs are 'stem changing'; irregular verbs change their stem but have the same endings as weak verbs. These stem changes are still seen in many English words which derive from the German; for example, I fall, I fell, I have fallen corresponds to the German *ich falle, ich fiel, ich bin gefallen.*

Conjugation in German changes along five dimensions: person (first, second, third), number (singular, plural), tense (present, past, perfect, pluperfect, future, future perfect), voice (active, passive) and mood (indicative, subjunctive). There are thus a possible total of 144 forms of each verb (with a few extras, such as the imperative), though not all of these are used and most are rather regular since they use the auxiliary verbs – *haben*, *sein* and *werden* – in much the same way as English.

Indeed, all that needs to be specified uniquely for each verb is the present and past tenses, together with the past participle and which of the auxiliary verbs (*sein* or *haben*) the verb uses. All the other information can be specified by rules which apply to all verbs.

We may thus draw an initial inheritance tree as shown by Figure 3.4.

The class 'verb' includes both the conjugation rules for all verbs and information about endings which are common to several categories of verb. It is possible to split the information about conjugation and endings into separate classes, but not much is gained, so we will not do it here. However, we will need to refer to the conjugation of the auxiliary verbs – *sein*, *haben* and *werden* – so these will be placed in the appropriate parts of the hierarchy (Figure 3.5).

The basic method, conjugate, in verb has five parameters: the tense, the voice, a single parameter which combines person and number, the mood, and the result, which is a list of one or more words. For simplicity, we will only show the active forms – the passive forms can easily be added in a

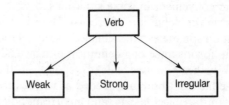

Figure 3.4 An inheritance tree.

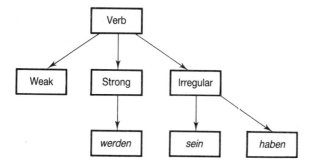

Figure 3.5   The inheritance tree extended.

similar fashion.

```
%conjugate(tense, voice, person, mood, wordlist)
conjugate(present, active, P, M, [V]) :-
    present(P,M,V).
conjugate(past, active, P, M, [V]) :-
    past(P,M,V).
conjugate(perfect, active, P, M, [A, V]) :-
    auxiliary(S),
    S <- present(P, M, A),
    pastParticiple(V).
conjugate(pluperfect, active, P, M, [A, V]) :-
    auxiliary(S),
    S <- past(P, M, A),
    pastParticiple(V).
conjugate(future, active, P, M, [A, V]) :-
    werden <- present(P, M, A),
    infinitive(V).
conjugate(futurePerfect, active, P, M, [A, P, S]) :-
    werden <- present(P, M, A),
    pastParticiple(P),
    auxiliary(S).
```

Much of the complexity of the conjugation process is handled here, leaving a much simpler interface for each of the verb types to handle. The specification of these is as follows:

```
    present(P,M,V) – the present form V for person P and mood M
       past(P,M,V) – the past form V for person P and mood M
       auxiliary(A) – the auxiliary verb A taken by the verb
pastParticiple(V) – the past participle of the verb
      infinitive(V) – the infinitive form of the verb
```

In each case, remember that there is an implicit self parameter which is the verb itself. To evaluate the call Prolog++ starts at self and scans up the hierarchy in order to find the appropriate method. Let us illustrate what would happen with a query to establish the third singular perfect of fallen – 'he has fallen', together with the top level of the proof:

```
fallen <— conjugate(perfect, active, s3, indicative, X) :-
    auxiliary(sein),
    sein <— present(s3, indicative, ist),
    pastParticiple(gefallen).
        ⇒ X = [ist, gefallen]
```

In this case, the main part of the conjugation is actually for the auxiliary verb sein, and not for the main verb at all. But the queries auxiliary and pastParticiple are evaluated with respect to fallen.

We now need to elaborate the subclasses to which these messages will be sent. Since the details of the conjugation process are not very relevant here we will simply show the smallest class, for weak verbs. The calls that are made from here are primarily to do with splitting words apart and gluing them together, which are mainly string processing, although the join procedure contains some domain specific rules (for example, the second singular of *senden* is *sendest*, not *sendst*).

```
class weakVerb.
inherits verb.

present(P, M, V) :-
    infinitive(I),              %defined by the verb class
    root(I, R),                 %remove 'en'
    presentEnding(P, M, E),     %get ending, inherited from verb
    join(R, E, V).              %join the word parts together
past(P, M, V) :-
    infinitive(I),
    root(I, R),
    pastEnding(P, M, E),
    join(R, E, V).

pastParticiple(Verb, P) :-
    root(Verb, R),
    concat(ge, R, Stem),        %direct join
    join(Stem, t, P).           %joins words, with special rules

end weakVerb.
```

Much of the other information can be a mixture of tables and procedures. For example, here is a fragment of the code which picks out the endings. The second parameter of person is a list which is indexed by the first parameter to yield the appropriate result.

```
presentEnding(P, indicative, E) :-
    person(P, [e, st, t, en, t, en], E).

person(s1,[P|_], P).
person(s2, [_,P|_], P)
person(s3, [_,_,P|_], P).
person(p1, [_,_,_,P|_], P).
person(p2, [_,_,_,_,P|_], P).
person(p3, [_,_,_,_,_,P], P).
```

We will return to this example later in this and the following chapter, to demonstrate more dynamic aspects. We would not, for instance, wish to define every German verb as a separate class: instead the relevant information would probably be stored in Prolog tables, with defaults, and an appropriate instance of one of the verb types generated on demand.

In some object-oriented systems, such as C++, it is necessary to indicate explicitly that methods are defined lower down in the hierarchy, by means of a *virtual* declaration. In keeping with the nontyped nature of Prolog this is not required, though there is one exception.

If a procedure is defined locally to an object, Prolog++ will assume by default that this is the required procedure, and not bother to look any further. However, you may wish this code simply to be a default, but to be redefinable in subclasses which inherit this class. In this case, it is necessary to write the self object explicitly. For example, the first clause of conjugate could have been written:

```
conjugate(present, active, P, M, [V]) :-
    self <- present(P, M, V).
```

The effect would have been identical, but it was not necessary in this case because present was not declared in verb (or its superclasses), so the Prolog++ compiler made the assumption that it had to start at the bottom of the hierarchy and search upwards. If there had been such a declaration, then the explicit use of self makes clear what is intended.

3.3.1 Non-overriding inheritance

One of the basic design choices with any object-oriented languages is whether an attribute or method should *override* an inherited definition or *augment* it. In the logical framework, the choice is often made that a local definition augments what is inherited. It is easy to see the reason. The value of a relation is normally seen as the set of values which satisfy it. Hence, if the same attribute appears at more than one level of the hierarchy, it is natural to consider the total relation as the union of the definitions at different levels.

Most object-oriented systems, however, use an overriding approach, and this is not simply because they work in a single-solution context. A method is normally complete in itself and supports software reuse by allowing parts of a definition to be redefined. Some authors (for example, Snyder, 1986) prefer to refer to this as *implementation inheritance*, reserving the name *specification inheritance* for methods based on specialization.

In most cases, the fact that a method overrides an inherited method is just what is needed, which is why Prolog++ adopts this approach. But there are cases in which one wants to *add* some information rather than replace it. An example has already been mentioned: suppose I can remember the name of someone's sister-in-law but not the intermediate relations. I want to add this information into the definition for that person. However, if I simply say

```
sisterInLaw(rachel).
```

then any inherited definition of sister-in-law (one is given a little later in the chapter) will be unavailable. If the person has other sisters-in-law that can be deduced using these normal inference methods, then they will be forgotten. One's immediate instinct is to say 'add another definition with a reference to the object with the generic definition'. In this case one would simply write:

```
sisterInLaw(rachel).
sisterInLaw(X) :- person <- sisterInLaw(X).
```

assuming that sisterInLaw is defined in the object person.

This doesn't work. The reason is that the identity of the self object is forgotten in the process. The person object should not normally be called directly, for this reason. So Prolog++ treats the object **super** in a special manner. Sending a message to super passes a message up the hierarchy in the conventional way but keeps the definition of self, so any procedures that reference it get the right value. A correct definition of sister-in-law then has two clauses, which can be written in either order:

```
sisterInLaw(rachel).
sisterInLaw(X) :- super <- sisterInLaw(X).
```

In this example we have passed on an identical copy of the original message, but we are not limited to that: we could have passed a different message. Passing a message to super can be used whenever we need to ignore a local definition of some method and depend instead on an inherited definition.

The super notation also allows us to control the search order exactly. In the definition above, the local definition is returned first, followed by the inherited definition. By simply reversing the order of the clauses the local definition can be returned *after* any inherited definitions. It is thus much more flexible than a declaration which says that a particular method uses an augmenting definition. It is also more efficient than the method derived from the *frame* notion in Artificial Intelligence which allows one to place conditions on the inheritance. The problem with that is that it is necessary to do a great deal of checking, some of which can only be done at run-time, to make sure that no superior methods have been ignored. With super, it is left to the definer of the lower-level class to stipulate when and how any inclusive inheritance is to take place. Any extra conditions are easy to add.

Overriding also has applications in knowledge representation. Let us take the classic example in this field: we want to know the means of locomotion of different animals. We know that birds can normally fly and walk. So we make the assertions:

```
class bird.
...
mode(walk).
mode(fly).
...
end bird.
```

We then wish to define a class for birds such as penguins, which can't fly but can swim. Since we only want to block the fly mode, we can define it like this:

```
class penguin.
inherits bird.
...
mode(swim).
mode(X) :
    super <- mode(X),
    X \= fly.
...
end penguin.
```

If we pose the relevant query to the system, we will then get the desired answer:

```
?- penguin <- mode(X).
X = swim ;
X = walk ;
no
```

In theoretical terms, overriding inheritance can be seen as inheriting a *name* rather than a *relation*. The name denotes a particular relation, so that we get back all of a particular definition, but do not inherit further definitions, unless we specifically request them.

3.3.2   Inheritance and the Prolog environment

Our first example was intentionally 'pure'. It didn't need any supporting facilities, whether they be arithmetic, string handling facilities or input/output. Real programming isn't like that. It needs support from a predefined environment. In the case of Prolog++, most of this is provided by Prolog but there are additional facilities which are only useful in the object-oriented environment. How are these integrated in the inheritance framework?

The answer is that every header class in Prolog++ (that is, a class with no super classes) has two implicit classes above it. One is referred to by its initials 'ppp', standing for Prolog Plus Plus. The other is Prolog itself. Thus the person class may be pictured as shown in Figure 3.6.

This has two effects: any call to a Prolog predicate can be placed in a Prolog++ program with no special annotation; and if a Prolog predicate is redefined within the class hierarchy, then that definition will be taken by default.

You may notice that we haven't divided the Prolog class into two classes: a user-defined and a system-defined sector. This is because there is no object-oriented distinction between the two. It is impossible to redefine a Prolog predefined predicate within a user program. As the facilities of Prolog compilers become more extensive, this is becoming a significant problem. When porting a program from one Prolog compiler to another it is not uncommon to find that the new system has used several of the predicate names in the system, so that a renaming process is necessary. Since Prolog is a symbolic language, there are probably efficient tools available for this process, but it is annoying nonetheless.

In Prolog++ one should not encounter this problem, since if a method is defined with the same name as a Prolog predicate, it will automatically take precedence over it. There are only two remaining limitations.

One is that names of objects themselves must avoid the names of predicates defined elsewhere in the system. The core of an object named person is compiled into the predicate person/2. In most Prolog systems, this only conflicts with another definition person/2, not person/1 or person/3, and so on. There are some systems, such as MacProlog, which do not distinguish predicates in this way and one must avoid any predicate named person.

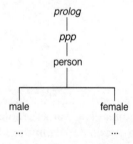

Figure 3.6   Inheritance tree for the person class.

The other is that, having redefined a Prolog predicate name somewhere in the class hierarchy, one then discovers a need to use that predicate. This is only likely in imported code, but there is an easy workaround for this: the message may be sent directly to the class prolog, avoiding any user-defined methods.

3.3.3 Class instances

Much of the power of object-orientation comes from the fact that one can group a number of related objects into classes which have similar attributes and methods. So far, we have illustrated one way in which this can be done – by declaring subclasses. A second method is by creating instances of a class. To do this we use a method called **create** which is built-in to every class in Prolog++ by virtue of being defined in the class ppp.

There are three forms of the create method, create/1 to create/3. All return as the first parameter a unique identifier of the instance which is used from then on as a 'handle' for the instance.

```
weakVerb <- create(P)
```

binds P to an identifier which is actually a term: it includes the name of the class and a unique identifier for this particular instance, which we may refer to as $weakVerb_1$, $weakVerb_2$, and so on.

The purpose of creating different instances is clearly that they should be distinguishable from each other. This is the purpose of the second parameter: to set the attributes of a particular instance. The second parameter is a list of pairs – attribute and value – separated by = operators.

```
weak <- create(P, [infinitive = machen]).
```

In order to use attributes such as these, they must be declared in the class of the object. This is done with the attribute declaration, which is similar in form to the inherits declaration, with the addition that it is possible to give default values to attributes. For example,

```
class weakVerb.
attribute infinitive, auxiliary=haben.
    ...
```

In this case there are two attributes: infinitive and auxiliary. There is no default for infinitive: it is precisely the infinitive that distinguishes one verb from another. But there is a default for auxiliary – because *haben* is used for the vast majority of verbs. Since there are a few weak verbs that are conjugated with *sein*, we could have:

```
weakVerb <- create(P, [infinitive = finden,
    auxiliary = sein]).
```

The value of attributes can be accessed in the same way as unary methods from inside or outside the class. Thus after the previous message, we could write the statement:

```
P <- infinitive(X)
```

which would bind X to finden. However, apart from the create statement, there is no way of directly assigning the value to an attribute from outside the class.

There is no need for the order of the list of assignments in the create message to match those in the attribute statement, or to be complete. If an attribute is not assigned a value, then an attempt to access the value of the attribute simply fails. We might wish the weakVerb class to check that infinitive has been assigned a value. One way to do this would be to redefine the create method, so that it checked for this. So inside weakVerb we could write the following:

```
create(_) :-
    writenl('Cannot create weakVerb without infinitive'),
    fail.
create(I, A) :-
    super <- create(I, A),
    (infinitive(_) -> true
    ; write('Error: weakVerb infinitive not assigned in'),
        writenl(I),
        fail).
```

The effect of this is to redefine the create method of weakVerb which is normally inherited from ppp. It disallows create/1 entirely and prints an error message and fails create/2 if it does not assign a value to infinitive.

This is such a common situation that there is another way to do this in Prolog++. After creating an instance, Prolog++ calls the method **when_created**, if one is defined. To achieve a somewhat similar effect to the example above, one would write:

```
when_created:-
    infinitive(_) -> true
    ; write('Error: weakVerb infinitive not assigned in'),
        writenl(self),
        fail.
```

If there is also a when_created method in a superior class, it is necessary to activate it explicitly using a super call. This allows the same degree of control over the ordering of initialization actions.

So far we have assumed that the identity of the created object is simply a value which can be used elsewhere in the program and may be stored temporarily as the value of another attribute. This does not tally with the concept of object identity as it was introduced earlier in the family relationships example. If we wish to identify an instance of an object with a specific real-world entity, we may need to talk about that identity in the program. Hence it is desirable to know in advance what the identity is.

The create method therefore allows a third parameter, which must be bound to an atom. If there are no attribute assignments, then an empty list should be given as the second parameter. For example,

```
female  <- create(X, [name='Jane Hindley', height=167,
    birth=1942], jane).
```

This call will only succeed if there is not currently an instance of class female with name jane. The variable X will be bound to a term which is the identity, which typically includes the class and name, but which should always be treated as a term, because there is no guarantee that the implementation will stay the same.

It may be desirable to send a message to an object of which you know the name but not the identity. There is a Prolog++ operator '$' which takes as its argument the name of the object and returns the appropriate instance. Thus after the use of create above it is permissible to make the following call

```
$jane  <- height(X)
```

If the call to $ fails, then the call will fail without attempting to send a message to a non-existent object.

It is a disputed question in object-oriented programming whether one should store object identities as the attributes of other objects. Instead, some of those concerned with object-oriented design have encouraged the use of associations:

'During conceptual modeling you should not bury pointers or other object references inside objects as attributes. Instead you should model them as associations to indicate that the information they contain is not subordinate to a single class, but depends on two or more classes.' (Rumbaugh *et al.*, 1991, p. 31)

Clearly an association is nothing more than a Prolog table! If this advice were taken, we might wish to restate the family relationship example given earlier. At this stage we merely point out that there is no prohibition in Prolog++ from storing either the names or the identities of objects as attributes.

In the family relationship example, the separation of the names and identities has a benefit. It may be that our genealogy is incomplete: for instance, we may have a reference to some person's father, but no object corresponding to them. In this case we are in danger of sending a message to a non-existent object. By using the identity function, we can ensure that the call simply fails, as it would if we had used Prolog.

This also simplifies the creation of objects: if two objects refer to each other then the identities of both will not be known until both are created. By using names one can delay the references until the model is complete. Since Prolog is a symbolic language, the object identity is in any case a symbol, not a pointer.

3.3.4 Multiple inheritance

In the family relationship example, each object inherits from only one other object. To limit inheritance to this style, normally called 'single inheritance', can lead to distortions in the way knowledge is encoded. Prolog++ supports a more powerful approach called 'multiple inheritance', which does not have this limitation. If an object has more than one inherits attribute, then each of them will be used in turn to find an applicable method following the normal Prolog 'depth-first' method.

To illustrate this, let us consider some of the properties of geometric shapes, such as triangles, squares and pentagons. If we need to compute areas and perimeters of various polygons the formulae for squares are much simpler and more efficient than those for an irregular polygon. For each class of polygon one can either include a special formula or inherit one from a more general shape. A small set of polygons is shown in Figure 3.7, which also shows where the attributes area and perimeter are defined.

Thus to find the area of an equilateral triangle we use the general formula for triangles, but to calculate the perimeter we can use the fact that

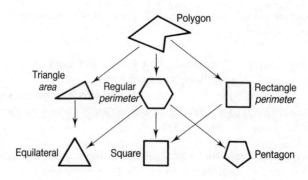

Figure 3.7 Multiple inheritance – a set of polygons.

it is regular. By inheriting from both of these (incommensurate) shapes the formula can be represented only once.

What follows is the Prolog++ code which specifies both the inheritance pattern and some of the attributes of the objects, given as methods. It uses the arithmetic predicate is which is part of the Prolog environment. First, we describe the shapes, starting with equilateral:

```
class equilateral.
inherits regular, triangle.
attribute base.
height(X) :-
  base(B),
  X is sqrt(3.0)* B/2.
end equilateral.

class triangle.
inherits polygon.
attribute base.
sides(3).
area(X) :-
  height(H),
  X is 0.5* @base * H.
end triangle.

class square.
inherits rectangle, regular.
height(H) :-
  side(H).
end square.

class regular.
inherits polygon.
attribute base.
perimeter(P) :-
  sides(S),
  P is @base*S.
end regular.

class rectangle.
inherits polygon.
attributes base, height.
sides(4).
area(A) :-
  A is @base * @height.
perimeter(P) :-
  P is 2*(@base + @height).
end rectangle.

class pentagon.
inherits regular.
sides(5).
end pentagon.
```

Note: in MacProlog the object square should be renamed (for example, to aSquare) to avoid conflict with a built-in predicate having the same name.

The attributes for particular shapes are not included in the above definitions: these simply demonstrate the aspects common to all triangles, or squares, and so on. To define a particular triangle we would normally create an instance of one of these objects, which defines attributes such as base and height.

For example, we might name an equilateral triangle and declare it as follows:

```
equilateral  <– create(I, [base = 2]).
```

To see the way multiple inheritance works in action it is worth tracing the inheritance steps in the evaluation of a query, such as finding its perimeter:

```
?- equilateral  <– create(I, [base = 2]), I  <– perimeter(X).
I =  $(equilateral, 11111), X = 6
```

The method for perimeter is found in regular using the second of equilateral's inheritance paths. To evaluate this it needs two values: base and sides. Base is found by referring back to the object e1, but to find sides the method in regular needs to follow the *other* inheritance path to triangle. This is illustrated in the proof below which spells out the inheritance paths followed using the notation explained earlier, where we refer to the instance name as e1 for convenience:

```
?- e1  <– perimeter(A).
++ equilateral  <– perimeter(A)  ++ e1
++ regular  <– perimeter(A)  ++ e1
    e1  <– base(B1)
        (B1 = 2)
    e1  <– sides(S)
    ++ equilateral  <– sides(S)  ++ e1
    ++ triangle  <– sides(S)  ++ e1
        (S = 3)
    A is 2 * 3
        (A = 6)
```

In this example, one path of the inheritance hierarchy contributed information to solve a problem on the other path. This is an elegant use of multiple inheritance. More often, it happens that an object naturally inherits properties from two different objects which explain different aspects of its composition. To attempt to force this into a single hierarchy requires one to put one object higher than the other in the same hierarchy. This can lead to distortions of the problem and it is consequently necessary to duplicate information.

It may also be the case that both inheritance paths provide a way of solving the problem. Consider the task of computing the perimeter of a square. Both regular and rectangle define this method, so which do we choose?

A number of alternative approaches have been taken to this problem: some systems try to find the nearest superior objects; others produce an error message if a method is defined on two paths; yet others, based on a logical approach, take the union of both paths.

We would suggest that, logically, methods inherited on both paths represent alternatives. Hence the question is which is to be chosen. Prolog++ takes the simplest answer, given the normal nondeterministic Prolog evaluation method. The inheritance path is evaluated left-to-right and depth-first (or if you prefer in this case, height first) and the first solution taken. So for square, objects will be searched in the following order:

```
regular
polygon
rectangle
polygon
```

Since it only inherits from one object, the search in this case stops at regular. Since both methods should give the same result, this doesn't much matter.

But consider another possibility. We have not suggested a definition for the top-level object polygon – because there was nothing useful to put in it – but in a real implementation it would probably contain a 'fall-back' algorithm for computing areas and perimeters to cope with situations in which there are no ready formulae. These would undoubtedly be less efficient than the methods given, presumably involving calculating the coordinates of the vertices.

The problem is that using the depth-first approach, the method for perimeter in polygon will be found before the call to perimeter is found in regular. It appears that a breadth-first search would be more appropriate in this context.

A great deal of theoretical study has been put into this question, and the basic, if over-simplified, outcome of this is that no method is perfect (see, for example, Cardelli, 1988; Touretsky, 1986; Selman and Levesque, 1991; Reiter, 1980). Suppose we depend on a 'nearest ancestor' approach (see, for example, Zaniolo, 1984). In the above example, we would therefore give rectangle priority over polygon because it is only one step removed even though it is found later in a 'depth-first' search. In this model, the ancestor which is found still depends critically on how many steps there are in the inheritance path.

Unfortunately, the number of steps is often related more closely to the amount of refinement in the model for the purposes in hand than to any deep semantic 'relatedness' of the ideas. By changing the structure of the inheritance path we can, perhaps inadvertently, change the method chosen. If the correctness of the result depends on this, we are on rather thin ice.

In the example above, the correctness of the result is not at issue. All the methods should give the same results for the cases to which they are applicable as they are genuine alternatives. What is at issue is efficiency. Hence the effectiveness of the search (particularly at run-time) is a relevant issue. If one wants to control the situation more carefully then the possibility of 'programming around the problem' is always available.

3.4   Prolog++ notation

Prolog is unusual among high-level programming languages in not allowing expressions that evaluate to values, except in a few well-defined contexts such as to the right of an is operator. Prolog++ allows a more 'functional' style of programming in which expressions are more freely used. In this section we will explore these extensions to the normal Prolog notation.

There is a basic difference between Prolog and most other languages, and in particular, the functional languages. In LISP-like languages, every term that appears in a program is 'evaluated'. Thus if I write foo in a program, the LISP system tries to look up the value of foo. In Prolog, foo means the atom 'foo', at least in most cases. The exception is in certain designated arithmetic contexts; for example, to the right of the operator is.

Prolog++ changes this rule in a carefully calculated way. There is a strictly limited set of Prolog++ atoms, the presence of which is interpreted in a special way. We have already come across one of them – the word 'self'. The full list of these reserved atoms is given below. Most of these are operators and the special significance only comes into play when they are used with the appropriate arity, which is indicated (by /1 and so on).

```
& /1 @ /1/2 + /1
all/1 ancestor_class/0/1 category/0/1 class/0/1
    composite/0/1 descendant_class/0/1 instance/0/1 self/0
    sub_class/0/1 sub_part/0/1 suchthat/2 super_class/0/1
    super_part/0/1
```

The effect of this policy is that the number of ways of interpreting a term increases from two to three: a Prolog term, a Prolog++ term and an arithmetic expression. The reason for the distinction between the last two is that Prolog++ is still a symbolic language: we may still want to treat $1+2$ as a binary term with two arguments, not as the value 3.

Let us consider these three contexts in turn.

(1) Prolog terms appear in two places: the arguments of the head of a clause, or method; and after the 'quote' operator &.

It is undesirable to have any form of function evaluation in the head of a clause in a Prolog-like language. The reason is that the mode of evaluation is unknown at compile-time – it may be input or output. The mode directly affects when the function evaluation would take place: on output it naturally occurs after the subgoals in the body of the clause; on input, the inverse operator should be checked before any other subgoals (for example, $I+3$ in the head when 4 is passed would lead to I being bound to 1, as is the case in Miranda).

The quote operator will be considered shortly.

(2) Prolog++ terms may occur in any other context. They may occur as parameters for any subgoal in a clause, within arithmetic expressions, and within declarations. They may also be included in part of the head of a clause designated as output. The resulting method is called a **function**. This gives the value of any clause after the attribute name separated by the operator =. For example, we could define a function which produces the name of the object:

```
name = self.
```

in which case the result would be the name of the current object, whereas

```
name(self).
```

would simply return the value self.

When the value of a function or attribute is required, the operator @ may be used. If it is a local function then it is used in unary form. That is,

```
base(X) :-
    side(X).
```

can be rewritten as:

```
base = @side.
```

The @ operator may be used as binary operator associating to the left so that it may be used repeatedly with the intuitively obvious interpretation. To pronounce it one can use the English possessive construction "s'. Thus, to return to the family example, we can write:

```
sisterInLaw = @spouse@sister.
```

and say 'self's spouse's sister' (the self is implicit), instead of the more verbose:

```
sisterInLaw(L) :-
    spouse(S),
    S <- sister(L).
```

and the other two definitions of a sister-in-law can be expressed in the same way:

```
sisterInLaw  =  @brother@wife.
sisterInLaw  =  @spouse@brother@wife.
```

There are three definitions here expressed in functional form (following the dictionary definition). In keeping with normal Prolog conventions, functions can be multivalued in Prolog++. There is no commitment to single values.

A word about syntax is in order at this point. The '=', '@' and '&' operators are conventional Prolog symbols, which means that they must be written separately from any other graphic symbols, or else they will elide with them. The space between = and @ above is not optional, since =@ is a perfectly good Prolog symbol. If it is left out, the compiler will give a syntax error message in this case, as in most cases. But in some situations whereby two graphic symbols have been elided it might be possible for the compiler to find a valid interpretation, so that it will accept the statement without giving an error message. In these cases it does not give the intended structure. You have been warned!

Only a single term is allowed after the = of a function definition, but this can of course be structured to return as much information as is required. Thus the function:

```
places  =  (1,2,3).
```

returns three values, but they are structured as a single term. If we called this in the nonfunctional form, there would be only a single argument and if we wanted to retrieve the values we need to place an extra pair of brackets round them:

```
places((X,Y,Z))
```

Sometimes we may wish to use one of the reserved Prolog++ atoms as itself, not as the value it generates. This is the reason for the unary quote operator: '&'. It removes the special interpretation of the Prolog++ term which is its argument. For example,

```
write(& self)
```

writes the word 'self' to the current output, not the name of the current object. The quote operator is less used in Prolog++ than in LISP, because in most contexts terms are *not* evaluated.

It is also possible to introduce an arbitrary Prolog goal into a term, using the suchthat operator. The first argument of suchthat is the term; the second is a Prolog goal which is evaluated prior to the goal in which the term occurs.

```
write(X suchthat (1>2 -> X=true; X=false))
```

will print the answer false.

There are a number of other Prolog++ terms which will be introduced in due course.

(3) Arithmetic contexts occur in Prolog++ in the same way as they do in Prolog, but there are a number of conventions that make them easier to use.

A function definition can be introduced by **is** to signify that the right hand side is an arithmetic expression. Thus in the definition of a regular figure in the polygon example, we might write the definition of perimeter as:

```
perimeter is base * sides.
```

instead of

```
perimeter(P) :-
    base(B),
    sides(S),
    P is B*S.
```

Names of functions and attributes may be introduced directly into arithmetic contexts without any use of @. The reason that this is possible is that any non-numeric term in an arithmetic context must be evaluated to a number – hence the distinction between symbols (which stand for themselves) and expressions (which stand for a value) can always be resolved in favour of the latter. In fact the value of expression need not be numeric, if it is not the argument of a numeric operator.

The arguments of any functions in an arithmetic context are themselves evaluated as expressions, but any variables are not. This is normally what is required, but it may occasionally be necessary to introduce the quote operator. Compare the following two definitions:

```
johnsAge is today@year — birth(&john).
age(X) is today@year — birth(X).
```

The second of these is the more common and is correctly interpreted even though the parameter X will probably be bound to a symbolic term. It is equivalent to:

```
age(X,A) :-
    today <— year(B),
    birth(X, C),
    A is B—C.
```

It is also possible to introduce arithmetic expressions elsewhere in Prolog++, as parameters of messages or embedded in data structures. The means for this is the unary + operator, which introduces an arithmetic context in an arbitrary term. Thus

```
write( + 1 + 2)
```

outputs the value 3, not 1+2. The precedence number of unary + is greater than that for arithmetic operators but lower than for the relational operators. Hence it dominates the whole expression in the above example.

Introducing this third context makes Prolog++ easier to write than standard Prolog programs. But we should emphasize that the effect is purely syntactic. All the facilities could have been introduced without any extra syntax. However, the result would have been burdensome. To achieve a better integration of relational and functional styles of programming than Prolog++ provides requires much deeper changes to the semantics of the system (for example, higher-order unification). There have been many attempts at this, and so far none have achieved a wide following. We think the balance that Prolog++ achieves is the best that can be expected from current hardware and compiler technology.

3.4.1   Other Prolog++ terms

A number of the special Prolog++ terms, known as **is-a links**, are designed to give information about the class hierarchy. Since Prolog is a symbolic language it is natural that it should have this self-referential capacity, which helps in writing programs that are very general in their applicability.

class	the name of the instance's class
super_class	a superclass of a class
sub_class	a subclass of a class
ancestor_class	an ancestor (superclass or its superclasses)
descendant_class	a descendant (subclass or its subclasses)
instance	an instance of the class

The is-a links can be used in two ways: with or without an object. When used by themselves, they refer to the self variable. If they are followed by an appropriate object they apply to that object: they are all defined as prefix operators binding tighter than the arithmetic operators.

Thus the following calls which refer to classes succeed within Prolog++:

```
super_class equilateral = triangle
super_class equilateral = regular
sub_class regular = pentagon
ancestor_class equilateral = polygon
```

while the following will succeed only if they occur within the body of equilateral or one of its instances:

```
super_class = triangle
ancestor_class = polygon
```

If X is bound to an instance of equilateral, then the following will also succeed:

```
class X = equilateral
X = instance equilateral
```

A common use of these expressions is for the receiver of messages.

3.4.2 The Prolog context

Our treatment of evaluable contexts in Prolog++ has skirted round some of the subtler points of the interaction of Prolog++ with Prolog. These we need to clarify before proceeding further.

The first is the exact relationship between the arithmetic operators and Prolog. There is always a slight tenson in Prolog between the need for efficient compilation and the need to express a uniform picture. A similar tension is found in Smalltalk, where all the arithmetic operators are conceptually messages sent to the numbers to which they apply. To achieve reasonable performance it is mandatory to compile sequences of arithmetic operations, at least as long as they apply to the normal arithmetic types.

In Prolog this may be seen in the following trivial definition:

```
add1(X, Y) :- Y is X+1.
```

What happens if we pose the following query?

```
?- add1(4+5, Z).
```

In this case the variable X in the arithmetic expression is bound not to a number, but to an expression. Early Prolog interpreters had a simple approach to their arithmetic predicates: they simply did a 'tree walk' of the expression which was held as a term. Thus there was no problem in handling the case in which a variable was bound to an expression at run-time. With a compiler this is more time-consuming. Although, because of the type-free nature of Prolog, it is still necessary to check whether the value X is real or integer, none of the other 'interpretation' overheads are necessary. Consequently, and for other reasons, a number of Prolog compilers impose the restriction that a variable in an arithmetic expression must be bound at run-time to a number.

In Prolog++, it is necessary to recognize the arithmetic expressions, not only for is, but for all the built-in predicates, such as >, =:= and tab. Though the evaluation is passed to the underlying Prolog system, in most situations the predicate is actually passed up the inheritance hierarchy.

For example, if the following expression is found somewhere in a method or function:

```
X > width+0.5
```

what is actually passed up the hierachy are the following two messages:

```
width(W),
X > W + 0.5
```

Thus, width has been interpreted as an attribute or function definition and is evaluated first, followed by the call to >, which will probably be compiled into Prolog, unless it has been redefined by the user.

The evaluable predicates may thus be redefined by the user, who must be aware that the arguments may be themselves expressions. The exceptions to this rule are the two operators is and =. Since any redefinition of these in Prolog++ would be treated as a function definition it is impossible for the user to redefine them and they are therefore sent directly to Prolog in all cases.

The other issue is the treatment of the Prolog 'control' primitives, such as !, or cut, \+, the negation operator, -> with ;, if-then-else and the set operators, including findall. Most of these require special treatment by the compiler. If '!' were to be regarded as a message to be sent to Prolog, it would not have the desired control effect within the method definition in which it occurs.

3.4.3   The units example

To illustrate the benefits of the Prolog++ notation, let us take an arithmetic example. We wish to have a set of functions for converting physical units, which should be able to work with hours, minutes and seconds, or with feet and inches, or kilometres, metres and millimetres. We will have two basic functions that apply to each unit: normal, which converts an integer into the normalized form (for example 4 hrs 17 mins 22 secs), and base which converts a normalized form back into the base unit. A third function, convert, takes the unit to be converted into and the value, and returns the normalized version of the conversion. The aim is to make the system modular so that extra units can easily be added without changing the existing objects. So we structure the inheritance network as in Figure 3.8.

Each of the particular units is named after its base quantity, such as 'secs'. A quantity with units can be printed as, for instance, 4 hrs 17 mins 22 secs. This is a structured value and we need some way of representing it.

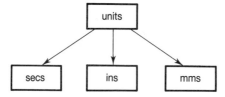

class secs	*class ins*	*class mms*
.	.	.
inherits units.	inherits units.	inherits units.

unitList = [60, 60, 24].
unitNames = [secs,
    mins, hrs, days]
	unitList = [12, 3, 1760]
	unitNames = [ins, ft,
	    yds, miles].
	factor(mms) = 25.4
		unitList = [1000, 1000].
		unitNames = [mms, m,
		    km].
		factor(ins) = 0.3937.

Figure 3.8 Structure of units program.

Since the number of entries is variable, the obvious representation is a list. When processing them we always need to access the least significant first, so this will be placed first in the list. So the internal representation for 4 hrs 17 mins 22 secs is simply [22,17,4], with the number of days omitted since it is zero. The conversion factors in the same format are then represented by the list [60,60,24] within the 'secs' object being the attribute unitList. Conversion factors to other units are given by the factor function.

The conversion into normal form is then given by a function definition within the object units as follows:

```
normal(Base) is toNormal(Base,unitList).

toNormal(Base, [A|B]) =
        [+Base mod A | +toNormal(Base // AD, B)] :-
    Base >= A, !.
toNormal(Base,) = [Base].
```

The first clause uses an is expression to signify that both toNormal and unitList are to be evaluated, with unitList being evaluated first. ToNormal however uses the = operator because its result is a list which is *not* to be evaluated, although the arguments of the list will be, as indicated by the + operators.

Possible calls to this routine are therefore

```
?- secs <− normal(3605,X)
X = [5,0,1]
?- secs <− normal(1234567, X)
X = [7, 56, 6, 14]
```

(These calls are made by the normal Prolog query mechanism which doesn't have the benefit of the @ notation. When used within a Prolog++ program one would naturally use the notation secs@normal(3065) and so on.)

If the recursive clause for toNormal was written in an entirely relational form, it would appear as follows:

```
toNormal(Base, [A|B], [C|E]) :-
    Base > =A, !,
    C is Base mod A,
    D is Base // A,
    toNormal(B, E).
```

The converse function is to convert a number in units into the base quantity:

```
base(Normal) is toBase(Normal,unitList).

toBase([A|B], [C|D]) is A + C * toBase(B,D) :- !.
toBase([], ) is 0.
```

The expression secs@base([3,2,1]) will then evaluate to $3 + 60*(2 + 60*1)$ = 3723.

To complete the example, let us consider the function to convert one unit to another. In this case a conversion factor is required for each pair of valid units. The obvious place to put this conversion factor is within the object which represents the unit from which the conversion is made. To convert a quantity we pass a message convert to the unit whose first argument is the new unit.

```
mms <- convert(ins, [0,1], X).
X = [3.369999999999999996, 0, 1]
```

that is, 1 metre $\approx$ 1 yard, 0 ft, 3.37 ins.

The code for the conversion function is shown below. Two cases are allowed for. The amount may be an integer in the base unit, or a structured value. The quantity returned is converted to the structured value according to the *target* unit definition.

```
convert(To, Amount) is To@normal(factor(To)*Amount) :-
    integer(Amount), !.
convert(To, Amount) is To@normal(factor(To)*base(Amount)).
```

Observe the obvious modularity of the system. Each legal unit conversion can be specified, using the name of the appropriate object as parameter to the factor function. For instance, the value for mms is defined within ins. These are local to the unit being defined and a new definition would be mainly concerned with providing conversions to existing units, although this definition would also involve updating some other definitions. Extensions can easily be envisaged to deal with new units automatically (see Exercise 3, p. 113). Other extensions could deal with compound units.

3.4.4 Refining the hierarchy

This far we have learned something about the utility of the Unix 'convert' program, which comes with an built-in database of useful conversions. The common factor to the vast majority of unit conversions is expressed in this program: they are straight multiplications. Object-oriented programming has however something more to offer for the other conversions that are not covered by this paradigm: for example, inverse calculations, such as wavelength and frequency, where division rather than multiplication is required.

The relevant thing about these conversions is that they are exceptions to the rule. The vast majority of conversions are straight multiplications (even those in more than one dimension) and therefore the Unix program covers most needs. One could imagine extending each of the definitions above to include other types of conversion, but it is annoying and unintuitive. The problem is not 'can we improve our coverage from 95% to 99% but 'what will happen when someone comes up with another type of conversion?' Will the user of your program need access to the source code to extend it in the way *they* want?

> Q: What other types of unit conversion can you envisage?
> Be imaginative. Make a list of three different conversions that have not been covered in this section, that might possibly be required.
> See Exercise 2, p. 113 for some suggestions.

Object-oriented programming provides a solution to this problem by means of dynamic binding. Since each unit is defined by a new object it is possible to redefine convert for an object for specified conversions. All the other routines, such as normal and base will still be accessible.

We will define two new objects to handle wavelengths and frequencies, which may be called 'kHz' and 'wave' respectively. These can inherit from another object called 'inverse' which defines the inverse function 'convert' for metres to kHz and vice versa. One possible implementation strategy may be pictured as shown in Figure 3.9.

In addition to any normal conversions, an object which inherits from inverse may define a function called inverse which takes the conversion unit as a parameter. The definition of convert within inverse has two clauses. The first queries whether there is an appropriate inverse definition for the required

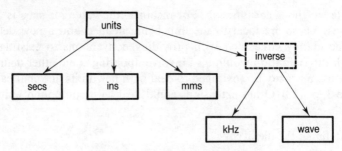

Figure 3.9   Refining the hierarchy.

unit. If so, it commits to that definition, using the cut and performs the calculation. If there is no such definition, the second clause simply passes the call up to the units object to take care of.

```
class inverse.
inherits units.
convert(Units,Value) is Mult/Value :-
    inverse(Units,Mult), !.
convert(Units, Value) = super@convert(Units, Value).
end inverse.

class kHz.
inherits inverse.
unitList = [1000].
unitNames = [kHz, mHz].
inverse(m) = 299792.
end kHz.
```

This example demonstrates the flexibility of the object-oriented approach in dealing with exceptions. The definition of convert in inverse effectively traps one specific case in which a different algorithm is to be used and allows other messages, including other uses of convert, to be handled in the normal way. Because other conversions do not reference inverse they are entirely unaffected by this exception. This makes a great contrast with other programming approaches in which introducing a new special case always tends to upset existing programs.

EXERCISES

1   Extend the units system with a print method, which provides a sensible printed representation of a value in the unit. For example, it should print the converted value of 1 m as:

   1 yd. 3.37 ins.

2   Provide modules to deal with the following types of units:
        (a) temperature, including Celsius, Fahrenheit and Kelvin scales, which
        have different zero levels;
        (b) logarithmic units such as decibels, converted to energy units;
        (c) years, months and days starting from 1900.

3   When a new unit of the simple multiplicative type is defined, each
        object that could convert to that unit needs an additional factor method.
        Rewrite convert so that if a factor is not found it computes the inverse
        from the new unit.

4   The units system as outlined in this section is naive about dimensions.
        Redesign the system so that derived units, such as area or
        power, can be converted automatically by specifying their dimension
        but without requiring specific conversion factors.

3.5   Parts hierarchy

To many people, inheritance means just the generalization/specialization
hierarchy which we have considered so far. But in program analysis and design
there is another important hierarchy: the way in which an object may be
broken down into its component parts. In 'conventional' object-oriented
languages, such as Smalltalk or C++, this hierarchy may be unnoticed,
because it is expressed via the type constructors (particularly record
definitions). But in database constructions and in a logic programming
context, it forms a new type of hierarchy.

   For example, let us suppose that we are modelling different forms of
cycle. An initial parts breakdown might be as shown in Figure 3.10.

   In other words, a bicycle has a pair of handlebars, a frame and two
wheels. The parts are declared by a **parts** declaration, which specifies each
of the parts, which are themselves defined by classes. Where there is more
than one instance of a part, this is indicated by following it with '*' followed
by a numerical expression. For example,

   parts frame, handlebars, wheel * 2.

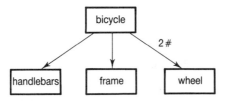

Figure 3.10   Parts hierarchy – a bicycle.

When one creates an instance of a class which has parts, each of the component parts is also created automatically. Unlike the specialization hierarchy, each of the parts has a separate instance, so that any attribute values are particular to the parts. A skeleton set of classes is shown below, each with a single method print which prints its name.

```
class bicycle.
parts frame, handlebars, wheel * 2.
print :-
    writenl(self),
    frame#1 <- print,
    handlebars#1 <- print,
    wheel#1 <- print,
    wheel#2 <- print.
end bicycle.

class frame.
print :- writenl(self).
end frame.

class handlebars.
print :- writenl(self).
end handlebars.

class wheel.
round.
print :- writenl(self).
end wheel.
```

Note that the parts do *not* inherit from the whole. If they did, then a create message would attempt to construct an infinite data structure. We could of course create another object from which they all inherit the print routine.

The print routine in bicycle demonstrates how the composite object refers to its subparts, using, for example wheel#2 to refer to the second wheel. We can demonstrate its use by sending a print message to a bicycle instance:

```
?- bicycle <- create(X), X <- print.
$(bicycle, 886488)
$(frame, 886490)
$(handlebars, 886492)
$(wheel, 886494)
$(wheel, 886499)
X = $(bicycle, 886488)
```

The body of the print routine in bicycle demonstrates a common situation in which one wants to send the same message to a number of different objects. To simplify this there are abbreviated notations in Prolog++.

The first is that any number of objects may be bracketed together on the left hand side of <− to signify that the same message is to be sent to each in turn. We could thus rephrase print as:

```
print :-
    (frame # 1,handlebars # 1,wheel # 1,wheel # 2) <− print.
```

A second notation utilizes the Prolog++ term **sub_part**. The term sub_part refers to any part of the current object (self). If we send a message to a subpart:

```
print :-
    sub_part <− print.
```

then the message will be sent to the first subpart. On backtracking the other subparts will be generated by sub_part. If we want to send a message to all subparts then it is possible to place the word **all** in front of this:

```
print :-
    all sub_part <− print.
```

The use of the word all replaces, or structures, a common use of failure-driven loops. Without using all, we would have to write:

```
print :-
    sub_part <− print,
    fail.
print.
```

to which one cannot give any declarative meaning, only an operational account. (One could also use the metapredicate forall which is not widely available.)

This technique is known as **message broadcasting** and is a powerful combination of the nondeterministic nature of Prolog and the message paradigm. It is achieved by repeatedly evaluating the left hand side, sending the message to each object found and then backtracking to find another.

It is also possible to send several messages at the same time to each of the objects generated by an expression on the left hand side. To do this, the messages are also grouped by means of brackets (to overcome the normal precedence of ,).

Suppose each of the sub-parts defined an attribute shape, then one can select the round components by selecting with the first. For example,

```
print :-
    all sub_part <− (shape(round), print2).
```

would print:

```
$(wheel, 886494)
$(wheel, 886499)
```

The use of composite objects will be demonstrated clearly in Chapter 5 where user interfaces are discussed. Graphical objects such as dialogue windows consist of a number of active objects each of which has its own state and methods. Objects in Prolog++ are otherwise 'flat' in the data structure sense. This does not mean that they cannot have structured attributes. But they are symbolic data items that can be listed in a roughly tabular form. The parts declaration provides the means for richer structures to be expressed in Prolog++.

3.6   The implementation of Prolog++

We have described the declarative features of Prolog++ informally up to this point in the chapter. To finish this chapter we wish to define them more precisely by giving a formal mapping from Prolog++ to Prolog.

But first a word of caution. Prolog++ defines a language 'on top' of Prolog and the mapping is up to the implementer. This may vary from system to system and there is no commitment that the exact details will remain the same. In particular, various optimizations are used to improve performance, some of which are described here but others are not. You should therefore avoid the temptation to 'go round the back door'. For example it is possible to call the Prolog implementation of a method directly. This is playing with fire! In fact, the way Prolog++ has been defined makes this unnecessary, in the author's experience, though it is certainly educational to inspect the compiled code as one is free to do using listing and clause.

Translation is the obvious way to make the meaning of Prolog++ more precise. Prolog is unusual in having, at least for the core of the language, a much better formal basis than most computing languages, because of its foundation upon logic – the Horn clause subset of the first-order predicate calculus. Instead of having a definition of meaning only in terms of what is done – an operational or proof semantics – it also has what is called a model semantics. In other words, one can give the set of all possible objects which satisfy any program quite separately from the proof steps required to establish them. This duality of declarative and operational semantics gives a very solid basis for reasoning.

Unfortunately, this attractive theoretical situation is compromised in practice in two ways. The proof which is necessary to find the model may not itself terminate (and Prolog's proof method is worse than many in this respect); and Prolog incorporates 'non-declarative' features to make it practical as a programming language: control features, such as the cut, and destructive features including i/o and changes to the database.

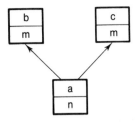

Figure 3.11   Example of dynamic binding.

However, it does mean that for simple situations at least, the mapping provides a clear semantics for aspects of inheritance which are otherwise vague. We can demonstrate that inheritance is an application of deduction at the metalevel.

To show the essential features of the inheritance schema used in Prolog++, let us take the simple definition of three classes, a, b, c in Figure 3.11.

```
class b.
m(A) :- n(A).
end b.

class c.
m(2).
end c.

class a.
inherits b, c.
n(1).
end a.
```

What happens if we have an instance of class a (assume this is bound to A) to which we send the message m(X)?

```
A <- m(X).
```

Since class *a* does not define method *m*, the message is first sent to *b*, where it finds a method and invokes a message *n*. This method is found not in *b* but the original class *a*, demonstrating the effect of dynamic binding. The net result is that X is bound to 1.

We will first take a very schematic translation of Prolog++ defined by the following rules:

(1)   Every class and instance of a class is named by a unique atom.

(2)   For each instance *i* of a class *c* there is a clause instance(i, c).

(3)   For each class *c* there is a clause of the form class(c).

(4)   For each instance of a class *c* inheriting from another class *s*, there is a clause of the form isa(c, s).

(5)   For each method *m* of arity *n* defined in a class *c* there is clause of the form defines(c, m/n).

(6)   For each clause of method *m* defined in a class *c*, having head *h* and body *b*, there is a clause of the form: method(c, h, S) :- message(S, b). with *message* repeated for each subgoal in the body. If there is a local definition of any subgoal *b* then the message that is sent is method(c, b).

If these rules are applied to the program above, the following Prolog clauses are obtained:

```
instance(a1, a).

class(a).
class(b).
class(c).

isa(a, b).
isa(a, c).

defines(b, m/1).
defines(c, m/1).
defines(c, n/1).

method(c, n(1), _).
method(b, m(A), Self) :-
    message(Self, n(A)).
method(c, m(2), _).
```

We may now define in Prolog an interpreter for these clauses which applies inheritance. It defines the predicate message/2:

```
message(Obj, Mess) :-
    class_of(Obj, Class),
    functor(Mess, N, A),              %Prolog built-in
    definition(Class, N/A, Cl), !,
    method(Cl, Mess, Obj).

class_of(I, C) :-
    instance(I,C).
class_of(C, C) :-
    class(C).

definition(Class, Name, Class) :-
    defines(Class, Name).
definition(Class, Name, Target) :-
    isa(Class, Super),
    definition(Super, Name, Target).
```

In this program, the predicate definition finds the appropriate inherited class for the message, by starting at the local class and searching all inherited classes. Message uses this to find the appropriate class to send the message to. An important detail is the cut ! in the message program. This restricts the number of solutions of definition to at most one, before invoking method, which can produce any number of solutions. The cut could be replaced by the application of the metapredicate oneof to the call to definition which would be logically clearer (corresponding to an existential quantifier); unfortunately this is not a standardized predicate.

The third parameter of method is crucial in this program: it names the *original* receiver of the message, the self variable. If this information was not passed, then the dynamic binding of n in the above example would not be possible. Messages in the body of the goal are sent to self, not to the local class, unless there is a local definition of the method.

It would be straightforward to modify this program to model other definitions of inheritance. For example, if we wished to model inclusive rather than overriding inheritance, it is only necessary to remove the cut in the definition of message. We have suggested earlier that this is not desirable, because for any method *m*, the different inheritance paths provide alternative implementations.

There are two aspects of the inheritance schema that we have not yet dealt with. The first is straightforward: rule 6 says that if a method is defined locally, then a call in the body is treated as a local goal unless it is specifically directed to the self variable. This is easily dealt with by substituting the self variable for the name of the local class.

The second is the use of super. This enables methods to be augmented with the contents of inherited definitions whose names are defined locally. In this case, instead of the body of a method being represented by a call to message, it will be substituted by a call to super/3. which is defined by:

```
super(Class, Message, Self) :-
    isa(Class, Super),
    functor(Message, N, A),
    getDef(Super, N/A, Cl), !,
    method(Cl, Message, Self).
```

3.6.1 The status of inheritance

What is the status of inheritance logically? Is it an axiom, a rule of deduction, a modal operator, or what? The clue comes from the definition of defines. The search is for the name of the method, not the method itself. Not until the class is found in which the appropriate method is declared is the message sent. This points to the fact that inheritance is actually a metalevel operation.

The notion of the metalevel was originally introduced to explain how the names of objects relate to statements directly involving those objects.

Logic becomes hopelessly confused if definitions of names take place in the same context as the definition of the contents of those names. Thus a 'chair' is something we use to sit on. Things with four legs and a back are examples of chairs, together with horizontal rock ledges with two verticals separated by approximately the length of an average human thigh. The introduction of the metalevel, originally by Tarski, separated out the definition of a word from the use of it.

We therefore characterize inheritance as **metalevel deduction**. It is a deduction which establishes the class of the method (class + name) to which a particular message is to be sent. Once the name is established, the message is sent to that class alone.

3.6.2   The implementation

The formalized account of inheritance given above is not, of course, the way in which things are done by the Prolog++ compiler. There are too many optimizations crying out to be done, and the optimizations are important for a number of reasons.

If the object-oriented level is significantly less efficient than the raw language, then people will not use it, or, just as bad, will try to program 'round the back' of the system. This is particularly important in the Prolog context where the procedure call is used at virtually every step of the program. If it is necessary to establish the inheritance path each time it is used, then the program could easily be slowed down by a factor of between 5 and 10.

Also, one is in danger of losing much of the effectiveness of the Prolog compiler. Prolog compilation is effective because in most cases one can spot at compile-time what steps are needed to perform unification, which is the heart of the Prolog 'engine'. This is not the place to digress into Prolog compilation. The interested reader is referred to Aït-Kaci (1991) for a very readable account of the techniques used. Two issues are particularly important. One is indexing: it is important to know the identity of the method used at compile-time, so that one does not waste time searching for it at run-time, and to preserve the position of whatever arguments are used by the Prolog compiler to choose the appropriate clause. The other is register allocation: the 'virtual machine' commonly used to implement Prolog is a register machine in which registers correspond to argument positions in the procedure head. Although knowledgeable Prolog programmers may use this to speed up their programs, this is not what we are talking about. What must be avoided is turning a list of arguments which would map directly into registers into a 'term' for which the naive unification algorithm would have to be used.

What we are talking about is the difference between the calls:

```
append([a,b,c], [d,e,f], X)
```

and

> method(list, append([a,b,c], [d,e,f], X), list)

In the second case:

(1)   Two sets of indexing are required even to identify the clauses for the
        append method, which in Prolog would be done at compile time.

(2)   The arguments of append are at the second level and in the normal
        abstract machine model these would be passed to a general unification
        routine, whereas in Prolog they would be optimized.

(3)   Most Prolog compilers use the first argument of append to select the
        correct clause of the definition to be tried, further speeding up the
        process.

(4)   In Prolog the second argument of append can be left untouched in its
        register during the recursive phase which executes the code:

> append([A|B], C, [A|D]) :- append(B, C, D).

This is the ultimate in compilation: no code is generated! It is
only picked up in the base case. In the 'raw' version, a new structure
would be generated on the heap for each recursive step, with the
necessity of copying all the contents.

In the current version of Prolog++ there are two modes of use: a
compiled mode and an optimized mode. The compiled mode is designed for
incremental development. Each class may be compiled separately without
needing any knowledge of other classes. The compiled clauses may be
inspected and used with the normal debugging tools. The optimized version
knows what is the inheritance hierarchy for the whole program and so can
produce better code which avoids inheritance calls in most cases.

Let us look at what these constraints allow in compiling the program.

Any calls to local methods can be made directly, including the
important case of recursion. Thus if we defined the append procedure within
an object:

```
class list.
append([], A, A).
append([A|B], C, [A|D]) :- append(B,C,D).
end list.
```

we would be able to generate almost the same code: the only differences are
a new and unique name for the clause (this would not be necessary in a
Prolog system supporting modules) and the extra argument at the end, which

is the self variable. In this case it is unnecessary but compilers need to be consistent.

```
'list<-append/3'([], A, A, _).
'list<-append/3'([A|B], C, [A|D], E) :-
    'list<-append/3'(B, C, D, E).
```

This is not enough to handle inheritance. If a class inherits lists, maybe at several places removed in the tree, then the message will be passed up the tree until it finds the right class. Hence there is in general a need for a stub, which defines the messages for the object. This consists of a predicate with the name of the class and arity 2. In this case it will be something like the following:

```
list(append(_1, _2, _3), _4) :-
    !,
    'list<-append/3'(_1, _2, _3, _4).
list(_1, _2) :-
    ppp(_1, _2).
```

The first clause is a simple 'dispatcher'; the second expresses the residual inheritance of this class which is from the predefined class ppp. The cut in the first clause prevents a message which is handled locally from being passed further up.

Nonlocal calls – from one object to another – must necessarily search the hierarchy of classes from self up to ppp. This includes calls to most of the Prolog built-in routines (except some arithmetic predicates). However this is not necessarily too much of an overhead. As is common in most object-oriented systems, it is possible to cache the names of methods which have been defined, to provide shortcuts in most cases. In logical circles this technique is usually known as **lemma generation**. For example, if no method of the same name has been defined anywhere in Prolog++, then the only possibility is to treat it as a direct call to Prolog, whether it is a user or system defined predicate. If there is no such predicate, an error message will be generated.

In the optimized case, more of the inheritance steps can be pre-evaluated at compile-time, so that many nonlocal calls can be made as efficient as local calls.

This description of the implementation is necessarily incomplete. We haven't described the provisions for private representations, dynamic attributes, and so on.

SUMMARY
- This chapter shows how programs can be organized around objects. Predicates become attributes or methods of objects. Two forms of hierarchy are allowed: the generalization/specialization hierarchy

associated with class inheritance; and the parts hierarchy which allows complex objects to be built up and manipulated.

- The class hierarchy allows a method to be inherited from a tree of classes and supports dynamic binding, so that different classes may refine calls in different ways. The default method of inheritance is overriding, but the use of calls to super allows a versatile and efficient form of inclusive inheritance to be provided. Multiple inheritance is also supported.

- Prolog++ provides a limited form of functional notation, designed in such a way as to respect the normally symbolic nature of Prolog computation. Various reserved symbols are used to access the hierarchy and to make the notation more convenient.

- It is worth noting that some of the examples in this chapter are rather forced: it would be much more natural to represent individual instances of an object dynamically using the mechanisms to be introduced in the next chapter. We have avoided doing it here to help make the declarative basis of the object mechanisms clearer. But read on!

4

Dynamic Prolog++

4.1 Introduction

In this chapter we enter a new dimension in object-oriented logic programming by considering the way in which objects may be dynamically changed. In Chapter 1, we discussed the rationale of this: logic programming is essentially 'declarative', in that it considers a static world in which objects do not change. Variables are like those in mathematics rather than those in programming: once they have received a value, that value cannot change. Of course, Prolog adds a new dimension to this with backtracking: if the value does not help to solve the problem under consideration, it may be possible to backtrack and find another binding. However this does not change the essential 'once-only' nature of assignment.

   With objects we move into a different world, in which the attributes of an object may change over time. This models our everyday experience in which objects do change over time: people change their appearance, their weight and height; we change the wheels on a car, and paint it a different colour; we replace the settee in the living room, though the new one is still 'our' settee. However introducing change is not without drawbacks. The 'microchanges' of conventional programming languages, in which each step normally changes the value of some register in the machine – this being reflected in the problem definition language – do not blend with the evaluation method of Prolog in which unification preserves the information at each step, so that at the end of a computation all the information that was used to derive the proof remains valid.

   There is, at this time, no entirely satisfactory resolution of these two perspectives. What we suggested in Chapter 1 as a methodology for object-oriented logic programming was to distinguish 'macro' from 'micro'-changes – dynamic from functional. Having performed a computation in a pure fashion, we then store the results of the computation within the objects so that next time it is these new values which define the computation.

In other words, the old attributes + a message from outside + a computation yields a new set of attributes. This corresponds to a state change in the object. Logic still applies in computing the new state; where it does not apply is in the ongoing sequence of changes in the interface between the different objects At this level we are frequently concerned with the interface of the program with the real world. This also is unpredictable in a creative way. We want to have the freedom to change the input parameters and to experiment in unforeseen ways. If the input data was predictable then there would be no need for it. Such data could be kept inside the program from its inception. In some cases, the data can be considered as 'completing' the program; but in other cases (such as resetting the input), it contradicts what has gone before.

One of the ways in which we are constrained is by the sequential nature of today's programming languages. When we loosen this constraint it becomes much easier to model a set of objects involved in updating each other, as we will see in Chapter 7. However the cost of this, in the versions of parallel or concurrent Prolog currently available, is that we lose other features: for example the ability to generate a number of solutions to a problem. Since most real programming is still done on sequential machines, these will remain prototypes for some time yet.

As we explore the dynamic nature of Prolog++, resist the temptation to treat it just like another Pascal: it isn't and your programs will not yield the productivity gains that Prolog gives if you treat it like that. Updates should generally be performed at the interobject level, not within the object method.

4.2   Mutable attributes

The notion of attributes was introduced in the previous chapter though for clarity we will repeat the definitions. Each instance of an object may have a set of attributes which are declared with the attribute statement which has the form:

```
attribute val1, val2.
```

Initial values may be set at instance creation time using the attribute list parameter as the second parameter to create.

```
simple <— create(T, [val1 = 1, val2 = −1])
```

In general, each instance of an object will have different values for its attributes. However it is possible to declare **default** values for the attribute which are associated with the class and are used if no assignment is made to the instance's attribute.

```
attribute val = 0.
```

The effect of this is almost exactly the same as if we declared an attribute and a function with the same name. If we declare an attribute with a default value *and* a function with the same name, then the attribute gets priority, though both values will be returned. That is, the above has the same effect as:

```
attribute val.
val = 0.
```

An attribute of an object instance can be given a new value by an **assignment** statement from within the object which uses the conventional symbol := . For example,

```
val := 2
```

After the assignment statement, the default value (or values) is inaccessible. In fact there are several different assignment statements. The statement above introduces an arithmetic context, so that expressions and function evaluations are permitted. We could, for instance, write:

```
val := val1 + val2.
```

since attribute names are evaluated within an arithmetic context.

The values of attributes are not limited to numbers. If we wish to assign a symbol, then one can use the symbol & = . This recalls the & operator which introduces a Prolog context: the value on the right-hand side of & = is *not* evaluated. Thus, if we wrote

```
val & = val1.
```

this would assign the atom val1 to the attribute val, not the value of attribute val1.

In addition to attributes associated with instances of objects, it is possible to associate an object with the class itself: this is called a **class attribute**. Its declaration is similar:

```
class attribute value = 0.
```

There is no way of changing the value of an attribute from outside the class. This is entirely intentional: it is one of the important differences between object-oriented programming and the use of *frames* in Artificial

Intelligence. An object is not simply a data structure that can be prodded and manipulated from anywhere. An object needs to be in control of its attributes and the best way to ensure this is to prevent assignments except from within the body of the class. For those attributes that it is safe to change one can easily supply an extra routine to do this, as we shall see.

It is also important to be able to control read access to attributes from the outside. One can declare an attribute **public** or **private**. This is done by placing either of the words public or private before the corresponding declaration, for example,

```
public class attribute total = 0.
```

The *default* for attributes in Prolog + + is that they are private and for methods is that they are public. Being able to access the value from outside has been proved to be the most practical for writing programs, as one otherwise simply ends up writing methods or functions with the same name, which tend to get confused with the initialization statement.

The full declaration of attributes is thus

$$\begin{bmatrix} \text{private} \\ \text{public} \end{bmatrix} \begin{bmatrix} \text{instance} \\ \text{class} \end{bmatrix} \text{attribute}$$

where the first option in each case is the default and may be omitted.

It is actually simpler in an interactive setting to demonstrate class attributes than instance attributes. A simple object whose only function is to remember a value using the method remember and return it on demand using the attribute total, can therefore be given by:

```
class simple.
public class attribute total = 0.
remember(V) :-
      total := V.
end simple.
```

The value of the attribute is retrieved externally using either method or function notation:

```
?- simple <- total(X).
X = 0
?- simple <- remember(3).
yes
?- simple <- total(X).
X = 3.
?- simple <- (remember(-26), total(X)).
X = -26.
```

One of the frequent uses of assignment is for accumulating totals. For this reason Prolog++ provides a set of operators similar to those in C, which combine arithmetic operations and assignment, written as $+ =$, $- =$, $* =$ and $/ =$. These add, subtract, multiply and divide the value of the expression on the right hand side to the existing value of the attribute.

Thus if we add method add and subtract to the definition of simple:

```
add(X) :- total += X.
subtract(X) :- total -= X.
```

then we can invoke it to keep running totals:

```
?- simple <- remember(3).
yes
?- simple <- add(5).
yes.
?- simple <- subtract(2).
yes
?- simple <- total(X).
X = 6
```

4.2.1   Initialization

When an instance is created it is usually desirable to perform some initialization actions. The most important of these are to set up its attributes, which we have already demonstrated: attributes can have static default values, or they can be assigned values with the second parameter of the create method. These dynamic values override the default values.

There may be additional actions which the object should perform at startup. For example, we might wish to keep a count of the number of objects in a class at a particular time, so that it is not necessary to count them when we want to know how many there are. One way to do this would be to send a message to the object immediately after it has been created:

```
object <- create(V),
V <- initialize.
```

There is, unfortunately, a danger that the user might forget to do this. Prolog++ has a set of predefined **handlers** for such situations. When various events occur in the course of executing a program, messages are automatically sent to the handler, if it exists. It is thus possible to prepare for various eventualities by placing a definition of a method with the name of the handler either in the class or in one of the classes it inherits.

After the creation of an object, the message **when_created** is sent to the newly created instance. We could use this in our simple example to keep track of the number of objects created by means of the definition:

```
when_created :- add(1).
```

This is an appropriate use of a class attribute: all instances of an object share a class attribute, so they would all have access to the same total value.

While the use of when_created has an advantage in reliability, there are limits to what it can do by itself. For one thing, the when_created message is only sent to the object itself, not to any superior classes it might inherit. Also, it has no parameters: the creator of the instance may wish to pass extra information to be used in initialization.

The first drawback is easy to correct using the super mechanism. The when_created message may be sent to superclasses either before or after the local initializations are done. In this way one can easily control whether initialization is performed in a 'top-down' or 'bottom-up' fashion, or somewhere in between. For example,

```
when_created :-
    super <— when_created,
    add(1).
```

The need to pass more information to the object at initialization time can be handled in two different ways. The simplest is to add parameters to a routine called immediately after initialization, such as initialize above. The other possibility is to redefine the create method, so that it still invokes the original create method in ppp to do the actual object creation. For example, we might wish to use the additional arguments to check that the object has not yet been created. If it has been, we simply return a reference to that object. If not we create the new object and send the arguments to initialize. If a method exists has already been defined which returns the object if it exists, the create method could be written:

```
create(X, Args) :-
    exists(Args, X) —> true
    ; super <— create(X),
        X <— initialize(Args).
```

If adopting this approach one needs to remember that it would be bad programming style to redefine the parameters altogether, so that, for example, the first parameter did not return the new instance. Also, it should be remembered that the two create routines, create/1 and create/2 are entirely different methods. In the above case one might wish to disable create/1, by redefining it as an empty and failing routine.

Let us now take a slightly more ambitious example to demonstrate the use of dynamic assignment. The example is the familiar eight queens problem: place eight queens on a standard chessboard so that none of the queens can attack the others. There is no simple known algorithm for this: we simply try placing queens in consecutive columns of the board until a proper configuration is reached. In Prolog this is usually taken as a standard example of backtracking (see Appendix C), but the solution we present here does not use backtracking. Instead, it creates each queen as a separate object that stores the queen's position locally and passes messages between the queens to check all the possibilities. The solution is adapted to Prolog++ from (Budd, 1991) where it is presented as a set of mainly Boolean functions in Object Pascal, C++, Objective-C and Smalltalk. A sample solution is shown in Figure 4.1.

The basic arrangement of the objects is shown below. Each queen is assigned a number which corresponds to its column on the board (since it is rather obvious that each queen must be in a different column). The queens each have three attributes: neighbour, row and column. The neighbour attribute points to the queen in the previous column, forming a one-way linked list (shown for four queens in Figure 4.2).

To set up the queens we call the method initial. This creates a list of eight queens, returning the last as a result. Here is the heading and implementation of the queen class:

```
class queen.
attribute row, column, neighbour.
class attribute last.

%call to initiate linked objects, returning last one
initial(LastQueen) :-
    create(First, [column = 1]),
    initial(2, First, LastQueen).

initial(N, Neighbour, Last) :-
    N > 8 -> Last=Neighbour
    ; create(Queen, [column = N, neighbour = Neighbour]),
        initial(+ N+1, Queen, Last).
```

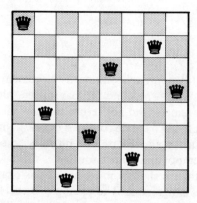

Figure 4.1 Eight queens: sample solution.

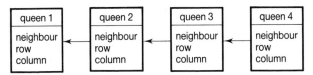

Figure 4.2   One-way linked list for four queens.

The work of searching for a solution is initiated by a method called first, which attempts to find the first solution. The message is given to the last queen (queen 8) who first delegates it to the previous queen to find a solution to the first seven columns. She then tries to find a row which is compatible with that partial solution. This is done by picking a row and passing the row and column back to the previous queens for vetting. If the message canAttack/2 succeeds, the queen tests the next column.

```
first :-
    (@neighbour <- first ; true),
    row := 1,
    testOrAdvance.


testOrAdvance :-
    @neighbour <- canAttack(@row, @column) -> next
    ; true.


canAttack(R, C) :-
    (@row = R
    ; R is row + column - C
    ; R is row - column + C
    ; @neighbour <- canAttack(R, C)
    ), !.


next :-
    @row = 8 ->
        @neighbour <- next,
        row := 1,
        testOrAdvance
    ; row += 1,
        testOrAdvance.
```

Note the use of the expression @neighbour as the target of messages. This picks up the value of the neighbour attribute in order to send the message down the line. In most of the procedures we have used the ->; conditional form here as it is just what is needed. We could also have used it in canAttack, but the cut (!) is just as appropriate: we only wish to know if one of the neighbours can attack; if several can we are not interested.

In arithmetic expressions (such as R is row + column − C), the @ symbol is not required before the attributes row or column. Since symbols are not meaningful in an arithmetic context, Prolog++ makes the necessary assumption that these must be evaluated either as attributes or functions.

One difference between the object-oriented approach and the conventional Prolog solution is that it is mandatory to provide an output routine to fetch the values of the generated attributes. This can also use a recursive routine in queen as follows:

```
print :-
    (@neighbour <− print ; true),
    writeseqnl(['Row ',@row, 'Column ',@column]).
```

It is necessary to provide a query or driving routine for the whole program, which is simply:

```
queen@initial <− (first, print).
```

When this is executed, the output is as follows:

```
Row 1 Column 1
Row 5 Column 2
Row 8 Column 3
Row 6 Column 4
Row 3 Column 5
Row 7 Column 6
Row 2 Column 7
Row 4 Column 8
```

All of these methods use a 'divide and conquer' problem-solving strategy. Get the remaining queens to build a partial solution and then add another brick to the pile. This leaves the question of how the foundation is laid. The conventional approach is to supply an extra test in every procedure: if this is the first queen, then react differently. In the program above, the attribute neighbour is not assigned for the first queen. Consequently, the expression @neighbour fails. This is precisely what is needed in testOrAdvance, canAttack, and next. But in first we need to make a special check in order to ignore the failure.

The object-oriented approach, however, provides an alternative solution: make the last object different. In this case it needs no internal state; the object simply needs to react appropriately to the different messages. This is simple in the case of first. It simply succeeds. But can_attack and next must fail. It is not enough to omit these: the Prolog++ system will generate an error message. It is therefore necessary to use the built-in predicate fail which does not produce such an error. The nullQueen object is therefore simply defined by:

```
class nullQueen.
first.
canAttack(_, _) :- fail.
next :- fail.
print.
end nullQueen.
```

The initialization routine is simplified; since nullQueen has no attributes it isn't necessary to create an instance of it. Initial then becomes:

```
initial(LastQueen) :-
    initial(1, nullQueen, LastQueen).
```

and first can also be simplified:

```
first :-
    @neighbour <- first,
    row := 1,
    testOrAdvance.
```

In this particular case, the difference between these two approaches is marginal. However, the use of a different type of object to represent the limiting case is a valuable technique.

Having demonstrated this solution, it is worth making some appraisal. How does this compare on the one hand with other object-oriented languages, and on the other with Prolog. There are two obvious ways of making the comparison: by the size of the code and the run-time.

If we rank the solutions in different languages by the number of tokens and (noncomment) lines of source code, we get the following result:

Language	Lines	Tokens
Prolog++	45	218
Smalltalk	48	231
C++	52	309
Prolog	24	338
Objective-C	59	358
Object Pascal	92	385

As one would expect, the Prolog version produces the smallest number of lines of code. However when one counts tokens, the other standard measure of the size of a program, the results are very different. Here the Prolog++ version is marginally superior to Smalltalk and Prolog is fourth. Evidently one reason for the small number of lines in Prolog is that it encourages a lot of information per line! The difference is accounted for by the repeated parameter lists in Prolog which are largely absent in the Prolog++ version.

Since the Prolog++ version is using the same approach as the other object-oriented languages, it is not surprising that there isn't a great deal of difference between them. It is to be expected however that a nonobject-oriented version would be significantly larger.

If we compare execution speeds of the two Prolog-based systems however (the results aren't available for the other systems), we see a different picture. The Prolog++ version runs significantly slower than the Prolog version. This might be surprising to those who have not used Prolog: surely the overhead of carrying around all the extra parameters must make Prolog slower. There are two answers to this: first, each step in a Prolog program tends to carry out a number of steps in the information transfer process, so that the number of unifications in a Prolog program is much less than the number of instructions executed in C++, for example. Second, the compilation process is able to reduce the amount of work by a significant proportion.

By contrast there is a significant overhead in processing assignment statements in Prolog++.

4.2.2   Multivalued attributes

So far there is a discrepancy between the treatment of Prolog++ attributes and the multivalued nature of methods and even functions. Part of the reason for this is notational. The assignment statement is a very convenient way of saying 'make this the value of the attribute and, by the way, forget the previous value'. Some object-oriented extensions of Prolog have used the assignment statement also for multivalued attributes, in which case the assignment statement means 'add this value to the existing values'. But since a perfectly good notation in Prolog exists already for this type of activity, which is also more precise, Prolog++ coopts and adapts it.

The primary purpose of providing the assignment operators in Prolog++ is to allow objects to be changed dynamically. One important application of this is to allow a database to change and evolve. Prolog is slightly awkward in this respect. Changes made with assert and retract are not reflected in the 'source' language of the program, so one must keep track informally of what are static and what are dynamic relations and program up the necessary housekeeping. Over the years, methods have evolved to signify this, such as the dynamic declaration in Quintus Prolog, but these are mainly to assist the compiler in generating the appropriate runtime representation.

The use of multivalued attributes in Prolog++ is designed to blend with the use of database updates in Prolog. The special facilities are provided by means of an additional class called **db**. This should be included in the inheritance path of any class which intends to use them using the declaration:

```
inherits db.
```

The class db provides new versions of the database primitives asserta, assertz, retract, which customize the names of predicates asserted into the Prolog database for a specific class or instance. Thus two instances of a class may both perform assertz(a(p)) and the results will be kept separate.

EXERCISES

1   Take the definition of family relationships in the previous chapter and redefine the individuals using instances. What are the advantages and disadvantages of this new approach? If you were constructing a family tree, which would you use?

2   Consider the geometric shapes example used in the previous chapter in the context of a drawing program which allows one to create and manipulate shapes. What extra information would be desirable? Extend the example to become a dynamic Prolog++ program.

4.3   Error handling

4.3.1   Assignment constraints

In our earlier example, we pointed out that the assignment statement := expected an arithmetic expression on the right hand side. You may therefore be surprised that it is not necessarily an error if the actual value is not a number. Take the following sequence:

```
?- simple <- remember('Something else').
yes
?- simple <- total(X).
X = Something else
```

As this shows, there is no intrinsic typechecking on the assignment statement: in the last example we have assigned a symbol not a number. Because in the assignment statement it appears as a variable, it is not interpreted as a function and is taken as a simple value to which no operator needs to be applied.

If this occurred in a program, then the mistake might not be discovered until some time afterwards and we might have tried to apply 'add' to this value. At this point it could be very difficult to establish where the rogue assignment was made. Because this is not an unusual situation, powerful typechecking systems are the norm in imperative programming languages, partly to catch this type of error.

Although Prolog is type-free and the benefits of a type system are not as pronounced as in other languages (and the disadvantages somewhat greater), Prolog++ does provide a means of trapping these types of errors by means of predefined handlers. **Invalid** performs a check before the actual assignment is carried out, and **when_assigned** is invoked immediately afterwards. The mechanism which invokes these, called a *daemon*, will invoke all such definitions in the scope of the objects. If any of the invalid routines succeed, then the assignment is not carried out. It does not matter whether the when_assigned routines succeed or fail.

The invalid routine takes two parameters: the first is the name of the attribute, the second is the value to be assigned to it. Thus if we wanted to ensure that no non-number is assigned to total in the simple example, we could write:

```
invalid(total, Value) :-
    \+ number(Value).
```

This acts specifically for one attribute; if we wanted to ensure that all attributes in that class were constrained to be numbers then we could leave the first parameter as a variable – all the power of unification can be used as normal:

```
invalid(_, Value) :-
    \+ number(Value).
```

Since the assignment has not been done, the old value is still available. Thus if we had an attribute salary and wished to express the constraint that it could not be increased by more than 50% we could add the clause:

```
invalid(salary, Value) :-
    Value > salary * 1.5.
```

There is no need to repeat the earlier check on numeric values, if they occur in the same class; the checks have a cumulative effect. They also apply to any assignments made within the class. So if, as earlier, assignments are made in three different routines, there is no need to change each of these; a single check will catch them. This makes the constraints particularly useful during the debugging of a program.

If we do not wish to stop the assignment then it is preferable to use the second handler, called when_assigned. By the time this is called, the old value does not exist, so when_assigned takes three parameters: the name of the attribute, the old value and the new value.

A simple but powerful use of this is to make a trace of all the assignments in the program execution. In the eight queens example, the following clause inserted into the class queen would be appropriate:

```
when_assigned(Attr, _, New) :-
    writeseqnl([Attr, of,@column,: = ,New]).
```

For the four queens problem, this produces the following trace:

```
:- queen@initial(4) <—first

row of 1 := 1
row of 2 := 1
row of 2 := 2
row of 2 := 3
row of 3 := 1
row of 3 := 2
row of 3 := 3
row of 3 := 4
row of 2 := 4
row of 3 := 1
row of 3 := 2
row of 4 := 1
row of 4 := 2
row of 4 := 3
row of 4 := 4
row of 3 := 3
row of 3 := 4
row of 1 := 2
row of 2 := 1
row of 2 := 2
row of 2 := 3
row of 2 := 4
row of 3 := 1
row of 4 := 1
row of 4 := 2
row of 4 := 3
```

Another use of this would be to store the values assigned for later use. To do this we will use the Prolog built-in predicate called asserta, which adds an assertion to the front of a relation:

```
when_assigned(Attr, _, Val) :-
    asserta(assign(Attr, Val)).
```

The effect of this is to store all the assignments to any attributes in reversed order. If this had been in place at the beginning of the chapter, then a simple inspection would reveal the following:

```
?- listing(assign).
assign(total, 'Something else').
assign(total, 6).
assign(total, 8).
assign(total, 3).
assign(total, -26).
assign(total, 6).
```

Useful as this facility is, there may be times when one wants to avoid the use of these constraints: maybe certain methods are well-checked already and calling invalid and when_assigned gets in the way of the other checks; also there is an inevitable performance penalty involved in making these checks. For these reasons, Prolog also provides a set of **quiet assignments** to match the 'noisy' assignments we have used up to this point. These look the same as the other operators except that they have an extra = at the end. That is,

:==	quiet arithmetic assignment
&==	quiet symbolic assignment
+==	quietly add arithmetic value to existing
-==	quietly subtract arithmetic value from existing
*==	quietly multiply arithmetic value by existing
/==	quietly divide existing by arithmetic value

One situation in which these quiet assignments are essential is within the routines such as when_assigned. Use of the normal assignments here leads immediately to a vicious loop: the assignment itself generates a recursive call to when_assigned.

So if we wanted to count the number of assignments which took place in the eight queens example, the following clause for when_assigned would be sufficient:

```
when_assigned(_, _, _) :-
    total + = =1.
```

where total is declared on a class-wide basis by

```
class attribute total = 0.
```

In the present implementation, the assignment := takes almost an order of magnitude more time than := =, so it is best to use the latter in situations where performance is important, with the noisy assignment used for debugging.

4.3.2   Dynamic typechecker

As a further example of the use of assignment checks we will be a little more ambitious and define a proper dynamic typechecker. This will allow the basic types (integer, real, atom and so on) and user defined types, including polymorphic data constructors. This may sound intimidating. Don't worry, it only requires about half a page of code (as there is no need for induction) and we will explain these terms.

First let us think of the object structure that is needed. When an assignment is done, the invalid message is sent to the class. Consequently the class should inherit, at some point, the class which defines the typechecker. It seems reasonable to declare the types of attributes in the user's class, using a function we will call type. Examples of possible declarations are:

```
attribute total, companies, today.
type(total)  =  integer.
type(today)  =  date.
type(companies)  =  list(atom).
```

What we have in mind are the following possible assignments:

```
total := 22.
today := date(1993, 12, 31).
companies := [ibm, univac, fujitsu].
```

Integer and atom are defined by the Prolog system, so all that is necessary to check them is to use the corresponding calls; for example, we generate the call integer(22) and if that succeeds then all is well. An extra type called any can match any data, and provides for an escape from the typechecking regime.

Date is a user-defined type consisting of a constructor date/3. Type definitions and constructors are more general than a particular class. Hence we need to create an intermediate object, which we will call types, in which the various type definitions are declared, using a similar function which we will call typedef. The declaration for dates will therefore be:

```
typedef(date)  =  date(integer, integer, integer).
```

Typechecker declares the invalid procedure. This may be pictured as Figure 4.3.

We have not dealt with the aspect of types which may be unfamiliar to some readers: polymorphic types. This is *not* the same sense of the word polymorphism which is often used in object-oriented programming, which we call dynamic binding. Essentially, a polymorphic type is a parameterized type. Lists are a good example: one can have lists of integers, lists of atoms, even lists of lists. The name of such a type takes a parameter which may appear

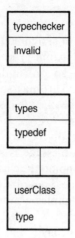

Figure 4.3   Typechecker declaration.

also on the right hand side. In the case of recusive types such as lists there will always need to be at least *two* definitions, to define the base and recursive cases. In the case of lists, these will be:

```
typedef(list(X)) = [].
typedef(list(X)) = [X | list(X)].
```

Unification takes care of all the details here. Our list of companies is given the type list(atom). This can be instantiated as either the nil list [], or the structure [atom | list(atom)]. The elements of this list are themselves types whose definitions are applied recursively to their arguments. We require that there are no variables in the type statement and that any variables on the right of the typedef also appear on the left (though the converse is not true).

Thus the definition of the types class for this particular situation is:

```
class types.
inherit typeChecker.

typedef(list(X)) = [].
typedef(list(X)) = [X | list(X)].
typedef(date) = date(integer,integer,integer).

end types.
```

Now we come to the definition of the typechecker itself. It is shown below:

```
class typeChecker.
%Type checker for variable assignments
%Include "type(Attribute)=" statement in all attributes to
    be checked
```

```
invalid(Var, Val) :-
    self <-type(Var,Type), !,
    (check(Type, Val) -> fail
    ; writeseqnl(['?Illegal assignment',Var,':=',
        Val,'in ',self]) ).
invalid(Var, Val) :-
    writeseqnl(['?Undeclared type for variable',
        Var,':=',Val,'in ',self]).

check(any, _) :- !.
check(Type,Val) :-
    self<-typedef(Type,TypeDef),
    functor(Val,Func,Arity),
    functor(TypeDef, Func, Arity),!,
    checkargs(Arity,TypeDef,Val).
check(Type, Val) :-
    atom(Type), !,
    call([Type,Val]).

checkargs(0, _,_) :- !.
checkargs(N, Type, Val) :-
    arg(N, Type, TN),
    arg(N, Val, VN),
    check(TN, VN),
    N1 is N-1,
    checkargs(N1, Type, Val).

end typeChecker.
```

We have included self as the target of two calls – type and typedef – for clarity, though it is strictly unnecessary to do so. Let us follow through a simple and a complex example. The simple example is

```
total := 22.
```

This gives rise to the following quasi-proof:

```
invalid(total, 22)
    userclass <- type(total, X)
    ++types <- type(total, X). ++userclass
    {X = integer}
    check(integer, 22)
            atom(integer),
            !,
            call([integer, 22])
    -> fail
```

Since invalid fails, the assignment succeeds. The use of call needs some explanation: a list of terms is not a valid Prolog query, so some Prologs (including MacProlog) convert this into the corresponding term using univ (=..), namely integer(22). Another way of expressing the same thing, defined in the Edinburgh Prolog library, is apply(integer, [22]) – this does a call using the first argument applied to a list of arguments which is the second argument.

Now let us take a more complicated example: the use of lists. To keep the discussion reasonable we will take the slightly shorter assignment:

```
companies := [ibm].
```

This gives rise to the following quasi-proof, which the interested reader may follow through:

```
invalid(companies, [ibm])
    userclass <— type(companies, X)
    ++ types <— type(companies, X). ++ userclass
    {X = list(atom)}
    check(list(atom), [ibm])
        userclass <— typedef(list(atom),[atom| list(atom)])
        functor([ibm], ., 2),
        functor([atom| list(atom)], ., 2),
        checkargs(2, [atom| list(atom)], [ibm])
            arg(2, [atom| list(atom)], list(atom)),
            arg(2, [ibm], [])
            check(list(atom), [])
                userclass <— typedef(list(atom), [])
                ++ types <— typedef(list(atom), []).
                functor([], [], 0),
                functor([], [], 0), !,
                checkargs(0, []. [])
            1 is 2—1,
            checkargs(1, [atom| list(atom)], [ibm])
                arg(1, [atom| list(atom)], atom)
                arg(1, [ibm], ibm),
                check(atom, ibm),
                    atom(atom), !,
                    call([atom, ibm])
                0 is 1—1,
                checkargs(0, [atom| list(atom)], [ibm])
                    checkargs(0,_,_), !,
    —> fail.
```

The main insights here are the use of functor in check to check the equality of the function symbols, or functors, and the use of arg in checkargs to visit every argument of a term. This is the Prolog form of a *for* loop, counting down from the number of arguments to zero. It is actually very efficient.

This example is a good use of pure Prolog functionality within an object. Though what it is checking is an assignment, the code does not itself use assignments.

A typechecker is an elementary form of constraint checking. Constraint checking has become a major aspect of logic programming in the last few years but its proper implementation requires significant changes to Prolog compilers. Checks must be placed on variables so that when a unification is attempted extra code is activated which checks whether the unification is acceptable. The danger with this is that these checks may take place at such a low level that they reduce the speed of the basic system to such an extent as to annul the benefit of constraint checking in the first place.

While one cannot compare the constraint system of Prolog++ to systems such as CHIP (Constraint Handling in Prolog) (Dincbas *et al.* 1988), or Prolog III (Colmerauer, 1987), it does provide some rudimentary facilities which can help control the most lasting forms of assignments: changes in the values of attributes.

4.3.3 Error trapping

The concept of an error in a logic programming system is sometimes doubted. Since any method, or predicate, can either succeed or fail, should not an error simply result in the failure of that method?

While this is logically defensible, it does not recognize the necessary distinction between logical falsity and programming error. The category of programming errors includes the following:

- Omission of a declaration of a method or predicate (undefined predicate),
- Generation of circular terms in the unification process,
- Incorrect parameters passed to built-in predicates,
- Failure of built-in predicates on particular data (for example, arithmetic exceptions).

There is also a category of unusual events (for example, end-of-file when reading a file) which do not count as programming errors but which are often treated as exceptions in programming languages. However, modern practice, including most Prolog systems, tends to handle these by other techniques, such as the extension of the type of objects read to include a special end-of-file token.

A well-designed logic programming system should be complete in the sense that none of its basic actions lead to a failure of the system. There is one glaring exception to this in Prolog: omission of the 'occur-check' in the unification process. This can lead to the generation of circular terms, as noted above, which will normally result in an infinite loop, or perhaps a stack overflow. This omission is justified by the enormous improvement it makes to the efficiency of the compilation process. In practice, there are few algorithms in which the occur-check is necessary, and these are normally handled by the use of the unify predicate which does include the occur-check. The experienced programmer is rarely bothered by accidental generation of circular terms and static checks will reveal most potential occurrences.

We therefore need to consider the other two categories of errors: undefined methods, or predicates, and exceptions occurring in the evaluation of methods. Neither of these can be detected infallibly at compile-time, partly because it is possible to construct a call at run-time and execute it with the call predicate, but also because many errors depend on the binding of variables in parameters, which is in general undecidable.

In Prolog, undefined predicates are normally treated as a special case of exceptions. Since it may be desirable for an undefined predicate to fail quietly, particularly if it is a proposition, most systems allow different possibilities by means of a built-in predicate.

In Prolog++ one is dealing with messages that are passed to objects. As has been explained in the previous chapter, most of these messages may be resolved at compile time into direct procedure calls. The exceptions are twofold: it is perfectly permissible to represent either or both the class or the message as a variable in the program – for example, X<−Y – provided, of course, both variables are instantiated to nonvariables at the time of the call. This corresponds to the use of call, or the metavariable, in Prolog.

The other exception concerns dynamic binding. Here a call is made in one class to a method defined in an offspring class, so that when compiling the class it is not possible to determine which of several methods is being invoked. Consider the set of four classes shown in Figure 4.4, where the dynamic binding is forced by the use of the self variable as the target of the message.

If the message a(X) is sent to class b, or to one of its instances, then X will be bound to b. Similarly it will be bound to a if sent to class a, or c if sent to class c.

The class d illustrates what happens if method b is not redefined. The inheritance mechanism ensures that the method for b in class a is found. This constitutes therefore a default mechanism, which ensures that the *undefined method* exception is never invoked. This is particularly useful when

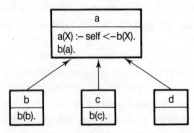

Figure 4.4   Use of dynamic binding with explicit self message.

standard messages, called events, are generated by the system and passed to an instance. The default actions (normally null) can be defined in a generic object and thus ensure that an object is always able to handle all the possible events.

In general, errors are handled by means of *exceptions*. This implies a break in the flow of the program and transfer to a recovery routine or general debugging mechanism. How this transfer is done and what process should be responsible for recovering the error are issues that have long concerned the software engineering community.

The facilities in Prolog++ build on those available in the underlying Prolog system and add some interesting refinements. When an error is detected, control passes to the error-handling module which determines what allowance the user program has made to deal with errors. If there is none, then it produces a standard error message and terminates execution of the program. If an error handler has been set up, it calls it as a procedure, passing the error number together with the goal that caused the error. The user's program can then decide what action to take.

The problem with an error handler is to know the right response to an error. For some errors, such as failure to find a file, it may be obvious locally what is the correct response. But when one considers the question of using an object system to provide modularity there are always some errors for which it is not within the capability of the local code to know what is an appropriate action. In these cases the whole invocation of the object needs to fail and pass responsibility back to the calling module.

These differing responses have shown themselves in two separate mechanisms: the first is an error-handling predicate with a predefined name which is called by the error handler (if defined). The second is the so-called 'catch-and-throw' method whereby a dynamic 'catcher' is set up by the calling program to field the error 'thrown' by the error. These methods can well be complementary. If the error-handling predicate cannot handle the error, it can then pass control to the other.

The normal problem with an error-handling predicate is that it is static: one predicate must oversee the whole program. Prolog++ allows this to be made local to the class being executed. Any class may define a method when_error which will be invoked when an error occurs, with two parameters. The first is a Prolog term indicating the type of error, such as an instantiation fault, a domain violation, and so on. The second is the actual message which caused the problem. Because when_error is a standard method there is a third, implicit, parameter, the self name of the object to which the message was originally sent.

The when_error method may be inherited like any other. It is thus possible to define the error handler at any generic level appropriate to the program.

The catch-and-throw method is not in fact part of the Prolog++ system: it is inherited from the underlying Prolog system. However since it has an important component of error handling in object-oriented languages we will describe briefly how it is implemented in MacProlog, which is close to that adopted by the ISO Prolog standard.

To provide an error handler when calling any procedure, including a Prolog++ goal, one calls the system-defined predicate **catch** which takes four parameters: the first is the goal to be called; the second is a goal which will be executed if there is an error during execution of the first goal; the other two parameters are the same as those for when_error – namely the error number and the goal in which the error occurred.

If the goal succeeds without error, then the call to catch succeeds and the recovery code is not executed, nor are the third and fourth parameters instantiated. However if an error occurs, then the whole of the call-stack is unwound to the point at which the catch predicate was invoked, and the recovery goal is called.

In languages such as C++ where a class invocation might terminate as a result of the error, it is necessary for the catch-and-throw process to perform any deletion actions in order properly to clean the stack; in Prolog++, object invocations are not kept on the stack and this problem does not arise. However, if any objects need to be deleted as a result of the error, this is the responsibility of the recovery code.

4.4   Managing objects

Prolog++ provides a basic but powerful set of capabilities for manipulating instances and classes. These include the ability to delete and reinitialize objects, and to save the current state in files in a similar fashion to Objective-C. But in addition, because Prolog++ is a symbolic language, it is possible for a Prolog++ program to create new classes with different behaviour. This makes it possible, for instance, to write a user interface package in which the user can describe the form and behaviour of an interface and have the program compile and execute this.

The instances and attributes of a class in Prolog++ exist independently of the program which defines their behaviour. In this sense, the objects have a true identity. When a class is recompiled, the instances and instance attributes are not deleted from the system. Clearly their future behaviour is dependent on the new form of the class: if an attribute is deleted from the class, then it cannot be accessed any more. But a new attribute can be assigned to an old object. This is the flexibility which arises from a symbolic system, compensating for its lower level of performance.

Most of these facilities are available via methods defined in the class ppp, so that they can be either invoked directly from within a Prolog++ program, or sent as messages to any instance or class, which will inherit the methods of ppp.

LOW-COST PROLOG++ COMPILER OFFER FROM
LOGIC PROGRAMMING ASSOCIATES

Congratulations! As the owner of *Prolog ++: the Power of Object-Oriented and Logic Programming* by Chris Moss you are entitled to a special offer on Prolog++ compilers from Logic Programming Associates, one of the world's leading suppliers of Prolog-based development tools.

As a bonus your disk will include full listings of all programs included in the book.

Available in both Macintosh[R] and Windows 3.1 versions, Prolog++ enables programmers to define object taxonomies and manipulate them with Prolog rules - a powerful and elegant combination of object-oriented and logic programming technologies.

Key features of *Prolog ++* include:

- dynamic objects with attributes, functions and methods
- class hierarchies with single and multiple inheritance
- private and local methods that can be easily edited
- full access to the underlying Prolog

- an interactive development environment with object browsers and inspectors

System requirements:

- MS Windows 3.1 with a minimum of 6Mb of RAM
- Macintosh System 7 with a minimum of 6Mb of RAM

Priority Order

I would like to order the following copies of the Entry Level Prolog++ compiler for (delete as appropiate):

No.   Cost

.... Windows 3.1 @ £29.95 in the UK / $49.95 in other countries   ....
.... Macintosh @ £29.95 in the UK   / $ 49.95 in other countries   ....
Please add VAT @ 17.5 % for orders from the UK   ....
Postage and Packing £5.00/$8.00 per copy   ....
                                                                       Total   ....

Name: _____ Job Title: _____

Organisation: _____

Address: _____

_____ Post Code: _____

Tel: _____ Fax: _____

Visa ☐   Mastercard ☐   Cheque ☐   (Cheques payable to **Logic Programming Associates Ltd.**)

Cardholder's Name: _____ Address: _____

_____

Card No: _____ Expiry Date: _____

Signature: _____

E-mail: lpa@cix.compulink.co.uk **Telephone:** + 44 181 871 2016
Fax: + 44 181 874 0449   US toll free 1 800 949 7567

Logic Programming Associates
Studio 4
RVPB
Trinity Road
London
SW18 3SX
UK

4.4.1   Deleting objects

The following procedures are available, in increasing order of severity.

reset/1	sent to an *instance* or *class*, removes the named dynamically assigned attribute value for that instance or class
reset/0	sent to an *instance* or *class*, removes all dynamically assigned attribute values for that instance or class
delete/0	sent to an *instance* deletes the instance and attribute values and local definitions
delete_all/0	sent to an *instance* or a *class*, deletes all instances of the class together with attribute values and local definitions
kill/0	sent to a *class*, does a delete_all and also removes the compiled definition of the class

When debugging a program, it is normal to include a delete_all or reset in the initialization routine as any previous attribute values are (deliberately) not cleared by the compilation process. This ensures that all instances and attributes start from their default values and there is no accumulation of dynamic entities.

Thus in the eight queens example earlier it would have been sensible to include a delete_all in the initialization routine, before the first instance creation:

```
initial(LastQueen) :-
    delete_all,
    create(First, [column = 1]),
    initial(2, First, LastQueen).
```

Sometimes it is only necessary to delete the dynamic attributes of an object. The method reset/0 deletes all dynamic attributes for the instance to which it is sent. To delete a specific attribute and restore it to its default value, give the name of the attribute as a parameter to reset/1.

4.4.2   Saving the state

Many dynamic processes have a lifetime longer than any single execution of the program. It is therefore important to be able to save these dynamic values in a file and recover them subsequently. This is called **object passivation** in object-oriented programming. Since programs are geared around classes, these routines save all instances of one or more classes together with all their values.

The following procedures take a file name and possibly a list of classes as parameter. A file name is simply an atom and its form will vary between different systems and we do not describe it in any more detail here.

dump/1   copies to the file the instances of the class given by the self variable, together with their attribute values, local database and component parts

dump/2   dumps all the classes given as a list in the second parameter to the file given in the first parameter

restore/1   copies from the named file all the instances, attribute values, local database and component parts previously dumped in that file

For example, to save the current state of the version

queen <− dump('Queen state', [queen, nullQueen]).

Note that with dump/2 it is necessary to include the current class in the list, as the self variable is ignored. The message can be sent to the class ppp, if preferred.

Because of the symbolic nature of Prolog, there is no difficulty in copying complex data structures into a file, whereas this is a novel concept in most pointer-based languages. However there are some nonobvious details. When dumping a group of objects, Prolog++ checks that any generated object references stored in the attributes of the class are resolved within the group of classes being saved. If this was not the case, then on restoring the instances, these references could not be resolved reliably. When the objects are restored, new unique identifiers will be generated for the instances. This does *not* apply to object names supplied by the user. Where the user supplies the name they are entirely responsible for ensuring that the necessary objects are loaded.

Any unbound variables are by their nature local to particular attribute values. When a compound object is dumped, all its component parts are also dumped.

Prolog++ provides one extra aid to grouping related classes. The class definition may include a category declaration. The name of the category may be used in the call to dump/2 instead of a class name.

4.4.3 Creating and modifying classes

The use of the create message to create a new instance of a class has been explained earlier. In some applications it is desirable to go beyond this to be able dynamically to create a new class, together with its associated attributes and methods. This facility is provided via a method called compile which takes two arguments: the first is the name of the class to be compiled, the second is the text of the class to be compiled, represented as a list of clauses.

For example, let us suppose we wanted to define a Help button which displayed a particular text. In Prolog++ this might be represented as follows:

```
class helpButton.
inherits button.
attribute text = 'Help'.
buttonUp :-
     display('This is a help message').
end helpButton.
```

To compile this in line, the following call would need to be executed:

```
compile(helpButton,
     [(inherits button),
     (attribute text = 'Help'),
     (buttonUp :- display('This is a help message'))])
```

Each of the statements in the definition is a term, which appears as normal. The class/end brackets around the class definition are not necessary. The brackets () around each statement are necessary when this is written directly in the program, because the binding number of the operators (for example, :-) is greater than that of the comma.

In practice, the second parameter to compile would probably be constructed at run-time from its component parts, otherwise there is little point in not using the normal compilation process. But the ease with which this can be done shows why Prolog-based languages are often used for defining compiler systems.

4.5   Control structures for objects

Some of the extra control structures available in Prolog++ were presented in the previous chapter. Here we collect all the features together.

4.5.1   Message broadcasting

It is often desirable to send the same message to more than one object. Therefore Prolog++ supports some powerful features normally referred to as message broadcasting. The simplest example is when the same message is to be sent to several explicitly named objects. They can be listed to the left of the message arrow using the sequence operator:

```
(a, b, c) <- message
```

The brackets are necessary to ensure the correct grouping, since <—
binds tighter than , . It is also possible to use the disjunction operator in
this position. For example,

    (a; b; c) <— message

would send the message to a, but if it failed, then it would be sent to b, and
so on.

The most powerful broadcasting operator is all. For example, if we
wished to send a particular message to all instances of a class, we can construct
a Prolog++ expression that represents all these instances:

    all instance employee

and then send a message to it:

    all instance employee <— print

It is worth noting that there is an implicit loop in this code. The left hand
side is evaluated repeatedly and the message on the right hand side is sent
to each instance that is found. The whole statement only succeeds if all the
messages sent to each instance succeed.

Because one might wish to choose some subset of the total generated,
Prolog++ also supports the suchthat operator in object expressions. This
is a binary operator: the left hand side is evaluated, and the message which
is on the right hand side sent to it. If this succeeds, then the whole expression
succeeds. For example,

    all instance employee suchthat salary > 20000 <— print

4.5.2   Prolog control structures

It is frequently desirable to send several messages to the same object. Hence
to the right of the <— operator it is permissable to use the conjunction (,)
and disjunction (;) operators. In this case it is necessary to place brackets
round the whole expression so that it is parsed correctly. For example,

    test :-
        foo <— (a, b, c),
        baz <— (d ; e ; f).

This sends the messages a, b and c to foo and either d, e, or f to baz.
If the brackets were omitted, then the b and c messages would be sent locally
to the self object. The case of a disjunction works exactly as in Prolog: if d
succeeds, then e will not be tried unless and until backtracking occurs.

In the example above, where the target object is represented by an atom, the effect is exactly the same as if it is repeated. That is,

```
test :-
    foo <- a,
    foo <- b,
    foo <- c,
    (baz <- d
    ; baz <- e
    ; baz <- f).
```

However, if the left hand side is an *expression* which evaluates to an object, then each of the messages will be sent to the *same* object, as long as the messages all succeed. For example,

```
all instance employee <- (eval, print, nl)
```

It is tempting to suppose that the first message(s) in the list can be used to prune the generated set. One might think of doing this as follows:

```
all instance employee <- (salary > 20000, print, nl)
```

Unfortunately this does not work; the first time the right hand side fails, the whole statement is aborted and fails. In this case, the suchthat operator introduced in the previous section should be employed.

As well as the conjunction and disjunction operators, a small number of other Prolog constructs are recognized by the Prolog++ compiler and treated specially. These include the cut operator (!), conditional operator (—> ;) and negation (\+). These have their normal Prolog significance and are *not* treated as messages to be sent to the object.

4.5.3 Repetitive control structures

Prolog++ offers a set of structured control statements that are clearer to use than the conventional Prolog control statements. They are primarily of use in dynamic rather than declarative situations: where statements are executed for their effect rather than to accumulate results. This style of programming is often useful when it is necessary to send a series of messages to a set of objects, which will then perform actions local to themselves.

The while statement is very close in meaning to that in Pascal or C. It takes the form:

```
while s1 do s2
```

where s1 and s2 are statements. First s1 is evaluated. If it succeeds then s2 is evaluated and the process repeated until s1 fails. There is no backtracking in this operation: both s1 and s2 are simply evaluated for their side effects – it is not even possible to carry across any variable bindings from s1 to s2.

A typical use of the while statement is in reading in from a file the definitions of objects. If we have defined the method readAndStore to read and create an object, then the evaluation of:

```
while readAndStore do total += 1.
```

will evaluate this repeatedly and store the total number of items created. This continues until the readAndStore routine fails. Whether the second statement succeeds or fails is immaterial. If several actions are required in either part, it is simply necessary to enclose them in brackets. Thus to read up to 10 elements one could write:

```
total := 0,
while total < 10 do (total += 1, readAndStore).
```

The repeat statement is similar, but makes the test *after* evaluating the first statement:

```
repeat s1 until s2
```

If s2 fails, the first statement, s1, is then evaluated again, and this is repeated until s2 succeeds.

By contrast to these, the forall statement is a syntactic variant of the forall predicate found in many, but not all, Prolog systems. It takes the form:

```
forall s1 do s2
```

where s1 and s2 are statements. s1 is evaluated repeatedly (by backtracking) and for each success s2 is evaluated. It succeeds if and only if s2 succeeds every time s1 is evaluated.

In the case of forall, any variable bindings made in s1 can be used in s2, though it is not possible to use them outside the forall construct.

As a simple example of forall, we will use the Prolog predicate member, which can be used either to select an item from a list or check whether it occurs in the list. Thus

```
forall member(A, [1,3])
      do (member(A, [1,2,3]), write(A), nl)
```

will succeed and result in the printing of:

```
1
3
```

whereas

```
forall member(A, [1,2,3])
    do (member(A, [1,3]), write(A), nl)
```

would fail and only result in the printing of:

```
1
```

None of these repetition operators collect together the results of the operations which they invoke. But Prolog++ does recognize the traditional Prolog set operations: findall, setof and bagof. These operations are not treated as messages to be sent to an object but as direct calls to Prolog.

The simplest of these is findall which has the same structure as the others, but produces a more simple result. It may be defined as follows:

findall(A, B, C) C is the list of all occurrences of A such that B is provable

The first parameter is a template. Often it is a simple variable which also occurs in the goal B, which is to be evaluated. But it may be a complex term including several variables in B. The result, C, is a list of all the bindings of A produced by evaluating the goal B.

For example, suppose that a method is defined by three clauses:

```
a(d).
a(c).
a(b).
```

then the effect of evaluating findall(X, a(X), Y) is

```
X = _
Y = [d, c, b]
```

Solutions are returned in the order in which they are found and the result is always a simple list.

Setof and bagof are somewhat more complex. The difference comes when there is a variable in the goal (B) which does not occur in the template (A). In this case, setof and bagof can produce (sorted) multiple solutions, each of which corresponds to a different binding of these variables. The difference between the two routines is that setof eliminates any duplicate solutions, whereas bagof retains them.

Suppose we have a definition

```
b(c, e).
b(d, e).
b(c, d).
b(d, f).
```

then the goal:

    setof(A + B, b(A,B), X)

produces the result:

    A = _,
    B = _,
    X = [c + d, c + e, d + e, d + f]

whilst the goal

    setof(B, b(A,B), X)

produces two results:

    A = c
    B = _,
    X = [d, e]

and

    A = d
    B = _,
    X = [e, f]

Although this has considerable appeal as a logical solution to the set problem, it may not be the intended result. To achieve a 'flat' list from setof or bagof, it is necessary to indicate to the system any variables in the goal which may be ignored using the operator ^, which takes the name of the variable and the goal as arguments. Thus the goal

    setof(B, A^b(A,B), X)

produces the result:

    A = _,
    B = _,
    X = [d, e, f]

Finally, the goal, which is the second parameter, may be itself a message passed to another object. If no message is indicated, then the normal inheritance pattern on self takes place.

For example,

    setof(B, A^ obj <— b(A,B), X)

There is a problem with defining similar 'metapredicates' using other Prolog module systems which does not occur in the same way in an object-oriented system, because of the availablity of the self variable.

Consider how one could define one of these predicates within a class definition. If the goal which the user specifies as the second parameter is one local to the call, the user will not naturally specify the (local) class or instance name in the call. Yet the definition needs that information in order to evaluate the goal in the correct context.

The solution to this is the self variable. Within the definition, the goal is sent explicitly to self:

```
self <— Goal
```

and the evaluation will automatically be made in the correct context. Most implementations of modules in Prolog have great difficulty at this point.

4.6   Prolog++ techniques

4.6.1   Metacalls

One of the powerful structuring techniques in Prolog is the use of the metacall, which is used in such predicates as findall. When modules are introduced into Prolog they pose something of a problem, because it is necessary to indicate in which module the metacall takes place. This is particularly true when the predicate being defined is itself encapsulated within a module.

One of the strengths of the object-oriented paradigm is that each call carries with it implicitly the class in which it originated as the self variable. This provides the information that is required, which overcomes the compromises that are used in module systems.

Suppose for example we wish to define a predicate set, which works like findall, but removes duplicate solutions. One simple and efficient solution in most Prolog systems is the following:

```
set(X, Goal, List) :-
     findall(X, Goal, Bag),
     sort(Bag, Set).
```

This takes advantage of the fact that the common routine sort removes duplicate instances by default (and sorting is as efficient a means of removing duplicates as the more direct method). It avoids the extra complications of the built-in setof when we do not want other arguments in the goal instantiated.

Suppose we define this in a module using a common syntax for modules in Prolog, which is as follows:

```
:- module(sets).
:-exports([set]).
set(X, Goal, List) :-
    findall(X, Goal, Bag),
    sort(Bag, Set).
:- end_module.
```

Note in this case that the predicates findall and sort are available directly from the Prolog environment.

Now suppose that we wish to call this from within another module m. We might issue the call:

```
set(X, livesin(X, london), List).
```

If the predicate livesin is defined within m, then findall actually must execute the goal m:livesin(X, london). There are two ways this can be communicated successfully. First, the user can specify the module name in the call.

```
set(X, m:livesin(X, london), List).
```

While this works, it means that when moving a piece of program within a module one must be careful to tag various function symbols with the module name (and this may not be at the direct point of use). The other way is to make special provision in the module declaration for this case, indicating which arguments of an exported predicate correspond to a meta-argument. (A third method, which implictly tags all functors with the module of origin has problems because it is possible to construct a functor at runtime.)

In Prolog++, a metagoal is evaluated relative to the object which generates the original call and inheritance takes care of any other dependencies. The code below defines a method called bag which is the equivalent of the standard findall. The second goal of this method is self <— Goal, which makes the dynamic binding explicit, although in fact this is the default translation if only Goal were specified.

```
class sets.
inherits db.

bag(_, _, _) :-
    asserta(ans(stop)), %allows nested queries
    fail.
bag(X, Goal, _) :-
    self<—Goal,
    asserta(ans(a(X))), %backwards to check markers
    fail.
bag(_,_, List) :-
    harvest([], List).      %get list right way round
```

```
harvest(A, List) :-
    retract(ans(X)),
    !,
    (X=stop -> A=List
    ; X=a(Y), harvest([Y|A], List)).

set(X, Goal, List) :-
    findall(X, Goal, Bag),
    sort(Bag, List).

end sets.
```

To use this suppose we have a class which defines a relation and inherits sets. For example,

```
class m.
inherits sets.
f(b). f(a). f(c). f(b).
end m.
```

This gives the following results:

```
?- m <- bag(X, f(X), List).
List = [b, a, c, b]
?- m <- set(X, f(X), List).
List = [a, b, c]
```

This example also shows the benefit of a local database. There is a tradition in Prolog of using unlikely names for dynamic relations which are used for local purposes. This is unnecessary when one can use a local database.

Local storage has other uses in defining what are conventionally metapredicates. An example is the map predicate which applies a relation to the members of a list. There are many variants to this predicate of which we will consider only one, which is able to accept an arbitrary relation of any arity and produces another list which contains the results. To do this we need to give the predicate the equivalent of a lambda-expression, for which we will use the symbol ^ as an infix operator.

An example of its use would be to specify an 'add 5' function:

```
?- map(X^Y^(Y is X+5), [1,2,3], Z).
Z is [6,7,8]
```

The obvious implementation of this does not work.

```
map(_, [], []).
map(A^B^Rel, [A|As], [B|Bs]) :-
    Rel,
    !, map(A^B^Rel, As, Bs).
```

The problem is that although the first time round the loop X^Y^(Y is X+5) matches against A^B^Rel to give the correct expression for Rel of Y is 1+5, on the second recursion the argument is already bound to 1^6^(6 is 1+5).

The solution is to save the lambda-expression and reuse it each time. This gives the Prolog++ definition:

```
class maps.
class attribute lambda.

map(X^Y^Rel, List, Ans) :-
    lambda := X^Y^Rel,
    !, map1(List, Ans).

map1([], []).
map1([A|As], [B|Bs]) :-
    @lambda = A^B^Rel,
    self <- Rel,
    !, map1(As, Bs).


end maps
```

Note that since we don't need to generate an instance of the class maps to perform this it is necessary to use a class attribute to store the value of the lambda expression.

While the same result could be achieved in Prolog by means of the database, the easy extension of these to a modular system encourages their more widespread use.

4.6.2   Abstract datatypes

One of the primary uses of encapsulation is to be able to hide the method of implementation of a datatype. This is hard to do in Prolog because all data structures are handled explicitly by the user. While this encourages a very pure type of programming, it complicates the construction of larger programs.

Let us take a classic example: a stack. This has many uses where it is necessary to retrieve information in the inverse order from which it is stored. That is, last-in first-out. Often this can be mirrored directly by a recursive program structure, but there are occasions when this is undesirable.

A stack can be modelled very easily in pure, or declarative, Prolog++, simply by encapsulating the corresponding Prolog program. There are four conventional operations required of a stack:

new	generate a new stack
push	add an item to a stack
pop	take the top item off the stack and return it
empty	test whether the stack is empty

We will use a list as the obvious representation for a stack in Prolog++. In the pure version, each stack manipulation (except the test empty) returns a new stack as its value. The definition of stack, using the Prolog++ functional style, is quite brief:

```
class stack.

new = [].

push(Item, Stack) = [Item | Stack].

pop(Item, [Item|Stack]) = Stack.

empty([]).

end stack.
```

To see how this works, consider a sequence of operations on the stack (Table 4.1). The operations using a sequence of variables are shown on the left hand side, and the binding of variables or result is shown on the right hand side.

The user of the stack is thus compelled to keep track of all the changes going on, by use of the variables S0 to S6. Also there is nothing to stop them looking at the representation and subverting the aim of the encapsulation by modifying the representation between two calls.

The program certainly meets the declarative aim, but it makes building larger systems difficult. Suppose that an algorithm has a number of data structures. These must all be passed around the program – and the data structure can get quite complex. Each time a component is changed, all of the ancestors up to the root of the data structure must also be changed. For

Table 4.1   Operations on a stack.

Operation	*Bindings*
stack@new = S0	S0 = []
stack@push(a, S0) = S1	S1 = [a]
stack@push(b, S1) = S2	S2 = [b, a]
stack@pop(X, S2) = S3	X = b, S3 = [a]
stack@empty(S3)	fail
stack@push(c, S3) = S4	S4 = [c,a]
stack@empty(S4)	fail
stack@pop(Y, S4) = S5	Y = c, S5 = [a]
stack@pop(Z, S5) = S6	Z = a, S6 = []
stack@empty(S6)	true

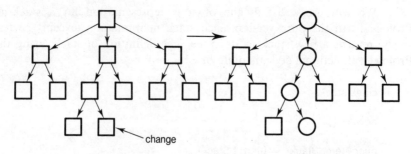

Figure 4.5   An arbitrary declarative data structure.

remember, in a declarative system, the elements of a data structure are *values*, not pointers to locations.

This is pictured in Figure 4.5, which represents an arbitrary declarative data structure. Each node of the data structure is represented as a small square, and if we wish to change one element we must also change the data structures which point to it. The cells that must be changed are indicated by circles.

Thus to change one element which is four levels deep in a data structure, we have to change four nodes in the representation. Each of these changes will involve copying all the elements (or, in practice, pointers to them) which have *not* changed into the new node. Instead of a unitary change we are faced with a change linear in the depth of the data structure.

Does a declarative system have an answer to these problems? The answer to this question is yes (except for the last one), but at the cost of giving up the very simple and efficient left-to-right evaluation strategy that makes Prolog so attractive. The answer lies in *coroutining* between the client and the user. In Chapter 7 we will look at this approach, which only becomes feasible when using parallel rather than sequential processing. But for the time being we will explore the more conventional route of using the assignment statement to hide the intermediate values.

Here is a version of the stack object using instances and assignments:

```
class stacka.

attribute val = [].

push(Item) :-
    val := [Item | +val].

pop(Item) :-
    @val = [Item|Stack],
    val := Stack.

empty :-
    @val = [].

end stacka.
```

The current contents of the stack are saved in the attribute val. The initial contents of val are nil. The same sequence of pushes and pops as in the previous example can now be performed using only a single unchanging variable:

```
stacka@new = S            S = (some constant)
S@push(a)
S@push(b)
S@pop(X)                  X = b
S@empty                   fail
S@push(c)
S@empty                   fail
S@pop(Y)                  Y = c
S@pop(Z)                  Z = a
S@empty                   true
```

It is interesting to note the similarity between this implementation and the previous declarative version. For example, in the pop method, unification is used in both cases to test whether there is an item currently on the stack and at the same time to extract the top value. If the stack is empty then unification, and thus the call to pop, will fail.

In the second version however, the user only needs to keep a single reference, S, to the stack and the contents of slot, S@val, are hidden, because an attribute is by default declared as *private*.

If we wish to establish the declarative validity of this implementation it is particularly simple because stacka does not refer outside itself to other objects. Take the second push message. The relation involved is between the value of the local variable before and after, and the message:

```
Before        Message        After
val = [a]     S@push(b)      val = [b,a]
```

In this case it is *only* necessary to take that one variable into account. There may be many other objects in the program, each with their own internal state, but these can be disregarded as they cannot possibly influence the result. In addition, only those parts of the program that have access to the binding of variable S can possibly change the state of this instance of val. So if this is limited, then the possible causes of change are also limited.

Although we cannot pretend that this is declarative programming, we have taken part in a damage limitation exercise. By keeping the effects of assignment within the object, the conceptual overhead in understanding the effect of a program is limited. Ultimately this shows up in the ease of making a correct program, and in providing tools for proving and debugging programs.

4.6.3   Change of representation

A further value in being able to conceal the representation of a datatype is that it is frequently desirable to be able to change it to deal with differing situations. For example, the effectiveness of multiprecision arithmetic is critically dependent on using the available single precision arithmetic of a particular machine to the full. If one is designing a multiprecision package, it is desirable to hide the representation from the user, so that it can be changed for different machines.

A particularly instructive example (adapted from Meyer, 1988, p. 136) is complex numbers. There are two common representations for a complex number: the Cartesian representation with a real and imaginary part and the polar representation using magnitude and angle (Figure 4.6).

The first representation is ideal for implementing addition and subtraction; the second for implementing multiplication and division. A division using polar coordinates requires only two divisions compared with five divisions when using the conventional algorithm with Cartesian coordinates. So which does one use in practice?

An elegant answer is to use both, as the occasion arises. In other words, if the value is specified in one form, store that; but if the need arises to use the other, then make the conversion and store that as well. In this way the internal representation acts as a local 'lemma generation' system.

This still leaves choice to the implementer in designing the form of the procedures. For example, if we wish to perform a binary operation on two complex numbers, should this form a totally new complex number or overwrite an existing value (of, say, the first argument)? Smalltalk takes the first approach, Eiffel the second. We follow the first approach here as it is more declarative, though it would be simple to add extra methods for the second.

The code for creating complex numbers and converting from one representation to another is shown in Program 4.1. The routines for minus and multiply are left to the reader. What is shown is enough to demonstrate the basic principles. For example, we can define a number in Cartesian coordinates and fetch its value in polar:

```
?- complex <- create(A, cartesian(1,1)), A <- polar(R,T).
A = $(complex,1111), R = 1.4142135623730 95049,
    T = 0.7853981633974483096
```

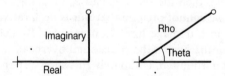

Figure 4.6   Cartesian and polar representations for a complex number.

Program 4.1 Complex numbers.

```
class complex.

attribute valc,valp.

new(cartesian(A,B)) = Inst :-
    create(Inst, [valc = cartesian(A,B)]).
new(polar(A,B)) = Inst:-
    create(Inst, [valp := polar(A,B)]).

cartesian(A, B) :-
    @valc = cartesian(A,B), !.
cartesian(A, B) :-
    @valp = polar(C,D),
    valc := cartesian(+C*cos(D),+C*sin(D)).

polar(A, B) :-
    @valp = polar(A,B), !.
polar(A, B) :-
    @valc = cartesian(C,D),
    valp := polar(+sqrt(C*C+D*D),+atan2(D,C)).

setCartesian(X,Y) :-
    valc :=cartesian(X,Y),
    reset(valp).

setPolar(R, Th) :-
    valp := polar(R, Th),
    reset(valc).

add(X) = Inst :-
    cartesian(A,B),
    X <-cartesian(C,D),
    complex <- create(Inst, +A+C, +C+D).

div(X) = Inst :-
    polar(Rh1,Th1),
    X <- polar(Rh2,Th2),
    Rh is Rh1/Rh2, Th is (Th1-Th2) mod (2*pi),
    complex <- create(Inst, polar(Rh,Th)).

pi is 3.1415926535.

end complex.
```

The messages polar and cartesian are used to fetch the value in the appropriate form. If we create, multiply and fetch the answer in Cartesian, then we need never be aware of the internal change of representation:

```
:- complex@new(cartesian(1,1))@times(X)@cartesian(C, D)
C = 0, D = 2
```

The messages setPolar and setCartesian not only record the representation but reset any previous alternative representation. Where both representations have been used, it is possible for them both to be recorded, but only if the values are consistent. Thus the effect of the 'lemma generation' is quite invisible to the user.

The overhead of object creation means that the alternative approach in which the operations are effectively 'add a complex number to the current number' is more practical in the context of Prolog++. In addition, it is easy to add code to handle complex constants without object overhead. Nonetheless, the implementation gives the advantage of private representation, which is an important factor in many contexts. It gives freedom to the implementer to review and change the representation, knowing that the users will not be affected.

4.6.4   Generic programs

Objects can be used effectively to provide programs which are customized to their use in several different ways. But it is worth pointing out that Prolog programs are already more generic than programs in most algorithmic languages. This arises partly from the fact that Prolog is usually an untyped system but more deeply due to the nature of unification.

Consider the standard operations on lists: to join two lists together, search for a particular value, find the last element, and so on. Many of them will apply to a list of anything. It is even possible to apply a type system to such programs which can eliminate many classes of errors. This is called a polymorphic type system (which should not be confused with the other use of the term in object-oriented programming) and typecheckers are available in most Prolog libraries.

The types for two standard list-processing operations – append and member – can be given as follows:

```
append(list(X), list(X), list(X))
member(X, list(X))
```

where the type list is defined by the recursive structure:

```
list(X) = []
list(X) = [ X | list(X)]
```

Here the variable X can stand for any type, and unification can ensure that it is consistently applied in as detailed a fashion as required on to the basic types such as integer, real and atom. Thus [1,2,3] has the type list(integer).

Some of the basic operations in Prolog are similarly generic in type. For example, the comparison operators, @>, @<, @=, and so on can be applied to any Prolog term and even give a predictable (if not so useful) result when applied between types (for example, on some systems, integers rank before reals, so that 2 @< 1.3, although of course 2<1.3 is false).

However this amount of flexibility is not sufficient in some applications. Take sorting: at the heart of the sorting operation is an ordering operation. There are many different ways of ordering: increasing, decreasing, various methods of lexicographic ordering (taking into account case, abbreviations, spaces, and so on). It is also common to sort on part of an item only, so that one may wish to specify access functions that will select the appropriate part of the item. Yet the same sorting algorithm might be used in every case.

One traditional approach to this has been macroprocessing. The source code of the procedure is supplied with generic arguments and the code is duplicated for each different use within the program. This is at the heart of generic modules in Ada, and is explicit in the preprocessor for C. Object-oriented programming provides what is often a more satisfactory solution by means of dynamic binding. Consider the following simple definition of quicksort:

```
class sort.
qsort([A|As], B) :-
    partition(As, A, Gs, Ls),
    qsort(Gs, G),
    qsort(Ls, L),
    append(L, [A|G], B).
partition([A|As], B, Gs, Ls) :-
    self <- order(A, B, O),
    (O = '>' -> Gs = [A|G], Ls = L
    ; Gs = G, Ls = [A|L]),
    partition(As, B, G, L).
order(A, B, O) :- compare(A, B, O).
end sort.
```

The call to order sets up the ordering O of its arguments to >, < or =. A default implementation is specified which uses the built-in routine compare. However, because the message is passed explicitly to self, then if the user who inherits this routine redefines order, the revised definition will be used in preference.

For example, suppose that we are sorting records of the form:

```
person(id, name, age, dept, salary)
```

and we wished to sort on people's age. Then we would need to provide a local definition such as:

```
order(A, B, O) :-
    A = person(_,_,AAge, _,_),
    B = person(_,_,BAge,_,_),
    compare(AAge, BAge, O).
```

which supercedes the default definition.

    Thus inheritance provides a way of parameterizing specific operations within a program, without the need for passing any extra parameters specifying the operation. Different programs can invoke the programs in sort with different effects and be interleaved arbitrarily without the need for keeping multiple copies.

    A final means of customizing the program is by means of the dynamic database and this can be appropriate in some circumstances where we wish to make the changes available on a wider basis. By including the directive inherits db and a clause such as:

```
comparison(NewClause) :-
    NewClause = (order(_,_,_):- _),
    asserta(NewClause).
```

it is possible for the user to provide a new version to augment or override the old version. Note the test in the above clause, which makes sure that this is only used for the purpose it was intended for.

    Each of these approaches can be of use in specific circumstances and it is up to the programmer to ensure that an appropriate method is used.

SUMMARY

- Mutable attributes of an object are declared using the attributes statement, are represented by Prolog names and are assigned with the assignment statement ($:=$). By default they are public and belong to an instance of the class, but they can also be declared public, when their value can be interrogated but not assigned from outside the class, and as a class attribute when the value is shared by all members of the class. Multivalued attributes can be obtained from the class db which specializes the conventional Prolog database predicates such as assert and retract.

- Errors are handled in Prolog++ by passing messages to the instance of the class in which the error occurs. These are handled by methods such as when_assigned and when_error . Thus generic error routines may easily be defined.

- A comprehensive set of built-in methods are provided for creating, deleting objects and re-initializing attributes. It is also possible to save the state of any or all objects in a file, to restore these at a later point and to create classes dynamically. The syntax of Prolog++ includes means of broadcasting messages to sets of objects which can be defined very flexibly.

● The chapter concludes with an examination of programming techniques. Prolog++ provides more powerful means of defining metapredicates than the simple use of modules. The implementation of abstract datatypes is illustrated, including the advantages of changes in internal representation. Finally, dynamic binding enables generic programs to be defined.

5

Graphical user interfaces

5.1   Introduction

The one area in which object-oriented programming has become practically
indispensable is in the provision of graphical user interfaces. The battle which
raged at one time about whether these were really necessary, or were just
aids for beginners, is fading as even the experts realize that these tools are
time-saving. With the arrival of Motif running under X-Windows on Unix
workstations, the Windows revolution has reached the workstation market
after having turned the PC market upside-down.

   As was noted in Chapter 1, the user interface is also one area in which
it is indisputably necessary to model change in the real world and track the
identity of changing objects. Because of this, many object-oriented tools in
commercial Prolog systems are primarily geared towards the user interface.
In this chapter we will demonstrate how the practical tools of Prolog++
can be put to use in this area by constructing a graphical user interface.

   Rather than concentrate simply on an application, we want to show
how the use of object-oriented techniques can improve a Prolog development
environment. It is an unfortunate fact that the portability of a program is
becoming hostage to the difficulty of porting it between the window systems
available under different operating systems. Without object-oriented
techniques it is nearly impossible to reduce these differences to manageable
proportions, and even when using them it is not possible to bridge the gaps
in all cases. We have therefore chosen three systems that are broadly similar
in their 'look and feel': the Macintosh user interface, Windows 3 on PCs and
Motif on Unix workstations. Not only does this cover a wide range of popular
machines, but these systems are widely considered among the best of those
presently available. There are many alternatives – for instance the IBM
Presentation Manager used with OS/2 and SunView used on Sun

168

workstations – but the two mentioned are currently being superseded by models closer to the three that we have chosen.

A Prolog development environment traditionally consists of a number of programs: on the one hand there are tools for editing, compiling, running and debugging Prolog programs; on the other are the predefined subroutines or 'built-in predicates' that are available to the programmer. These are not part of the language itself but are indispensable to the practical use of it. The core predicates, summarized in Chapter 2, are in the process of being standardized by an international committee, but they include little in the way of graphics or user interface.

Take, for example, the development environment available on the Macintosh with MacProlog. In addition to approximately 150 standard predicates, the system contains approximately 150 predicates concerned with graphics and another 120 concerned with windows. This represents a significant learning load for the programmer, though the 'declarative graphics' system, in particular, has some very nice features, which we will outline later. The reason for this multiplicity is not hard to see. There are a number of basic operations which must be performed on each of these categories of objects: create, delete, select, rename, and so on. But there are many different types of objects: pictures, windows, tools, menus, dialogues, and so on.

Thus as a first approximation, the number of predicates required is the product of the number of operations and the number of objects. Systematic naming reduces the memory load, but does not eliminate it, as the operations tend to have small but significant differences between each object.

This is a paradigm for the use of 'messages'. The same message can be sent to different objects and have differing effects. Discrepancies between the objects can be handled partly by allowing sensible defaults and partly by providing for additional messages which change these defaults. Before we see how this works, we need to review some of the basic features of a user interface.

5.2   User interfaces

The organization of a program with a graphical user interface is very different from the conventional 'main loop' of other programs. The reason for this is the basic ergonomic constraints on user interfaces.

A traditional computer program consists of several prompt-input and computation-display loops: the program outputs a prompt to request input; inputs data; does a computation; outputs the results; then repeats the loop. The program is expecting some particular input at every point and it is difficult for the user to do something different – the program is very much in command.

One requirement of a graphical user interface is that the user can at any point perform any reasonable action: input with keyboard or mouse, choose an item from a menu, etc. If there is a form to fill in they should be able to complete the items in any order and go back and make corrections at any point. 'Modal' situations, in which the user is constrained to do things in a fixed order, should be kept to an absolute minimum.

A second requirement is that there should usually be some visual clues for the actions that are possible at any stage, so that the memory of the occasional or new user isn't overburdened. These visual 'signposts' are an essential element in making the program 'user-friendly' and it needs considerable skill to design them successfully. Some of the cues are iconic – such as the shape of a window, with its scroll bars and 'go-away' boxes. Others are textual, including the conventional 'pull-down' menus which permit a large number of choices without overwhelming the user. A third category of cues are conventional: they belong to the style of the interface so that a user will very quickly remember them: for example, the insertion point for text (or cursor) can usually be moved to another point on the screen by using the mouse and clicking.

Many of these characteristics are not related to any particular program; they can and should be consistently implemented across many different programs using the same basic 'interface style' – such as Macintosh, Motif, Windows, and so on. The programmer has a lot to gain by following these guidelines closely: not only do they reflect major results of research and testing, but the users of the program will probably understand the conventions already and be able to use the program more easily. Indeed, if the programmer *doesn't* follow the guidelines, for no obvious reason, then the user will probably be irritated rather than intrigued.

One of the consequences of the graphical approach to interaction is that raw 'input/output' (to and from the terminal, at least) becomes less important. Most input is directed to a predesigned dialogue, and the amount of raw typing by the user is reduced. Many actions are initiated by menu options, and the corresponding key sequences act basically as shortcuts.

At any point the input to the program is any one of a number of labelled 'events', such as a button-click on a menu button. It makes sense to treat these in a uniform manner so that the programmer does not, for instance, need to program all the actions involved in tracking where the pointer is on the screen, the change in appearance of a button when it is clicked and so on. A number of standard events such as 'quit the program' are also needed which may be generated by conventional activities such as clicking in a certain place in the window.

At the heart of this process, and preferably 'out of sight' in a high-level language such as Prolog, is an 'event loop' which is the corollary of the display-input loop of the traditional program. This provides the basic control in such a way that the keyboard need not be at all closely connected to the computational process.

Thus the Motif system (Berlage, 1991) is designed for use with X-Windows on workstations. It is assumed that the keyboard, pointer and display may be separated by a network from the processor executing the program, which may use entirely different hardware from the computer providing the interface. The event loop runs on the display processor and passes events over the network to the program processor which will also be executing an event loop. Because most pointer movements can be handled locally, network traffic can be kept to a minimum, with only significant events, such as a buttonclick, being notified to the processor running the program.

Events arising from pointer movements can be generated extremely rapidly and cannot always be handled immediately. So the event *loop* is in practice an event *queue*. Pending events are piled up until they can be serviced and if the servicing is not quick enough, some events, typically the oldest, will be discarded. Certain events must be handled immediately if the user's perception of the system is not to suffer. Activities such as the movement of the pointer on the screen in response to a mouse movement are generally handled by the system using interrupts in the most efficient manner possible. 'Knock-on' effects, such as redrawing an area when its appearance is changed, may not be handled so quickly.

In this context some compromises are necessary in order to balance the conflicting requirements of efficiency, versatility and ease of programming. The event mechanism is the basic means of providing these compromises and it should provide different information at different levels. Consider, for instance, the action of pressing a button on the screen. This consists of the following actions:

(1)   The pointer moves into the button area,

(2)   A button is pressed,

(3)   The button is released.

This description abstracts from the actual behaviour considerably. The exact position of the button is irrelevant and whether it moves slightly within the area defined by the button between actions (2) and (3) also does not matter. It is a characteristic shared by the three systems (Macintosh, Windows, Motif) that the 'action' of the button only happens when the button is released, but usually a visual effect (highlighting) is provided when the button is pressed. This effect may be under the control of the window system or the program.

A number of variants are possible even with this simple action. If the user changes their mind after pressing the button, then moving the pointer out of the button area before releasing the button cancels the effect (and the highlight). But if the pointer then moves *back*, before release, the highlight is restored.

These actions can be conveniently abstracted into three events: *arm*, *activate* and *disarm*. Arming happens when a button is pressed, activation when the button is released inside the area of the button, and disarming if the pointer is moved outside the button area while depressed. Visual effects will occur at all three stages to give the user some feedback. Arming causes an inversion of the colour of the button, or the '3-D button-press' effect in Motif. Activation and disarming both cancel this, with possibly some other subtle effects thrown in.

These events occur at a higher, more user-oriented level than the raw events provided by the system because they deal with conceptual objects such as buttons and are the only events that require the attention of the user process. They are not the events that the Macintosh or Windows programmer normally deals with, though they are recognized in Motif.

Other events might be important in a display area of the screen. For example, pressing a button over an object corresponds to selecting it, moving the pointer with the button depressed means dragging it to another position and releasing the button drops it at the current position. Between these events, all the movements of the pointer would be important since the program would need to represent those movements, by moving some representation of the object on the screen.

It is highly desirable to provide standardized event-loops which works with widely differing programs. This means that the programmer does not need to rewrite this code for each program and this provides a useful division of labour. The event-loop needs a certain amount of information about the objects on the screen: which areas correspond to which objects, and what events are significant to each object. Given that information, it is a simple matter to turn *events* into *messages* which are sent to the correct *objects*.

The basic organization of a program written with a graphical user interface in mind should therefore respond to each cue with the appropriate action, complete it in a reasonable period of time, and wait for the next cue. This involves restructuring the normal method of writing the prompt-input loops which we have already mentioned, namely:

- output a prompt (or dialogue box)
- wait for the input
- dispatch on the result (by means of, say, a case statement)

Take for example, a simple question to the user, which requires a yes/no answer (Figure 5.1). Using a graphics interface, this should not be written 'on the fly', as a call with a side-effect, because there is no one point of control after the dialogue is displayed. Instead, one must designate entry

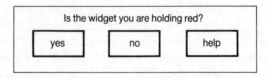

Figure 5.1   A simple question to the user.

points accessible from the outer level of the program, that can be invoked from the event-loop. It is no bad thing that the conventional organization is challenged, as recovering from errors deeply embedded in a program when performing such an action is tricky, to say the least. But the process is a radical change from common procedures, affecting the structure of the program significantly, since the local context of the program is lost (and remember that in a pure logic program there is no other).

In its place must be put the following organization:

- set up the procedures to be called at the end of the dialogue
- display the dialogue box
- send a message to the object chosen

The messages might be implemented as procedure calls in a non-object system (as the *call-backs* in the Windows and Motif systems), but then one has to define a separate set of call-backs for each object. Also one does not have the advantage of inheritance in defining objects which are based on system defined objects (such as buttons) but differ from them in certain respects. Thus the number of different procedure calls tends to proliferate.

In the approach we have outlined, objects that appear on the screen are *active* in the sense that each object has its own behaviour and associated program. There is another style of graphics interface, which is primarily used for drawing and painting programs, in which the objects on the screen are *passive*, and a *tool* is selected from a palette and applied to the object. For example, selecting an eraser object and clicking it on an object will make the object disappear. In this case, it may be the tool which is active and not the object.

Since the main domain of programs written in Prolog++ is knowledge intensive rather than graphical manipulation, the emphasis in the treatment of windows in this chapter is on active rather than passive objects. The passive objects that need manipulating are typically text (but may be pictures or sounds), for which the editing features are normally provided by the underlying system.

5.2.1   An interface toolkit

An object-oriented approach makes the writing of interfaces much more intuitive because it is easier to take an existing set of components and adapt them to a different use instead of specifying each dialogue and component from scratch. This is a natural use for the specialization hierarchy.

But it is possible to get confused by the different forms of hierarchy available. The individual components of a dialogue box, for instance, do not stand in a specialization relation to each other, but as parts of a component hierarchy.

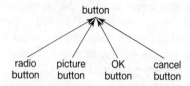

Figure 5.2   Specialization hierarchy.

In Figure 5.2, different types of button are refinements of the generic form, button. Radio and picture buttons have different forms, 'OK' and 'Cancel' buttons have the same form but different, conventional, code associated with them. A dialogue, however (Figure 5.3), is composed of a number of elements which may be similar but are components, not refinements.

The difference is obvious when one considers the way in which an event is handled. A 'button up' event will be passed up the generalization hierarchy if it is not handled at the lowest level as is any other message in that hierarchy. It does *not* make much sense to pass such an event up from a button in the dialogue to the dialogue itself: there is no presumed shared behaviour.

A confusion of the two hierarchies mars the otherwise excellent Hypercard system which is distributed with all Macintosh systems. In Hypercard, a message which is not handled by a component is passed successively to the 'card', the 'background', the 'stack' and the 'Home Stack'. While some of those may be regarded reasonably as generalizations (the relationship between card and background, for example), the rigid nature of the 'inheritance' and the fact that it is impossible to have any other forms of real inheritance means that many of those working in object-oriented systems would not regard it as an example to be followed.

What we will try to present in the rest of this chapter is therefore a set of classes which will make the standard features such as buttons, menus and fields easy for the programmer to specify and also portable between different systems. These can have both a graphical and a symbolic representation. We will suggest that, as long as it is possible to convert between the two, the difference between them is not important. One might construct an interface with graphical tools or expect it to be constructed automatically from a symbolic description. Having the two forms gives a great deal of flexibility.

Although this chapter is about graphical user interfaces, it is not

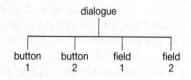

Figure 5.3   Component hierarchy.

primarily about graphics. While it will be possible to incorporate pictures in the windows, we will assume that these are mainly imported from outside the Prolog++ environment. But it is still necessary to understand the basic features of the graphic system in order to be able to lay out these components. We will therefore start by describing how windows are laid out, before presenting the windows toolkit.

5.3   Window basics

A screen on current machines is formed by a two-dimensional grid of points normally called pixels. Measurements are made in pixels starting at the top left-hand corner of the screen, following the normal scanning direction of the screen. A typical size is 640 by 480 pixels, but the screen notionally extends to $\pm 32K$ pixels, and in some systems it is possible to make the screen focus on any part of this extent. An item such as a window occurring on the screen is identified by the coordinates of its top left corner. Within the window, we forget the global coordinates and work strictly in a local system, starting again at (0,0), so that moving the window does not affect any of the local calculations that are made. The coordinates themselves refer to the gaps in between the pixels, so that they correspond to the geometric ideal of infinitely small points and thin lines (Figure 5.4).

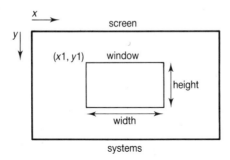

Figure 5.4   Window basics: systems.

Two of the essential requirements of a window system are to provide automatic *clipping* and *overlapping*. Any object drawn within a window that extends past the edge is automatically clipped at the edges (Figure 5.5). This provides a dramatic simplification in programming from which the user can

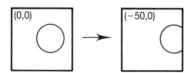

Figure 5.5   Scrolling and clipping.

also benefit. Scrolling a window can be reduced simply to adjusting the zero point of the local coordinate system and redrawing the contents of the window.

Overlapping is used at all levels: pictures are built up progressively hiding unwanted details. Pictures can be either 'raster images', in which painting on top destroys what is underneath, or 'objects' which retain their structure even when hidden. The latter involves more work for the display system but has a number of advantages for regular shapes, particularly in dialogue situations. For windows, overlapping is used to overcome the inevitable size limits of the screen itself. By showing a number of windows, even if they are partially obscured, the user can easily choose any of the other windows and bring it 'to the front' (Figure 5.6); in all the models we are considering, this is simply done by clicking with the pointer anywhere inside the area of a currently unused window.

When a window is exposed after having been partially covered, part or all of the window will need to be redrawn. To reduce the memory overhead of the windowing system, this responsibility is left with the program. The window system generates a message indicating which area of the window needs redrawing and passes it to the program to enact. This is an example of the 'housekeeping' which makes windowing systems so tedious to program unless the responsibility of the different parts of the system is carefully defined. Providing a general 'redraw' routine for one part of the picture is often no harder than doing the drawing from scratch – it is simply different.

Often the underlying window system only bothers about objects the size of windows: if the user clicks a button, for instance, the window system simply determines which window it is in and sends the appropriate message to the process controlling that window. We will follow instead the pattern set by Motif and X-Windows, which recognize the structure within a window and so can react more appropriately, when, for instance, the user presses a button which appears within a window. This is essential on a window system which uses a network, as the likely lag due to transmission of messages across the network would be unacceptable for a user interface, although it also provides a welcome simplification to user programming. On systems such as Windows and Macintosh, which do not handle this at a system level, it is easy to add this functionality into the 'event loop' which drives the user process.

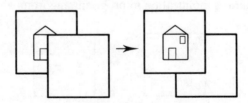

Figure 5.6 Overlapping and exposure.

Objects which have both a graphical representation and programmed behaviour are called 'widgets' in the X-Window system. We will sometimes use this word when it is necessary to distinguish them from objects in the object-oriented sense. That coining new words doesn't solve all problems is shown by the fact that Motif has to use another one – gadgets – for widgets that don't yet have a graphical appearance. The word 'view', used in Borland's Turbo Vision system, can unfortunately be confused with the use of the word in a database context.

To keep things efficient, widgets are limited to simple right rectangles. This is not as restrictive as might be thought, since the rectangles can overlap in arbitrary ways and the system knows which is 'on top'. In addition, the system needs to know which events each widget is interested in. As was pointed out earlier, a program is not normally interested in every movement of the pointer, and the desired performance would not be achieved if the system had to pass messages right through the system every time any movement was detected. But in some applications (for example, a paint program) this information is vital to achieve the desired result.

The events that widgets pass to the program are a consequence of the raw events it receives from the window system. The application does not normally have to duplicate the visual effects, such as the changes in colour when a button is pressed and released (though the user's program might provide extra effects). They are at a higher level: the level of functionality represented by the widgets. For example, if the user selects an item from a menu, the widget sends back a message to the menu which includes the item which was selected. In this case the menu is a composite item which contains a number of more primitive items which must be handled together.

Much of the definition of a widget is declarative: it can be specified simply by entries in a table. In all three of the window systems being considered, this is recognized by the use of a *resource file* (also called resource database or resource fork). These specify not only the geometry of the widget, but also much of its standard behaviour, such as the reaction to various exceptional conditions.

The advantage of using resource files is that they enable the *distributor* or *user* of a program to customize the program without tampering with the program itself or its logic. For example, the strings which make up the program's 'prompts' can be placed in the resource file so that they can be substituted by strings in a foreign language. Similarly, the layout and colouring of windows and dialogues may depend both on the available hardware and personal preference and so need to be easily changed for different circumstances. In the Motif system, which is designed for a multi-user environment, a user can have his or her own resource file which is separate from the program's resource file, so the same program can appear differently to each individual user.

In the case of Prolog++, the system may or may not compile the information given in object declarations into a resource file: this depends on the mode of use of the program. The power of a symbolic language means that it is easy to convert the information from graphical to symbolic form, and from symbolic to program. It can be both more efficient and more useful for presentation purposes to use the resource file layouts. Using an object-oriented approach, it is possible to hide the storage details from most parts of the program.

5.4   Components

A typical dialogue is shown in Figure 5.7. This is used to set printing options for a particular printer (and its details are thus supplied by a different company to the applications programs under which it runs) and contains a number of the elements that appear in many windows, which are labelled in the figure.

Note that some of the options are already set when the window appears, and others are 'greyed out' to indicate that the option is currently unavailable. By leaving some evidence of the option, the user is reminded of other possibilities, even though some change must be made before they can be chosen. These evidences of 'state' are important in helping users locate themselves.

To create such a window structure we will use both types of hierarchies: aggregation and classification. The components of a dialogue – buttons, menus, text boxes, and so on – form a natural aggregation hierarchy. But the objects themselves form a classification hierarchy that is shown in Table 5.1.

Since the interest in this chapter is on techniques for the user interface, we will not consider other necessary parts of the definition, such as the top levels of the application which include facilities for opening documents, printing and other activities. The description here is necessarily simplified, since practical window systems have a multiplicity of features which obscure the basic principles. However, these aspects can be unified into the same framework, as is shown by the Motif system. The treatment derives in part

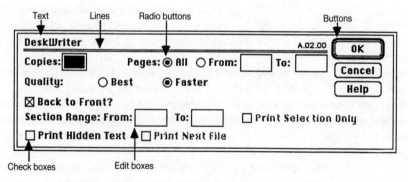

Figure 5.7 A typical dialogue to control printing.

Table 5.1 Classification hierarchy for objects.

Macintosh	Windows	Motif
Button	Push button	Push button
–	–	Arrow button
Picture	–	Drawn button
Check box	Check box	Toggle button
Radio button	Radio button	Toggle button
Static text	Text	Label
List box	List box	List
Popup	Popup	Cascade
–	Rectangle	Frame
Edit text	Edit box	Text
Icon	Icon	Label
Scrollbar	Horizontal scrollbar	Scrollbar
	Vertical scrollbar	
	Custom	

from the lead given by the MacApp system (Schmucker, 1986), an object-oriented programming environment which extends the toolbox built at a low level into the Macintosh which handles mouse movements and drawing on this system.

The predefined objects for windows come in two basic categories: windows and items. Windows are standalone objects which appear in various conventional forms, whereas items are subparts of these windows. The items are the basic components of any interface. They include buttons, text boxes and scroll bars. Composite objects are made up of primitive objects, but have common functions which means they must be treated together. For example, a group of radio buttons might be constrained so that just one is turned on at any one time.

The terminology of these three systems is broadly similar, but differs in detail. A summary of the terms for primitive objects which approximately corresponds is shown below. The visual details of the graphic representation varies in a number of ways, partly to avoid violations of claimed copyright. Motif, for example, uses 'sculpted' buttons with a 3-D effect produced by shadowing. This causes slight problems in that 'arrows' need more complex shadows than other buttons.

(1) **Push buttons** are either rounded rectangles or, in Motif, use a '3-D' effect (see Figure 5.8). When they are pressed they have a highlighted or 'depressed' look. These are the standard method of initiating an action. The 'default' button is also usually distinguished visually.

Variant types of buttons use either 'icons', which are small bitmap pictures, or have access to all the graphics facilities. This is called a *picture*

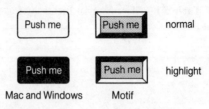

Figure 5.8   Isolated button styles.

on the Mac, but the 'Custom' equivalent in Windows (see (8) below) does not have the same default button action. Motif also has a special category for arrow buttons, as already noted.

(2) There is another type of button, called a **toggle button**, which indicates its current setting – off or on. There are two styles, called 'check boxes' and 'radio buttons' respectively, which are illustrated in Figure 5.7. They both represent Boolean states, such as whether pages should be printed in a back-to-front order, but the circular radio buttons draw on the folk memory of buttons which control a fifties-style radio: when one is pressed, any others in the group which are on are turned off. Radio buttons are therefore used to represent a one-out-of-many choice. Motif represents the toggle buttons by square and diamond shapes respectively.

(3) **List boxes** (see Figure 5.9) are a means of making selections and are normally used where the information is transient or may have a variable number of items, such as a list of files of which one is to be selected. A number of strings can be displayed, one per line. **Popup** menus are another form of selection, where only the current option is normally displayed, but a full list appears when the button is pressed. A downward arrow is used to draw attention to the fact that it is a button.

(4) **Edit boxes** are designed for text which can be entered and updated. The programmer needs to be able to control what is entered and this can be done either by call-backs when each character is entered, or by checks when control enters or exits the field using the appropriate means (for example, the pointer). Normally the 'focus' of a window is centred on one such box, where the cursor appears. There is a distinction in several systems between short and long texts, although the limits vary. These boxes need to be distinguished from primary windows, which do more of their own display management.

(5) There is a group of static text and picture elements which can optionally be used for control purposes. **Icons** are small bitmaps which easily fit into resource files, whereas pictures (drawn buttons) can be of any complexity and may be controlled by the program. **Text items** have font information attached to them. Rectangles are used as visual dividers: if they have a height of 1 they are simply lines.

(6) **Scrollbars** are normally incorporated in other elements such as scrolling windows and the analogue type of scale, but are defined by themselves so they can be incorporated into other designs.

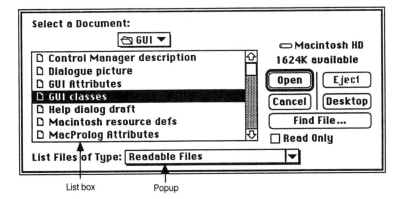

Figure 5.9 List boxes.

(7) Pulldown **menus** are not themselves part of the dialogue box, but often work closely with them and therefore need to be included in the catalogue. Where these menus appear – at the top of the screen on the Mac, at the top of the window in Windows and possibly floating in Motif – does not make much difference at the programming level. However, new menus may need to be installed, or the contents of existing menus changed, and the events generated by them must be handled.

(8) Another type of button is entirely user-defined, called **custom** in Windows. The user is responsible for drawing the contents and handling any events within the area of the object. This serves as a convenient escape mechanism for any special-purpose functions which cannot be conveniently handled by the other primitives.

This relatively small catalogue includes all the basic elements needed in creating an interface. But elements of a window are not necessarily independent of each other. For example, a group of radio buttons needs to be managed together. Another example is the 'tabbing order' of data entry fields. When one finishes entering data into a field, such as the 'From' fields in Figure 5.7, by entering some conventional key such as a tab, one expects the cursor to move to the 'next' field. But in a graphical environment it is not necessarily obvious which field should be handled next, so the form designer should be allowed to designate the order in which fields are visited.

Though the question of tabbing order can be settled at 'compile-time' (the time at which the window's layout is decided), radio buttons need a 'run-time' manager, to ensure that when one button is turned on, others are turned off. There are several ways of organizing this: either the whole area containing the radio buttons is treated as one area and the manager is responsible for sending signals to the buttons, or each button fields the signal and sends a message to another manager object which decides which action to take. Since the way in which the different systems handle this aspect varies, we will use the Prolog++ object system to express these dependencies and allow the differences to be dealt with at a system level.

The most complex objects are the windows themselves. These contain a number of standard features, such as titles, means of resizing and making the window disappear. Most systems have several different styles of window to convey information about the status of the window: a dialogue window may look different from a document window, and a 'modal window', which must be attended to before anything else is done, also needs a distinctive shape. However, these differences are superficial. Underneath, most of the behaviour is shared and it is the components within the window that differ.

In addition to the items that have already been discussed, there is a need to define composite items. These include groups of radio buttons and multipaned windows. They share the property that they themselves have components and often need to intercept the messages sent them. The way in which this is done varies from system to system: for example, a radio button is normally part of a group, such that when it is switched on, any other button in the group must be turned off. This can be handled by the group intercepting the button press and computing the appropriate messages to send, or by the individual button passing a message to the group which then transmits a message to switch off the other button which is currently in the on position.

When we come to design the classes for window objects there is a significant amount of shared behaviour which can usefully be inherited. For example, the rectangular shape of all window objects, together with the methods for manipulating them, can be included at the highest level and shared by all the objects. We can derive a hierarchy as shown by Figure 5.10.

There are several advantages to using an object-oriented approach compared with the conventional procedural approach:

(1)   It is easier to separate the static and dynamic information present in the dialogue. The static information can potentially be compiled into a resource fork, or file. With existing Prolog techniques, all the information is supplied at run-time, which means that it cannot be recompiled and is not available to the distributor for customizing.

(2)   Any element of the window can be given its own behaviour. This feature is available already in MacProlog, using extended dialogues. However, the user is required to generate the appropriate dispatch table. In an object-oriented environment, the dispatching operation can be supplied by the system.

(3)   It is possible to inherit the behaviour of standard components. For example, a *Cancel* button normally has the effect of annulling the effects of the current dialogue. In MacProlog this is signalled by the failure of the call which generated the dialogue with the automatic

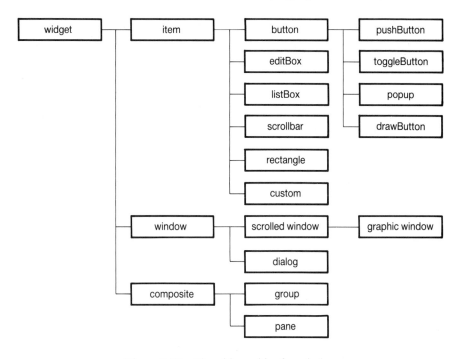

Figure 5.10 Class hierarchies for windows.

disappearance of the dialogue. In Prolog++ this will typically cause the window to disappear, but otherwise leave the user of the program to make the next move. However, it is perfectly possible to program other behaviour.

5.5 Specifying the user interface

In order to specify the behaviour of a windowing interface one needs the following:

(1) A geometric description of the windows, menus, and so on that make up the interface.

(2) A definition of the procedures that are invoked by user actions in these windows.

(3) Procedures to display and change the graphical objects.

Let us examine each of these elements, in turn.

5.5.1   Geometric description

There are three main approaches to describing the geometry of a window:

(1)   Use a display editor, such as the DIALOG program supplied with Windows 3.

(2)   Describe the components of the window by means of their contents and let the system decide the layout.

(3)   Describe the layout explicitly, using the coordinate system.

Each of these have their advantages. Many people find the first approach the most intuitive. Buttons, fields and headings are laid out and changed with a drawing program and then linked into the program. Several Prolog vendors supply tools for this purpose. This can be tedious for simple layouts, particularly if the number of items is dynamically varying. So the second approach also has its place. Elements can be laid out in rows and columns, with particular attention given to margins around each group of elements.

Motif provides some elaborate layout management. This is partly justified by the wide variation in screen size and capabilities in the systems for which it was designed. Its design was influenced by the desire to be able radically to resize any Motif window, although algorithmic layouts are unlikely to look as professional as purpose-designed layouts. Since these facilities can be provided in a relatively orthogonal manner to the other aspects, we will not elaborate on them here.

In most cases, the results of either of the first two methods will be computed in advance and expressed in the resource file in the third, explicit, form. In Prolog++ most of the information will be expressed as attributes in the corresponding class definitions. The basic information for this – size, position, colour of background and foreground, text fonts, sizes and styles – is common to most of the widgets and can therefore be defined at the top level of the hierarchy.

5.5.2   User events

In a window 'package' it is necessary to leave provision so that application-specific code can be invoked at various stages. For example, when the user has filled in a text box, there may be other parts of the display that need to be updated to reflect the new information. This is a classic use of an 'overriding' definition in an object-oriented system. The user supplies a routine which overrides a default definition, which in many cases will simply do nothing.

This corresponds to the provision of slots for 'call-back' routines in systems such as Motif. The programmer provides the name of a routine which is to be called when a particular event occurs. However it is implemented, it is this call-back structure which provides a new level of abstraction for the application programmer. In designing a user interface, much of the programming starts from these 'events' which are generated by a specific action, such as a mouseclick. Because of the geometric structure of the dialogue these can be interpreted in specific ways.

5.5.3 Displaying the window and handling input

A typical dialogue will have a number of fixed items (such as buttons) and other items, such as text boxes, whose contents will be different for each use. Provided that one is sticking to the predefined elements, there is not a great deal that has to be done by the user. The state of various controls changes their appearance: for example, if an option is inappropriate in the current state, this can be indicated visually by 'greying out' the appropriate button. Then the user is not surprised either when the option does not work, or by its absence from the display.

Much of the programming of a user interface derives from the need to redisplay parts of a window after they have been obscured by other windows, or moved around the screen. Most of this can be handled 'automatically' so that it does not trouble the application programmer. There is clearly a trade-off here: the more complex the interface, the more control the programmer has. Although the object-oriented approach means that one can add incrementally to an existing structure, it cannot hide the complexity totally. Special behaviour means special programming. However, there is a large proportion of shared behaviour that need only be programmed once: this is the benefit of reusable code.

5.5.4 MacObject

To illustrate an approach to constructing interfaces, we will briefly describe in this chapter a tool available in MacProlog called MacObject. This follows the first approach in allowing the user to lay out a window using a display editor. It then generates a *program* which is a set of Prolog++ classes which can generate a dialogue. In addition, it has features allowing one to represent and manipulate the object hierarchy, add methods to each of the items in the window using an interactive editor and change the value of the default attributes for each object.

As an example, we will use an interface for the conjugation of German verbs demonstrated in Chapter 3. This is a testbed that allows the user to produce any person, tense, voice or mode of any of the verbs in the database. This has a title, four sets of radio buttons to select the person, tense, voice and mode respectively of a verb, a list box to select the root form of the verb to be declined, a text box in which the verb is displayed and two buttons to trigger actions (Figure 5.11).

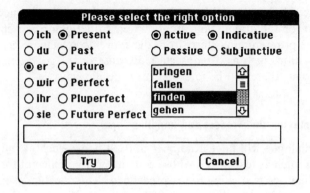

Figure 5.11   Dialogue in MacObject for the conjugation of German verbs.

The editor which produces the dialogue is shown in Figure 5.12. This is a graphics window, which uses a grid (shown dotted) to allow easy regular placement of items. The area on the left is the tool pane: clicking on any of the icons allows one to create or edit the corresponding type of object. The nearly completed dialogue is in the main panel. Each of the vertical sets of radio buttons are distinct groups which may be set individually. The list box on the right is used to select the root form of the verb – the actual list of verbs will be adjusted at run-time. The edit box underneath will display the result when the *Try* button is activated.

The output of the editor is a Prolog++ program in the form that will be discussed shortly, consisting of a composite object whose parts are objects which define the items within the window.

The classes themselves which make up the application can also be displayed and edited in MacObject, which includes tools such as the hierarchy

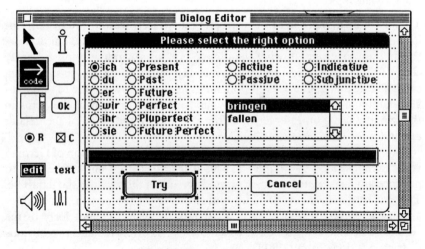

Figure 5.12   Dialogue editor.

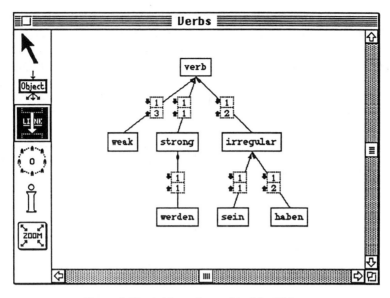

Figure 5.13   A hierarchy tool in MacObject.

tool in Figure 5.12 for setting up the inheritance network, and dialogues for inspecting and changing the attributes of the objects.

5.6   Prolog++ windows

The structure of the program to handle windows in a language such as Prolog++ should now be somewhat clearer. The process is essentially as follows:

(1)   A set of classes is provided which corresponds to the components of the windowing system. For each item in the window, the user defines either an instance of one of these components, or a new class which inherits from one of them.

(2)   The major class, for the window, will have as subparts instances of all the items.

(3)   The appropriate attributes of all the items are assigned values corresponding to the geometry, appearance and contents of each item. Methods are defined to handle the call-back events.

(4)   A method 'draw' is invoked for the window, which recursively invokes the drawing procedures of all its subparts and displays the window on the screen.

(5)   Events occur which pass messages to any of the components of the window. These may result in changes being made to the contents or form of the window.

The biggest departure from normal practice is in the control of the program. The program does not in general simply call a subroutine to do some input/output and carry on. The window itself and its associated objects become the organizing entity around which the control of the program is organized.

Let us take a simple example to see how this works in practice. We will use the example of the conjugation of German verbs in Chapter 3, with the interface, shown in Figure 5.11, discussed in Section 5.5.4.

The user is free to select a verb and specify the person, tense, voice and mood that is required by using the radio buttons. Then by pressing the 'Try' button, they can see the correct declension of the verb.

The class that sets up this dialogue has as its heading:

```
class verbWindow
inherits window, verb.
parts tryButton, cancelButton, personGroup, tenseGroup,
      voiceGroup, moodGroup, editBox, listBox.
```

The parts declaration gives all the components of the dialogue; some of these are predefined (for example, editBox, listBox), others are defined as subclasses of the predefined classes. The components may themselves be structured, as in the case of the groups of radio buttons, which are subclasses of the group class. The two classes tryButton and cancelButton derive their basic behaviour from the predefined class button. When an instance of verbWindow is created, all the aggregation hierarchy is automatically set up, and the relevant attributes set up by passing setValue messages to the components, as demonstrated in Program 5.1. This shows representatives of the different classes (see Appendix B for a full listing).

The dimensions of the window are given as a set of conventional attribute names: position specifies the top left coordinates of the box as an (X,Y) pair; size similarly specifies the width and height. These are used indirectly by the implementation code contained in the window class and thus achieve a high degree of system independence: the code can easily be varied for different situations, because the parameters are available when required.

The declaration for the radio group contains an element of layout for this rather simple situation: instead of providing individual dimensions for all 6 buttons, it is only necessary to provide the overall size of the group and the implementation code can easily lay them out within that area, using the height parameter which gives the only other dimension needed, the height of each individual element. In this way it is only necessary to provide a total of 9 sets of dimensions for the window rather than the 21 sets that would otherwise be required.

We will examine the attributes shortly, but let us first look briefly at how the methods work. The main action of the window occurs within the

Program 5.1 Interface for verb conjugation.

```
class verbWindow.
inherits window, verb.
part tryButton, cancelButton, personGroup, tenseGroup,
    voiceGroup, moodGroup, editBox, listBox.
attribute position = (78, 72), size = (356,198),
    title = 'Please select the right option'.

when_created :-
    editBox # 1 <-
        setValues([position = (10,130),size = (322,16)]),
    listBox # 1 <- setValues([position = (170,50),size = (124,68),
        text = [bringen, fallen, finden, gehen, haben, helfen,
        kennen, machen, müssen, reden, rufen, schreiben, sein,
        tragen, wechseln, werden], selected = [finden]]),

try :-
    personGroup # 1 <- on(Person),
    tenseGroup # 1 <- on(Tense),
    voiceGroup # 1 <- on(Voice),
    moodGroup # 1 <- on(Mood),
    listBox # 1 <- on(Inf),
    conjugate(Voice,Verb,Tense,Person,Mood,String),
    editBox # 1 <- (set(text, String), redraw).

end verbWindow.

class tryButton.
inherits button.
attributes position = (60,160), size = (60,20), text = 'Try'.
activate :-
    super_part <- try.
end tryButton.

class personGroup.
inherits radioGroup.
parts radioButton*6.
attributes position = (5,5), size = (45,120), height = 16,
    texts = [ich, du, er, wir, ihr, sie], on = er.
end personGroup.
```

class verbWindow. which inherits its domain-specific behaviour from the class verb and its interactive behaviour from the class window. The window components do *not* inherit from verbWindow (never inherit from a super_part – your program could immediately go into a loop trying to create an infinite size object!). Because the verb class is essentially declarative, the window components could inherit directly from that class, but it is better practice to pass domain-specific requests through the main window, using messages sent to super_part.

A button being pressed in the Try button causes an activate message to be sent to the instance of the tryButton class and this is immediately passed up the line to the routine try. It is then necessary for the main window to find out the settings of all the radio buttons. It does this simply by querying the current setting of the on attribute for each of the relevant components. After calling the conjugate method to find the new form of the verb, it sends the result to the edit box via the command:

editBox#1 <— (set(text, String), redraw).

Each of the window classes will respond to a set message for one of its known attributes. The last requirement is to display the new state of the edit box – and for this a redraw message is sent directly to that component, avoiding the need to redraw the whole window.

This arrangement of windows shows the complementary nature of the two forms of hierarchy – inheritance and aggregation. Passing a message up through the aggregation hierarchy is sometimes confusingly called inheritance. In the Hypercard system (Apple, 1990) it is called the *message-passing order* and is relatively inflexible: messages are passed by default from buttons to cards to other stacks. In Prolog++ there is only one built-in message-passing order, based on inheritance, working between more specific and more general objects. To provide alternative behaviour one must code specific handlers using the constructors such as super_part as used in the definition of calcButton. One can write generalized buttons with these which can be used in different contexts; where the message is sent depends on what object it is part of, not its inheritance structure.

Having considered one example, let us look at definitions of the different elements. First, the attributes of the different classes are shown in Table 5.2.

Both position and size are pairs of numbers, constructed with the comma operator. Since the comma can be ambiguous in Prolog it is normally necessary to enclose this in brackets. Thus (200,100) can represent the position $X = 200$, $Y = 100$, or alternatively a size, of width 200 and height 100. The dimensions refer to the overall size of the object, including any framing which may surround it.

Colours consist of either an atom such as black, white or red or a term representing the red, green and blue components of a colour, such as rgb(60000, 1000, 1000). In addition, the atom transparent is allowed.

Since most items can include text or pictures, or in some cases both, the attributes defining both of these are declared at the level of items. It isn't necessary for the attributes to be repeated at lower levels because all inheriting classes share attributes. In particular, all styles of buttons share the same attributes.

Table 5.2 Classes and attributes for windows toolbox.

Class	Attributes
widget	position, size, bgColor, fgColor, pattern
item	itemNumber, name, textSize, textStyle, textFont, alignment, icon, text, visible
button	dimmed, hilite
toggleButton	state
editBox	focus, keyVerify
listBox	items, multiple
popup	items
rectangle	lineThickness
scrollbar	value, minimum, maximum, increment, page
group	texts, on, height

Attributes are set by the message setValues which takes a pair-list of attribute names and values as arguments, as demonstrated in the example above. There are two basic messages that are accepted by both windows and items: show and redraw. A window is not drawn when the object describing it is created, as one usually wants to change some of its attributes. The act of drawing a window automatically causes a draw message to be sent to all its component items. Also a window isn't changed when one of its attributes is changed – only when a redraw message is sent to the item or window. In this way, a number of changes can be made which only result in a single redrawing of the image.

In most cases, the user does not need to bother about drawing or redrawing either windows or items. The one exception to this rule is the custom item. Here the user is responsible for almost everything: both show and redraw do not have a default action.

All items have both an item number and a name. The item number is derived from the order in which objects are declared in the *window* object, is used internally for several purposes (including the layering of items front to back and tabbing order) and is fixed – it cannot be changed by setValues. As it is inconvenient to refer to an item by this number, which may be changed in different versions of a program, a name is also provided for each item, which is simply an atom. For a button, the text defaults to the name if this is not set. This can be changed, but its main purpose is to simplify programming by being the tag by which the item is known.

For the programmer, it is vital to know what messages the item must expect and be able to handle. A brief list is shown in Table 5.3.

The messages to buttons have already been explained. For edit boxes, messages are sent when the user enters or leaves the field, and a newValue message whose parameter is the new state of the text. In addition, each time

Table 5.3   Messages sent to items.

button	activate, arm, disarm
field	enter, leave, newValue, changeVerify
popup	entry, map, unmap
listBox	selection
custom	buttonDown, buttonUp, enter, leave
scrollbar	newValue

the user presses a key within the box, a changeVerify message is sent: if this does not succeed and the attribute keyVerify of the box is set to on, the action of the key is not used.

For popups, it is necessary to check their state when the user activates them and before they are shown, so that the unavailable states can be shown accurately. The map message allows this, with unmap being called afterwards.

List boxes can either permit single or multiple choices, depending on whether the multiple attribute is set to *on*. In either case, the selection method has an argument which is a list of atoms, one per line of the box.

For scrollbars, all movement is translated into a single number which is the new position of the scrollbar. If the user moves to the top, the minimum value is returned, if they move to the bottom, the maximum value is returned. If they click in the area above or below the scrollbar, the value of page is subtracted or added to the current value (subject to the limits).

Finally, for custom areas, all button actions are sent back with a parameter (the number of the button on the mouse), which has a maximum of 1 for Macintosh systems to 3 (normally) with Unix systems, though it may be a larger number.

Each class must handle the following types of action:

(1) Display (or redisplay) itself. This is defined at the top level for each type of widget and it is not normally necessary for the user to change the definition. How the item is displayed will depend on whether it is highlighted, or 'greyed out', (which indicates an option that is currently unavailable).

(2) Return its current value and attributes. The value depends on the type: it may be on/off, a piece of text, or perhaps some other type such as a picture or sound.

(3) Set the current value or attributes to a new value. There may be internal checks imposed on what value is set and the user can add to these by means of invalid assertions.

(4) Item-specific code. Since each item is potentially a full Prolog++ class it is possible to add both responses to events and any extra Prolog++ methods that are used by these.

The code for any particular item may query and update other items by means of these routines.

Let us look more closely at the requirements for the particular items.

5.6.1 Items

This most generic class includes a large number of attributes common to all the items, such as name, text and visibility attributes.

The item number is fixed at creation time by the order in which the items are declared in the parts hierarchy. It fixes both the way in which overlapping items are displayed (lower numbers on top of higher) and the 'tabbing order', the order in which control passes from edit box to edit box by default when the box exit key is hit.

It can be convenient to have an item that is invisible. It provides a means of optionally displaying something without the overheads of adding and removing it from the window. Instead one simply toggles the visibility index. There is in fact no means of dynamically changing the components in a Prolog++ aggregate. Hence it is necessary to include all possible items.

Now that differing typefaces and styles are allowed, specifying the type is rather complex, particularly if cross-platform portability is required. Names of typefaces and styles vary considerably.

5.6.2 Push buttons

Push buttons typically cause actions. Apart from the arm and disarm messages, which are usually handled by built-in actions, the main action takes place in response to the activate message which occurs on 'mouse up'. There are two special actions for any window: a normal and abnormal termination.

5.6.3 Toggle buttons

Both check boxes and radio buttons have an internal state which is either *on* or *off*. This state is represented visually by conventional means.

Radio buttons have an additional aspect. When one button is pressed, any other button in the group will be turned off. Hence, it is necessary to have a group item separate from any of the individual buttons. The simplest arrangement is for this group item to cover all the buttons so that when any button in the group is pressed, the action is intercepted by the group item, which then passes on appropriate messages to the buttons below it: to turn off any button currently on and turn on the button clicked.

What is the relationship between the group and the buttons? It is certainly not an inheritance relationship: they don't have a great deal in common. The relationship only appears within the component hierarchy, and then only because of the spatial arrangement of the different components. The group is a distinct component which can usually be calculated easily from other information within the dialogue description.

We will take the simplifying assumption here that the group is itself a rectangular shape, though it could in general be several discrete rectangles.

5.6.4   Edit boxes

Edit boxes are potentially the most complex type of item. They require a rather full set of editing operations, including the ability to move the insertion point freely, to cut and paste from the clip board. Most of this behaviour is directly inherited from the built-in features of the operating system. At any time, one edit box at most can be active: this is indicated by the attribute focus being set to *on*.

Characters typed into a box should not always appear directly. For example, if the box is being used to type a password, some other character, such as '*' will normally be typed in place of the characters.

5.6.5   List box

A list box is a scrolling box with preset contents. A list box can be *single* or *multiple* selection. If the attribute multiple is off, then clicking on another item will cause any currently selected items to be deselected.

The attribute items is set by the class to a list of all currently selected options, as a list of atoms with their names.

5.6.6   Scrollbars

Scrollbars are typically seen as controlling a scrolling window full of text, but they are in fact rather more general. They can be used for any purpose which requires a variable 'empty to full' display. This might be a thermometer, or something recording the progress to completion of a task, or a control to set a variable value in a simulation.

5.7   Designing an application

To be successful in using a graphical interface, a complete change in the approach to writing the program is necessary. Whereas traditionally logic programmers tend to start from function and add the necessary controlling functions afterwards, this really doesn't work with windows. It is particularly hard to port an existing program to a windowing environment. It is tempting simply to take the interactive parts of the program and try to put the windows interface in there. This inevitably leads to frustration and possibly eventually to a total rewrite of the program.

An alternative approach has become popular in the last few years, as is well described in the *Turbo Vision* manual. Turbo Vision is a set of C++

classes designed for much the same purpose as the set of classes in this chapter. It warns against the danger of trying to adapt an existing interface or put a graphical layer on top of an existing application, and suggests that:

> 'The better approach to porting an existing application is first to write a Turbo Vision interface that parallels your existing one, and then scavenge your old code into your new application.
>
> You need to spend some time thinking about the essence of your application, so you can divide your interface code from the code that carries out the work of your application. This can be difficult because you have to think differently about your application.
>
> The job of porting will involve some rewriting to teach the new objects how to represent themselves, but it will also involve a lot of throwing away of old interface code.' (Borland, International, 1991.)

This approach is particularly appropriate to the mix of logic programming and object-oriented programming being considered in this book. The logician is far more interested in the form of the solution than in the way in which a program meets the particular need of the user. Unfortunately, an elegant solution is wasted on the user if it is not presented in a way that helps them get on with their real business. Their activity is typically represented not by a particular algorithm, but by the integration of knowledge about a problem, the algorithms necessary to solve it and a convenient interface which provides a cost-effective means of identifying the solution. This is what is meant by an application.

How to combine input/output (i/o) – an essentially undeclarative aspect of computing – with the declarative approach has never been resolved properly. Prolog provides an elegant description of grammatical formalisms, the bread and butter of linear language, but cannot account for the effect produced by an output on the subsequent input produced by the user. This involves deep issues of causality which are beyond a logical and necessarily abstracted account. They remain as 'open research issues'.

The traditional Prolog approach has therefore been unashamedly pragmatic: provide a full set of built-in i/o 'predicates' which the user can incorporate into his or her programs. Prolog textbooks normally recommend the separation of i/o and declarative predicates, but this fails to be a consistent methodology.

Some Prolog-like systems, such as Trilogy (Voda, 1988) have a more systematic approach. Trilogy has three types of building blocks, with identical syntax but different capabilities: functions, predicates and subroutines. Functions (and subroutines) are limited to single solutions, which gives performance advantages. Neither functions nor predicates can perform any input/output, only subroutines. Predicates can call functions and subroutines can call either of the other classes, but calls in the other direction are not permitted (though functions can invoke predicates via set operations).

From a methodological point of view this has big advantages: the temptation to include some little piece of nondeclarative programming in the middle of a declarative program is overridden. Consequently the meaning of a program is strictly delimited by its set of arguments, without having to consider any hidden side-effects which the program performs, either in i/o or changes to the internal database. This, in turn, makes debugging programs by declarative means much simpler.

For various reasons, this approach has not become widespread. Yet it captures the essence of the new approach to the construction of application programs. The collection of windows, buttons, menus and displays becomes the organizing component for the program, which is now a collection of facilities which can be invoked by the user in whichever way they choose. Many of these components, such as those which query a database or perform a calculation, will be entirely declarative. Others will perform state changes, taking the database from one context to another.

There is a significant difference in perspective between declarative and imperative code. Declarative code answers a question: what is the square root of 2, what is the largest country in Europe, and so on. Imperative code does something: display a map on the screen, compile a program, and so on. Inevitably with imperative code, the data is objectified and the code is active:

> 'In traditional programming we tend to think of the program from the perspective of the code. We are the code and the data is "out there", something on which we operate.' (Borland, International, 1991.)

Writing imperative code in Prolog brings exactly the same mentality. Yet Prolog is a perfectly good structured language, and it adapts well to the imperative approach even though it does not make the best use of the paradigm. The use of event-driven programming in Prolog++ is a much better basis for this type of i/o programming. It works alongside the more declarative code so one can state what are the program's responses to external stimuli. Rather than the problem domain, or particular data manipulations becoming the focus of the program, the application itself takes on this role:

> 'It makes more sense in the integrated environment to make the application itself the organising object. After all, what is an application but something that binds things together? If we had continued to look on the application as just a lump of data that should be "out there" somewhere, we might have been tempted to put the center of the application elsewhere. We would then have had to carry a burden of excessive and strained communication among parts of the program.' (Borland, International, 1991.)

It is precisely at the application level that the imperative actions of the user are most apparent. We create and modify documents – which in this context might be text, pictures, logical assertions or sounds – and use

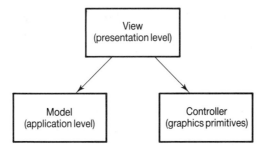

Figure 5.14   Model-view-controller (MVC).

these to produce the output which solves the problem we have in hand. This might include the retrieval of facts from a database, some intricate algorithm expressed in an algorithmic language or, more typically, a combination of both.

This type of interface has been christened the model-view-controller (MVC) paradigm at the Xerox PARC laboratory. The logic of the application is called a *Model*, the conceptual definition of the interface is the *View*, and the *Controller* is the set of graphics primitive routines which implement the user interface. These may be visualized as three separate layers as shown in Figure 5.14.

It is the presentation layer which is in charge, and it has an asymmetric relationship with the model: the view can receive information about the model, but the model does not need to reference the view, indeed it should not be in any way dependent on it. Similarly, the controller is simply a set of (predefined) subroutines which knows nothing about a particular view.

5.7.1   Mushroom finder

To demonstrate these principles in a live application, we will use a very simple expert-system type of application: the mechanization of a dichotomous key to identify an unknown living species, in this case mushrooms. Such keys are printed in most field guides and take a certain amount of practice and skill to use them effectively. The beginning of such a key is shown in Figure 5.15.

(1)	Cap with pores or tubes underneath. **Key a.**
	Cap with gills or ridges underneath. **2**
(2)	Stem eccentrically or laterally attached to cap or absent. **Key b**
	Stem centrally attached to cap. **3**
(3)	Gills free or narrowly attached. **4**
	Gills broadly adnate to decurrent. **5**
(4)	Gills free. **Key c**
	Gills narrowly attached, adnexed or shortly adnate. **Key d**

Figure 5.15   The start of a key for identifying mushrooms.

The key is divided into major sections, by letters, and into individual choices by number. The user must consider each pair of statements and pick the most appropriate one, and follow to the next key indicated. This continues until the genus or species is found.

Although the main purpose of this example is to show the user interface, we will demonstrate that a computerized version has advantages over the paper version. For example, it is sometimes not possible to answer a question uniquely. The key might, in the case of mushrooms, ask for the colour of the spores. It is only possible to ascertain this by placing the mushroom cap uppermost on a piece of paper and leaving it overnight – an inconvenient diversion if one is faced by a crop of seemingly delectable mushrooms! The Prolog++ version allows you to follow both branches of the tree in the hope that some of the other questions will eliminate one of the branches. Similarly, one might wish to retract a decision taken earlier which seems, with hindsight, to be mistaken. The bookkeeping for both of these is simple on a computer, but not so easy with pen and paper.

Representation of the key in Prolog++ is simple. We represent it as a 5-ary predicate, mk, consisting of the label for a particular pair of questions, and two pairs of conditions and actions:

```
mk(1, 'Cap with pores or tubes underneath', to(a1),
    'Cap with gills or ridges underneath', to(2)).
mk(2, 'Stem eccentrically or laterally attached to cap or
    absent', to(b1), 'Stem centrally attached to cap',
    to(3)).
mk(3, 'Gills free or narrowly attached', to(4),
    'Gills broadly adnate to decurrent', to(5)).
mk(4, 'Gills free', to(c1),
    'Gills narrowly attached, adnexed or shortly adnate',
    to(d1)).
```

There are essentially two types of action, corresponding to branches and leaves of the classification tree. The standard way to represent these in Prolog is to use different function symbols for each type of action, using the arguments to specify the value. Here we have used the symbol to to represent a branch, having as argument the label of the next pair of questions. To avoid duplication of numbers, we specify a1 for the first question in key a, etc.

There are three possible leaves of the tree: either we have arrived at a species, which is specified by a pair of words – genus and specific; or the key simply gives a genus, leaving further identification outside the key; or it may yield several alternatives, which are either species or genera. These are coded as follows:

```
genus(X)      genus named X
species(X,Y)  species named X Y
or(X,Y)       either X or Y (which are in turn one of the 3 alternatives)
```

To search this tree, it is simple to describe the logic, by constraining all user input/output within a predicate agree which succeeds if the user concurs with the statement that is the parameter and fails otherwise.

```
class key1.
search(From, Result) :-
     mk(From, Cond1, Act1, Cond2, Act2),
     (agree(Cond1), act(Act1, Result)
     ; agree(Cond2), act(Act2, Result)).

act(genus(X), genus(X)).
act(species(X,Y), species(X,Y)).
act(or(X,Y), or(X,Y)).
act(to(Node), Result) :-
     search(Node, Result).
end key1.
```

Normally, we would expect the call to agree to invoke some i/o to compute its answer. This will be a side-effect of the search algorithm, a 'modal' event which must be completed before the next part of the program is elaborated, not an event in the GUI (graphical user interface) style. (This need not be modal in the sense used in the Macintosh guidelines, where the system software prevents the user doing other activities. But it is modal in the sense that the user's program is 'suspended' until the activity is completed.) However, we can consider the result of all the calls to the predicate conceptually as a new relation which is simply elaborated by this process. This approach, known as Query-The-User (QTL), has a long history in logic programming (Sergot, 1982) and neatly avoids difficult semantic issues concerning i/o.

Unfortunately, we normally want a more elaborate i/o system than a series of unconnected and possibly mysterious questions, and QTL is not easily extended to explain these. In the above case, we might wish to take special action if the user replied 'no' to both branches of a particular point in the tree; but this requires changes to the algorithm (by adding a third alternative in the code for search), not to the (invisible) QTL system. As these changes multiply, users of QTL have realized that a different method of separating the algorithm from the i/o component is required.

Let us therefore consider the form of the user interface. The simplest form might be as Figure 5.16.

What is wrong with this? Here is a partial list of faults:

(1)   There's no sense of context: why is this question being asked now?

(2)   Pictures would be much better than sentence descriptions.

(3)   There's no indication of what decisions have already been made.

(4)   Though an opportunity has been given to 'cancel' the dialogue, it's not clear what the effect of this would be, and there could be other options.

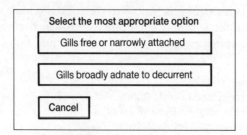

Figure 5.16   A simple user interface.

A second attempt is shown in Figure 5.17. This shows the *previous* description that was picked, so giving the user some context (earlier decisions can be accessed via the pulldown menu arrow). Pictures show what 'free', 'adnate' and 'decurrent' mean, in terms of a profile across the mushroom. One might think it better to dispense with the English descriptions altogether, but this is not necessarily an advantage: almost any picture can give a different set of messages: here it is quite plain that it is the attachment of the gills (to the stem) which is at stake. Other incidentals of the picture (for example, the shape of the cap) can be safely ignored.

The buttons at the bottom allow some more powerful manipulations: if the user is unsure of the answer to a question, they can follow *both* branches in the hope that subsequent questions might be decisive in narrowing down the choices to a single alternative. If it subsequently happens that both choices are clearly inapplicable to the specimen in question, then the user can answer *neither*. The *undo* option can be invoked repeatedly to retract incorrect responses, and *quit* merely allows the user to abort the current identification.

This picture reminds one of a branching tree and suggests another improvement. If space on the screen permits, there is nothing to prevent the

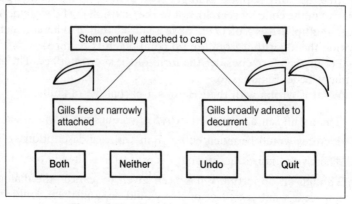

Figure 5.17   Graphical user interface.

Program 5.2   Key follower with Prolog interface.

```
class key2.
search(gen(X), _, gen(X)).
search(spec(X,Y), _, species(X,Y)).
search(or(X,Y), _, or(X,Y)).
search(to(Node), D, Result) :-
     mk(Node, Cond1, Act1, Cond2, Act2),
     choose(Cond1, Act1, Cond2, Act2, D, Act),
     D1 is D + 1,
     search(Act, D1, Result).

choose(Cond1, Act1, Cond2, Act2, D, Act) :-
     dialog('Choose appropriate response', 50,50,100,500,
        [button(70,10,20,60,'Both'),
        button(70,90,20,60,'Neither'),
        button(10,10,20,480,Cond1),
        button(40,10,20,480,Cond2)],
        B),
     decide(B, Cond1, Act1, Cond2, Act2, Cond, Act),
     writeseqnl([D, Cond]).

decide(1, Cond1, Act1, _, _, Cond1, Act1).
decide(1, _, _, Cond2, Act2, Cond2, Act2).
decide(3, Cond1, Act1, _, _, Cond1, Act1).
decide(4, _, _, Cond2, Act2, Cond2, Act2).
end key2.
```

presentation of several decision levels at once, or allowing more than two options at any one level. The eye can scan far faster than the pointer can be positioned or buttons clicked. On the other hand, presenting too much information at once can be confusing. So if several levels are presented simultaneously, it is probably worth allowing this as an 'advanced' option, which the user either turns off or on.

Let us first elaborate the search to allow several branches to be searched. For reasons which will become apparent later, we will not include the *undo* option. The algorithm above needs to be changed to that shown in Program 5.2, which uses the Prolog backtracking mechanism in significant ways.

Here we have used the built-in dialogue predicate available in MacProlog to generate the result. To simplify the programs we have omitted the pictorial and historical elements. The call to dialog binds the variable B to whichever of the four buttons the user presses. It produces a dialogue box such as that in Figure 5.18: the details of this are not important, but it should be remembered that it is still a 'modal' event.

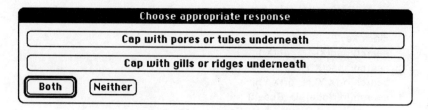

Figure 5.18   Dialogue box for mushroom identification.

Let us consider what happens when the user cannot make a decision between two alternatives. It may happen that when they try to follow two branches, one of the branches is subsequently 'blocked off' because neither possibility applies to the specimen in question. In this case, we might represent the search of the tree of possibilities as shown by Figure 5.19.

Here the thick lines represent choices which were accepted, and the thin lines, terminated by X, those choices which were rejected. At point A, the user was unable to make a decision and therefore took both branches. On the left branch, they subsequently rejected both branches, whereas the right branch led to a leaf (marked O).

This is not the only possible outcome. It may happen that several leaves are reached, so that there are several possible candidates. In this case, it is necessary to resort to descriptions and pictures which contain information not in the identification key.

The second parameter D of search2 is used to print out the depth of search, which is useful in following a trace of the search process. Here is a simple example with the depth shown at the beginning of each line:

```
:- key2 <— search(1, 1, R)

1 Cap with pores or tubes underneath
2 Spore print dark brown to blackish, cap with thick dark
    scales
No1        R = species('Strobilomyces', floccopus)

2 Spore print yellowish brown or pinkish
3 Stem very swollen, up to 5–15cm diam, with network pattern
    on upper surface
No2        R = gen('Boletus')

No more solutions
```

In this case the user answered *both* to the second question, so that there were two possible answers: either *Strobilomyces floccopus* or the genus *Boletus*.

The heart of the change is in the procedure decide, which selects one or the other pair of condition and action. The dialog procedure returns the

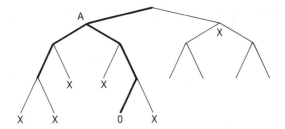

Figure 5.19   Search tree for mushroom identification.

number of the button and this is used to select the appropriate action, as follows:

1   Both

2   Neither

3   Condition 1

4   Condition 2

Since there are two clauses for 1, backtracking will ensure both of these are found eventually. There are none for 2, so it fails (in fact, the second button is conventionally a cancel action, and the call to dialog fails, which amounts to the same thing). Action 3 selects the first condition/action pair and Action 4 the second. So it is very easy to express and Prolog takes care of all the housekeeping.

It is not so easy to implement the undo action using the Prolog backtracking method. For although backtracking undoes previous decisions, it is always moving inexorably on through the 'search tree' of possible solutions. But an undo action needs to go back, whether the last action was a success or failure – if it was a failure it will need to rebuild what has just been destroyed. Hence, ironically, many systems implemented in Prolog don't support any type of undo facility.

Yet the ability to undo an action is rightly seen as a critical element of a 'user-friendly' interface. Everyone makes mistakes at some point, and the ability to take back an action encourages the user to experiment and use a program boldly. How many steps can be undone varies between systems: the Macintosh guidelines only call for one significant action to be undoable, and this is often perfectly adequate and is easier for the implementer.

In order to handle this it is necessary for the program to remember its actions and the obvious data structure for this problem is a stack. To undo an action we simply pop the most recent action from the stack and redo the previous one (assuming there are no other side-effects). Having done this, we can't rely on the backtracking points introduced by the both action being simply implemented by Prolog: it is necessary for the program to handle the backtracking information explicitly. It is perfectly possible to use the same stack to store this information.

The result of this is shown below in Program 5.3.

There are two types of items stored on the stack: the first is a pair: D-Act, consisting of the depth D and action Act, which is one of the four function symbols found in the head of search. One item exists for each action performed. The second has a functor back/2 and a similar pair of arguments and records the other branch of choice for which the *both* option was taken and which has not yet been explored.

There are two occasions when the backtracking objects are sought: one is when the *neither* option is selected by the user (this corresponds to a failure of dialog in the procedure above); the other is when a solution has been found and it is necessary to check whether any other solutions have to be found. The searchback procedure finds the stored action, if one exists. Note that in this implementation one cannot undo these backtracking actions.

But this approach still assumes the use of a modal i/o procedure: that is, the Prolog++ program is reckoned to be suspended at the point of invocation of the dialogue and it can't do anything else until the dialogue is complete. It can't be used to drive an 'event-driven' i/o system. However, the key3 program is still useful because it shows us clearly what information needs to be maintained and how it is manipulated. It thus serves as a useful prototype for the version of this program which we will now explore.

In order to implement an event-driven approach, the program has to be split up into sections which do not include interactive events. Each section is thus effectively a state transition: it takes the program from one state to another. In Prolog++ the state is stored in the attributes of the objects making up the program. This follows the approach of dynamic logic advocated by Harel (1987).

Once represented in this way, the program can be effectively isolated from the underlying i/o system. We will illustrate this by showing two different implementations in terms of the i/o primitives of MacProlog. One uses exactly the same dialog primitive as was used in the previous program. The other uses an event-driven interface called 'control windows' which is available in the newer versions of MacProlog. The 'user' part of the program is identical in both approaches: the differences are confined exclusively to the inherited classes which implement the interface.

In object terms, the program is structured around an object called keyDialog which is a composite object having a number of buttons as subparts. It inherits from two other classes: the search object contains application-specific code, whereas window provides the implementation of the windowing actions. Each of the button classes also inherits from a class button, but they do not inherit from search as they pass their message up to the composite object keyDialog (Figure 5.20).

In keeping with the aim of separating the application content from the interface, let us examine first the class search, which is shown in Program 5.4. It defines four parameterless procedures – start, nextstep, backtrack and

Program 5.3   Key follower with backtracking.

```
class key3.

search(gen(X), _, Stack) :-
    result(genus(X), Stack).
search(spec(X,Y), _, Stack) :-
    result(species(X,Y), Stack).
search(or(X,Y), _,Stack) :-
    result(or(X,Y), Stack).
search(to(Node), D, Stack) :-
    mk(Node, Cond1, Act1, Cond2, Act2),
    D1 is D + 1,
    choose(Cond1, Act1, Cond2, Act2, D1, Stack, New),
    New = [E-Act|_],
    search(Act, E, New).

result(Type, Stack) :-
    writeseqnl(['Result is',Type]),
    backtrack(Stack).

choose(Cond1, Act1, Cond2, Act2, D, Stack, New) :-
    dialog('Choose appropriate response', 50,50,100,500,
        [button(70,10,20,60,'Both'),
         button(70,90,20,60,'Neither'),
         button(10,10,20,480,Cond1),
         button(40,10,20,480,Cond2),
         button(70,160,20,60,'Undo')],
        B), !,
    decide(B, Cond1, Act1, Cond2, Act2, D, Stack, Cond, New),
    writeseqnl([D,Cond]).
choose(_,_,_,_,_, Stack, [D-Act|Rest]) :-
    searchback(Stack, D, Act, Rest).

decide(1, Cond1, Act1, Cond2, Act2, D, Stack, Cond2, [D-
    Act1,back(D,Act2)|Stack]).
decide(3, Cond1, Act1, _, _, D, Stack, Cond1, [D-Act1|Stack]).
decide(4, _, _, Cond2, Act2, D, Stack, Cond2, [D-
    Act2|Stack]).
decide(5,_,_,_,_,D,[_|Stack], 'undo last choice', Stack).

backtrack(Stack) :-
    searchback(Stack, D, Act, Rest),
    search(Act, D, Rest).

searchback([back(D,Act)|Rest], D, Act, Rest) :-
    nl, writenl('continuing another branch').
searchback([_|Rest],A,B,C) :-
    searchback(Rest,A,B,C).
end key3.
```

Program 5.4 Key follower with object interface.

```
class search.
inherits stack.

start :-
    initStack(0-to(1)),
    nextstep.

nextstep :-
    topOfStack(D-Act),
    step(Act, D).

step(gen(X), _) :-
result(genus(X)).
step(spec(X,Y), _) :-
    result(species(X,Y)).
step(or(X,Y), _) :-
    result(or(X,Y)).
step(to(Node), D) :-
    mk(Node, Cond1, Act1, Cond2, Act2),
    D1 is D+1,
    condButton#1 <- set(Cond1,D1-Act1),
    condButton#2 <- set(Cond2, D1-Act2),
    redraw.

result(Type) :-
    writeseqnl(['Result is',Type]),
    backtrack.

backtrack :-
    pop(Item),
    (checkback(Item) ->
    nextstep
    ; writenl('no more solutions')).

checkback(back(Act)) :- !,
    nl, writenl('continuing another branch'),
    push(Act).
checkback(_) :-
    pop(Item),
    checkback(Item).

undo :-
    pop(_),
    topOfStack(Item),
    (Item=back(_) -> pop(_) ; true),
    nextstep.

end search.
```

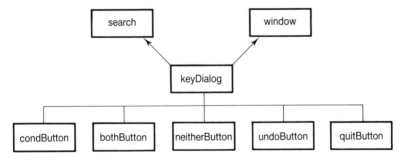

Figure 5.20   An inheritance tree for keyDialog.

undo – which break down the previous algorithms into their component steps. The stack-handling procedures are conveniently separated into a separate class.

It is worth comparing the procedures here with the implementation in key3 (Program 5.3). The similarities will be obvious, but the differences are worth noting: although the number of lines isn't very different, the number of tokens per line is generally far less, because data is generally only referred to when it is actually used. The extra parameters carried around in recursive procedures, so characteristic of Prolog, have largely disappeared.

In addition, the separation between application and interface has been largely achieved. There is one notable exception (apart from the trace calls): in the last clause of step it is necessary to set up the new conditions and actions for the display, and redraw the display. It would be possible to remove this dependency by storing the information locally and subsequently fetching it, but this seems pedantic. This type of dependency is relatively harmless and, with care, can be defined in an implementation independent manner.

The contents of the stack are stored in the class stack:

```
class stack.
attribute val = [].

initStack(Val) :-
        val := Val.

push(Item) :-
        val:= [Item|@val].

pop(Item) :-
        @val = [Item|Rest],
          val := Rest.

topOfStack(Item) :-
        @val = [Item|_].

end stack.
```

Now let us look at the classes which define the 'view' (Program 5.5). Don't be put off by the apparent length of these definitions: in practice most

Program 5.5   Interface for key follower.

```
class keyDialog.
inherit windowC, search.
parts bothButton, neitherButton, condButton*2, undoButton,
    quitButton.
attributes position = (50,50), size = (500,100),
    title = 'Choose appropriate response'.

init :-
    delete_all,
    create(W),
    W <- (initialize, start).

initialize :-
    condButton#1 <- initialize(1),
    condButton#2 <- initialize(2).

end keyDialog.

class condButton.
inherits buttonC.
attribute position,     size = (480,20), text = '', act.

initialize(N) :-
    setPosition(N).

setPosition(1) :- position & = (10,10).
setPosition(2) :- position & = (10,40).

set(Cond, Act) :-
    text := Cond,
    act := Act.

activate :-
    writeseqnl([@act,@text]),
    super_part <- (push(@act), nextstep).
remember :-
    super_part <- push(back(@act)).

end condButton.

class bothButton.
inherits buttonC.
attribute position = (10,70), size = (60,20), text = 'Both'.
activate :-
    super_part <- ( part(condButton,2,remember),
                    part(condButton,1,activate)).
end bothButton.
```

```
class neitherButton.
inherits buttonC.
attribute position = (90,70), size = (60,20), text = 'Neither'.
activate :-
     super_part <- backtrack.
end neitherButton.

class undoButton.
inherits buttonC.
attribute position = (170,70), size = (60,20), text = 'Undo'.
activate :-
     super_part <- undo.
end undoButton.

class quitButton.
inherits buttonC.
attribute position = (250,70), size = (60,20), text = 'Quit'.
activate :-
     super_part <- quit.
end quitButton.
```

of this can be automated and it is rarely necessary to look at anything but
the methods within each class. Each class corresponds to a visual object
(widget) and the attributes are mainly concerned with the physical dimensions
and the labels on the buttons. The only exception is the action associated
with the condition buttons, which uses an attribute act.

The method init in keyDialog is the class method which sets up the
entire dialogue. It has to perform one small piece of setup: there are two
instances of condButton, corresponding to the two choices available, and there
could be many more. Though they are in other ways identical, they must
necessarily occupy different points on the screen, so this change must be
made dynamically and the easiest way to do this in the current version of
Prolog++ is as shown.

The main actions of each button are invoked by the message activate
sent to the instance of the button. To achieve their purpose, they generally
send messages to their super_part, the class which owns the dialogue,
keyDialog. Thus to choose one of the stated conditions, two messages are
sent up: a push message, pushing the appropriate action on the stack, and
a nextstep, advancing the computation.

If the user wants to follow both paths, the effect is rather like pressing
both condition buttons, and this is exactly how it is implemented here. The
necessary data is held locally in the objects which define those buttons, and
it is undesirable to replicate it. The messages sent to each button are slightly
different: to set up the backtracking point a back item must be created on
the stack, so a remember message is sent to carry this out, whereas the other
action is simply activate. To send a message to another part of the same

object, a method part has been defined. This takes three parameters, the class and number of the item, and the message to be sent to it. It is defined (in an ancestor of keyDialog) by the clause:

```
part(P,N,Message) :-
    P#N <- Message.
```

What remains to be shown are the two alternative implementations of the underlying window management system. First we will look at the dialog implementation in Program 5.6.

The main procedure is to redraw the dialogue, which in this case is a call to the dialog built-in predicate. The dimensions of the window are defined as attributes of a subclass of the window class. It is therefore mandatory in this case to use the self variable explicitly – for example, self@position – as happens when invoking the dynamic binding of a method.

The sixth parameter of dialog describes all the buttons and other components of the dialogue and is typically a long list (see earlier programs). Here the responsibility is devolved to a function, defined within button, which generates an appropriate description from the attributes of the corresponding class. The Prolog++ expression all sub_part @ description sends the message description to each of the subparts of the current object in turn and forms the result into a list.

There is one oddity of the dialog primitive that should be noted: the order of the buttons is significant. When the call returns, the final parameter (B in this case) is bound to a number which signifies the position of button in the list which terminated the dialogue. In addition, items 1 and 2 have special significance: item 1 is assumed to be the default (and is drawn with an extra line around it) and item 2 is assumed to be a 'Cancel' action. If the 'Cancel' button is invoked, the call to dialog fails, rather than binding B to 2. This is the reason for the second clause of redraw which generates a call to dispatch(2), and thus avoids the asymmetry in the implementation. The call to dispatch then chooses the *n*th of the list of instance names of the subparts of the dialogue and sends an activate message to it.

Finally, there is one program action which is implemented within the window object rather than within the search object. The quit action normally involves more cleaning up of the environment (for example, deleting windows) than of the application. In this case, it is only the program itself which needs to be stopped, since the dialogue is displayed repeatedly each time round the loop, and this is done by using the built-in abort predicate.

This is a particularly simple example of the use of dialog. If the dialogue contained edit fields, then any changes are returned via variable bindings in the list of descriptions, so these would need to be inspected. It's also impossible for the program to make any changes while the dialogue is in process, using the simple scheme here. MacProlog supports an extended form of dialogue which attempts to overcome these limitations, but it is not as flexible as the

Program 5.6 Implementation of windows using dialog primitive.

```
class window.

redraw :-
    (X,Y) = self@position,
    (W,H) = self@size,
    T = self@title,
    dialog(T,Y,X,H,W, all sub_part @ description, B),
    !,
    dispatch(B).
redraw :-
    dispatch(2). %a peculiarity of dialog

%sends message to nth component of the window
dispatch(N) :-
    nth(N, all sub_part, Instance),
    Instance <- activate.

nth(1, [A|As], A) :- !.
nth(N, [_|As], B) :-
    N>1, nth(+N-1, As, B).

quit :- abort.

%send a message to another part of this object
part(P,N,Mess) :-
    P#N <- Mess.

end window.

class button.
attribute position, size, text.
method description//0.

description = button(Y,X,H,W,T) :-
    self@position=(X,Y),
    self@size=(W,H),
    self@text=T.

end button.
```

proper event-driven approach represented by the newer control windows system. An implementation using these is shown in Program 5.7.

The first difference one needs to notice is that the procedures are discrete entities. Unlike the earlier implementation, there is no thread running between and linking the different methods. Whereas, for example, the redraw method in Program 5.6 ended with a call to dispatch, and this generated a message to activate the appropriate button, the redraw method here terminates, leaving only the created window on the screen, and the underlying

Program 5.7 Implementation of windows using control windows primitive.

```
class window.

redraw :-
    clause(win(T,self),true), !,          %window already drawn
    forall (I= sub_part, class I=condButton)
        do cw_add_item(T,I@name, I@description).
redraw :-                                  %here to draw window first time
    (X,Y) = self@position,
    (W,H) = self@size,
    T = self@title,
    wkill(T),                              %in case there's one already
    cw_create(T,Y,X,H,W, [dialog]),        %creates window
    asserta(win(T,self)),                  %remember this for cwc
    forall I= sub_part
    do cw_add_item(T,I@name, I@description),
    cw_click(T,cwc),                       %declares name of handler
                                           %program
    wfront(T).                             %make it visible

activate(Component) :-
    part_name(Component,Class,Num),
    Class#Num <- activate.                 %send message to subpart

quit :-
    clause(win(T,self),true),
    wkill(T).                              %must delete the window

%send a message to another part of this object
part(P,N,Message) :-
    P#N <- Message.

is_part_num(Self,Num) :-
    Self= $(Class,_),
    nth(Num,1,9),
    Class#Num = Self.

nth(A,A,B).
nth(A,B,C) :-
    B<C, nth(A, +B+1,C).

part_name(Name, Class, Num) :-             %convert name of item to term
    name(Name, List),
    append(L, [N], List),
    name(Class, L),
    name(Num, [N]).

end window.
```

event handler, which is not represented directly in Prolog. The window is not dependent on the executing program, which is why it is necessary to delete an existing window (using wkill) left by any previous execution of the program.

The first clause of redraw is all that is necessary in most cases to change the display: it calls cw_add_item to add (in fact to change) the two conditional buttons only. The second clause is invoked only the first time round, and it uses an entry in the Prolog database (using the clause win) to detect whether the window has been created. The reason for this, rather than using a Prolog++ attribute, arises from the way in which control is passed back to the Prolog++ program after the first program is terminated. This is done by the predicate named as the second argument to the call to the built-in predicate cw_click, namely cwc. This is defined below and is conventionally called with two parameters: the name of the window (W) and the name of the button or other item in the window that has been pressed (Item).

```
cwc(W, Item) :-
    clause(win(W,Instance),true), !,
    Instance <− activate(Item).
```

Cwc picks up the name of the instance of keyDialog currently in use and sends a message activate/1 to it. The name of the item in the window is required to be atomic. This is derived from the class name and item number by the method name in class button (Program 5.8) and restored to its original

Program 5.8   Implementation of button class with control windows.

```
cw_add_button('Choose appropriate response', condButton2,
    button(40,10,20,480,'Spore print yellowish brown or
    pinkish'))

class button.
attribute position, size, text.
method description//0.

%generate atomic name for button
name(Name) :-
    super_part <− is_part_num(self,Num),
    concat(class,Num,Name).

description = button(Y,X,H,W,T) :-
    self@position = (X,Y),
    self@size = (W,H),
    self@text = T.

end button.
```

form by the method part_name in window. For example, condButton, 2 is converted to condButton2. The details of this process are not important, and involve several common Prolog predicates. A typical call to cw_add_button is shown in Program 5.8.

This example has only illustrated a few of the basic features of the event-driven approach. It doesn't deal with edit fields, or signals other than 'button-up' activation messages. But it does illustrate two important points: first, that a continuous user program has to broken up into its component parts, each of which is available separately to the user, in order to be usable under a graphical user interface. Second, that this process makes the resulting program much less sensitive to the style of programming system used to supply the user interface. The extra abstractions introduced allow an interface to be supplied which can be much more flexible.

EXERCISES

1   If you have a version of Prolog++ using another version of Prolog other than MacProlog, adapt the implementation of window and button to use the primitive calls available on that system.

2   A third approach to dialogues available in MacProlog uses the so-called 'extended dialogues'. This avoids redrawing anything except the new condition buttons in the dialogue, though it is not as general as the control windows approach. Rewrite the window and button classes to use this approach.

3   The 'undo' feature is incomplete in that it does not undo actions which involve backtracking. What additions need to be made to handle these?

SUMMARY

- The chapter defines a set of classes which implement an interface toolkit to simplify the writing of graphical user interfaces. The basic mechanisms of constructing a graphical interface are described, including the handling of events, the graphical layout and the components of a dialogue including buttons, fields and menus.

- The user interface involves the definition of a geometric description, handling the events generated by the user, and the means of displaying the window and handling input. Prolog++ is provided with a graphical toolkit, called MacObject, which allows one to construct these components in an interactive fashion.

- A worked example is given of a mushroom identification interface, involving all of these elements, to illustrate the way in which a program can be constructed.

6

Program design

6.1 Introduction

Program design operates at a different level to that of programming. The aim of program design is to produce an overall structure which is prior to, and more stable than, the concrete details of an implementation. To achieve this, abstraction is an important tool. But abstraction has the danger of bringing vagueness with it, and vagueness is the enemy of the precision needed at the lower levels of design and implementation.

Program design is traditionally the second step in the software engineering process, coming after systems analysis. Analysis is a much broader field, encompassing organizational issues wider than design and applicable to approaches other than computers. The distinction between the two phases was reinforced in the past by the different techniques, methodologies and formalisms used.

Program design has conventionally started from function. Requirements definition has developed as a number of techniques for clarifying the details of functional organization, including dataflow analysis, functional analysis and structure charts. In this approach, commonly known as Structured Analysis and Design (SA/SD), data is seen in rather passive terms, consisting primarily of schematic file layouts.

At the same time, a different tradition has arisen within the database community, variously known as information modelling and Entity-Relationship analysis. Instead of concentrating on function, information modelling started from an analysis of the structure of a concrete situation. In Chen's (1976) classic analysis, this involves identifying the *entities* involved in a situation and the important *relationships* between them.

To express these, Chen developed a simple graphical technique which has been widely imitated and extended in various directions. The entities that are described can include people, who initiate various actions, physical objects, such as products, components and places, and events. Relationships mainly deal with organization – management structures, space and time distribution, attributes of objects.

Because any set of processes can be defined in terms of the events which characterize them, there is an overlap between the concerns of the information modellers and those of the structured analysts. A priori, one might expect this to be a fruitful area of collaboration. In practice this has not always been the case. An example is given by Coad and Yourdon concerning a major air traffic control project:

> 'One team of analysts (the "DFD Team") started their project using data flow diagrams to develop an overall functional decomposition... Meanwhile a second team of analysts ("Data Base Team") started by focusing on the information the system needed to do its job and then building an information model... Over time, the DFD team continued to struggle with basic problems of domain understanding (e.g. the details of what happens when one controller hands off responsibility for an aircraft to another controller). In contrast the Data Base Team gained a strong in-depth understanding of air traffic control. Yet the results of the two teams did not mesh together; worse they contradicted each other. ... under pressure of schedule and budget, the results were pushed into preliminary design, with the hope of resolving the discrepancies at that time. Sadly the Data Base Team was perceived as irksome, even somewhat as troublemakers; people (and their careers) paid the price for this major rift and its untidy resolution.' (Coad and Yourdon, 1991a)

Why are there such conflicts? At least two reasons can be cited. The first concerns the differing time scales on which these two processes operate. The database viewpoint is essentially static and within that constraint it is able to develop much richer structures with which to deal. These are available in the query languages, such as SQL, which are essentially declarative in nature.

By contrast, the process modellers (the DFD team) are more usually concerned with deadlines and performance targets, which are the 'hard' limits within which a development schedule operates. The richer structure provided by the information specialists may be seen within this context as a source of overheads with insufficient pay back.

The second reason is because relations are the major organizing dimension in the relational view. This doesn't blend too well with the process view. Take for example the design of a transaction system for a bank. Given a transaction for a single customer, the system may need to access the balance, withdrawals over a particular time period, credit limit, maximum withdrawal amount, expected pay-in levels, and so on. This information will probably be scattered over a number of different relations, when the process view would dictate that they are grouped together as this is the most common use of the data.

Objects, with a combination of data and procedures, are an obvious escape route from this dichotomy. For the first time, procedures can begin to exploit the richer structures that are not immediately dictated by processing requirements. Conversely, the data structures benefit from the procedures which can be tailored to specific needs rather than depending on general purpose query systems with their inevitable inefficiencies.

These may be the immediate reasons why object-oriented analysis and design are popular. But it is important to ask whether there are deeper reasons. When one looks for these, they are not hard to find.

One of the design methods popular, particularly in Europe, is Jackson System Development (Jackson, 1983). A distinctive feature of this method is its treatment of multiple transactions. For example, Jackson analyses a set of bank accounts as a set of long-lasting processes. For each account that is open a process is initiated which conceptually continues to run until the account is closed. Given this perspective, the operations on the account – deposits, withdrawals, addition of interest and subtraction of charges, and so on – become very simple to specify and to check for accuracy. In many batch-oriented transactions, these operations are frequently scattered over many different programs and may depend on these programs being executed in a correct sequence.

In the Jackson method, the simple program can then be restructured semi-automatically into more complex operations, required to service a large number of accounts and transactions, by semiformal methods, which help to preserve the truths of the original conception.

In a traditional data processing program one has the loop:

```
for all updates
    apply update to the corresponding record
```

in which the control is kept in a general purpose procedure which has to know about every type of record, whereas in the object-oriented approach one has the loop:

```
for all updates
    send update message to the instance of the object
```

where the real work is deputed to the particular object being considered.

The net effect of this is that in the object-oriented approach, all the operations on an entity are grouped together textually and logically. One can indeed consider the set of operations applied over time to a specific instance to be a single process, even though they are separated into many separate runs of different programs. Indeed, in a properly constructed object-oriented operating system, there would only need to be one set of procedures for operating on the accounts, which could be referenced by processes implementing many different day-to-day operations.

Today, most such systems are 'on-line' rather than 'batch'. This encourages the move towards the object-oriented approach, as the programs are increasingly operating in a truly concurrent manner in which the exact order of operations cannot be predicted in advance.

At the same time, the importance of system evolution is increasingly recognized. It isn't possible in practice to specify in advance all the requirements that a system must meet. Changes in technology, expectation and the organization that runs a system serve to defeat the most perspicuous analyst. Consequently what is required is not merely an effective solution to currently perceived problems, but a structure which will adapt easily to the unexpected.

The critical issue in this case becomes one of program structure. It is important to be able to structure the problem and its solution so that the interface between code written in different languages is clear and independent of the data representation used, which will probably change with the precise algorithms and language used. This is what has given rise to concepts of data abstraction in software engineering and is a prime motivation behind object-oriented programming.

In addition, there is a key requirement for *reusability* of code. Earlier attempts at providing this purely using function were less successful: the combination of data and function in data abstraction proved to be the key to providing this quality.

The formalist approach to program design was largely seen in terms of a *specification* expressed in rigorous language. While this can be successful in uncovering inconsistencies in the requirements and proposed solutions it is usually difficult to complete a specification ahead of the actual implementation. Consequently the use of formal specifications has been limited to demonstrators and safety critical situations where the extra costs are justified.

Attention has shifted to modelling, with obvious analogies to the types of models used by architects and engineers to show to customers, test out critical design decisions and clarify details in the context of the overall design.

> 'A good model captures the crucial aspects of a problem and omits the others. Most computer languages, for example, are poor vehicles for modelling algorithms because they force the specification of implementation details irrelevant to the algorithm. A model that contains extraneous detail unnecessarily limits your choice of design decisions and diverts attention from the real issues.' (Rumbaugh *et al.*, 1991)

Yet models also gravitate to one of two poles: the static or the dynamic. Logic demonstrates one pole: the static description is accepted as an exhaustive description. The other pole may be illustrated by simulation, the field in which Simula arose, which looks at the dynamic interaction between relatively simple objects. This provides entirely different insights.

The designer, who needs to produce tangible results in a finite time, must use both insights. Modelling provides the necessary approach. When dealing with software, modelling can provide more than a prototype. A prototype is a model which is thrown away. If one is building a bridge, then this is quite reasonable. Even if a model costs a million dollars, it still has to be superseded by the real thing.

Software is different. A model might be a toy: something which cannot be scaled to a complex and embracing structure. Or it might be the right framework for the full-scale solution. If the latter is the case, then the later stages of design and implementation consist of an elaboration and filling out of this structure. The main outlines carry through to the final project and the model becomes the outline of the eventual system.

This leads naturally to the re-evaluation of the role of *prototypes*, particularly those that can be developed in a high-level languages such as Prolog or Prolog++. Providing the kernel of a system as a prototype, or *exploratory program*, serves as a communication device between designer and client helping to clear up misunderstandings and showing what is and is not possible. Of course, using a higher-level language such as Prolog++ does not by itself prevent the designer becoming bogged down in extraneous decisions. It has to be used judiciously.

But while many people consider Prolog excellent as a prototyping language, they fear that they must throw away all the results of their development when it comes to producing the final product. This has not been the experience of many users. For example, Scandinavian and Swiss Airlines run a reservation system for flight arrival and departure slots that will accept in real time bookings via telex. This is almost entirely written in PDC Prolog and runs on a PC workstation with minimal additions in a low-level language.

However it is clearly the case that Prolog is not as efficient as many lower-level languages when it comes to dealing with large quantities of information. This does not mean that it is necessary to recode the whole program, but only those parts which are critical to efficiency, in terms of either time or space. Because of this, most commercial Prolog systems allow mixed language working using commonly available languages such as C, Pascal or COBOL.

But it is the structure of the overall solution that is critical. If that is right, then issues of optimization are obvious. In software, a model is not something that is built to scale but rather something that will scale.

There have been several approaches to an object-oriented design methodology, among which should be mentioned those of Booch (1991) and Coad and Yourdon (1991b). These do not emphasize the role of modelling. In this chapter we will primarily follow the Object Modelling Technique

(OMT), a methodology described in Rumbaugh *et al.* (1991). It is currently the most comprehensive technique, and deals well with relational aspects of program design, an issue rather neglected by other approaches.

6.1.1   Program modelling: an example

To demonstrate the issues of program modelling, we will throughout this chapter use an example which combines issues of databases, transaction processing and information retrieval. This concerns the handling of a library catalogue. The initial task, which often justifies the installation of a computer system in this context, is the administration of borrowing books from the library. Many systems have been built simply to handle this one function. But to do this properly (including, for instance, the issue of meaningful renewal notices) requires entering full author and title details of all the books in the library.

Once that large task has been done there is an inevitable pressure to make these details available to all the users of the library in place of the existing catalogue of books. Efficient means of searching such a database mean a total reorganization and inverting of the files describing the bibliographic details. To find a book can itself be a multistage process involving Boolean queries and being able to narrow and broaden the search. From there the next step is to use Artificial Intelligence techniques to provide conceptual searches.

The number of tasks associated with even such a relatively simple set of tasks can be very large: new records for books and borrowers have to be created, details have to be changed and records deleted. Summaries have to be printed in many different forms and graphical interfaces provided for every step that are simple enough for the total outsider and efficient enough for the professional. In addition, if the system is to be useful in libraries which have different cataloguing systems and borrowing regulations, it needs to be able to be configured in nontrivial ways. Some of these can be predicted in advance, but others may need to be added afterwards.

In order to get some idea of the requirements of the system, let us first of all sketch out some main functions that the system may need to support. These lists are in no way exhaustive, but give some idea of the complexity of an average package for this purpose.

Activities relating to library loans:

- Withdraw a book, or other item, allowing for borrower-specific limits
- Register a new borrower and update details for existing borrowers
- Inspect a borrower's current lending record and update it
- Generate overdue and other periodic notices
- Handle book reservations and renewals

- Allow for recording and video collections
- Keep track of fines and payments
- Report on current borrowing levels according to various criteria and historical borrowing levels over a period

Activities related to catalogue enquiries:

- Look up a book according to author, title, subject
- Provide a full Boolean search capability on fields
- Allow for multiple steps in broadening and narrowing the search
- Print list of books found in a search
- Generate a new index for the catalogue, ignoring 'noise' words

Activities generated by the existence of both functions in one system:

- Looking up a book in order to issue or renew it
- Controlling access to different facilities according to type of user

Configuration and maintenance tasks:

- Define borrowing limits for different classes of users
- Define any penalties that must be imposed
- Register a new book in the catalogue
- Define the format of bibliographic entries and the indexing system, including special collections
- Backing up of all files

This list is not of course a specification. It is not a design for a system. It is merely a rough sketch of some of the functions that the system is expected to perform. In the course of development some might be omitted, and many more will be found to be necessary. But it corresponds to the requirements document, or problem statement, that is the first stage of conventional analysis and design methods.

The conventional approach has been essentially task-based. Each task within the system generates dataflows and the flows of data are then represented by diagrams, which form the basis of the design.

The dataflow approach is several levels more abstract than a program, or the early flowchart method. It is not necessary to represent the precise conditions under which one branch or the other is taken – a dataflow diagram simply records what information is used by different parts of the system, and correspondingly what is independent of each other.

The problem with all of these methods is that over the lifetime of a product, or even the design period, the tasks often change. What one ideally wants of a design is that it is more stable; that as the requirements, hardware and software environment develops, changes can be made within the context of an overall design.

Experience has shown that it is the data which should form the centrepiece of the design. The data is in most cases the largest and most expensive component of an information system. In the case of a library, which might have 50 000 books and 20 000 subscribers, the acquisition and maintenance of these two databases is a substantial investment. Most of the functionality of the system will in turn depend on the attributes or fields of this data and it is very difficult to substantially change these once the system has been in operation for any length of time. We are not referring here to the physical form of the data: this might well change. But the logical dependencies may be deeply built in to the software.

But we are not simply talking about a database. The essence of most of the functionality of the library system is the changes that are being made. These changes need to be analysed and performed in an efficient manner and the generalized approach of a database management system has not proved adequate in most cases. This is where the object-oriented approach scores heavily. For the first time it is possible to combine a rich data description technique with the functionality which characterizes highly reactive systems.

6.2   Object Modelling Technique

The Object Modelling Technique (OMT) advocated by Rumbaugh *et al.* (1991) divides the design process into three stages: object modelling, dynamic modelling and functional modelling. Let us consider each of these in turn.

Object modelling

Object modelling identifies the identity of the basic objects involved in the process, together with their attributes and associations. It corresponds rather closely to Chen's Entity-Relationship analysis and to conventional approaches to database definition. However, to these it adds notions of classes, generalization and aggregation, which come from object theory.

In OMT, there are two basic diagrams to represent objects: rounded boxes represent individual objects, rectangular boxes represent classes of objects. The boxes which represent classes are divided into up to three areas: name of class, names of attributes and names of operations that may be applied to objects of the class. For example, we might represent the widgets discussed in the previous chapter by Figure 6.1.

It isn't always necessary to include all three parts of the box. In the early stages of the design, only the name of the class may be used. As the design proceeds, attributes will be added, and finally the methods to which the objects can respond. So one- and two-part boxes are also used.

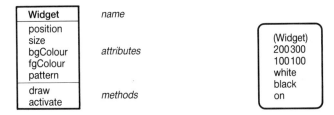

Figure 6.1 An object diagram.   **Figure 6.2** An instance diagram.

Note that we have *not* included in this definition an attribute, such as *id* which uniquely identifies the object. We may easily have several widgets with the same attributes, but it is not necessary to distinguish them. In an object model each object is unique. There is thus implicitly a unique identifier associated with each object, and which is most conveniently supplied by the system.

It is often useful to be able to represent specific objects, or instances of classes. These are represented in rounded boxes, with the name of the class in parentheses and the specific values of the attributes underneath. For example see Figure 6.2.

OMT allows one to represent links or *associations* between different objects. Links are connections between specific objects. Associations are sets of links which exist between classes of objects, or in other words, relations. Associations may be one-to-one, many-to-one or many-to-many and are represented by straight lines joining the objects, with bullets to represent multiplicity. For example, a one-to-one association between a country and the city which is its capital may be represented by Figure 6.3, whereas a many-to-one association may be represented by Figure 6.4.

Associations are not limited to the binary case. To represent an

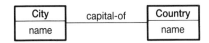

Figure 6.3 A one-to-one association.

Figure 6.4 A many-to-one association.

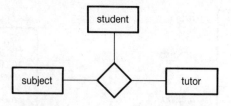

Figure 6.5   A ternary association.

association of more than two objects, a diamond is used to join the boxes (Figure 6.5).

   An association can itself be modelled by an object which can itself have attributes. These are known as *link attributes* and are drawn below the association (Figure 6.6).

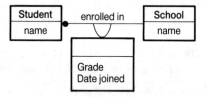

Figure 6.6   Use of link attributes.

   The association class is implicitly identified by both objects which identify the association. This provides a unique identification in the case of a one-to-many or many-to-many association, so that it is not necessary to repeat information within the link object.

   OMT supports two principle characteristics of object-oriented methodology as special cases of association: generalization and aggregates. They are represented by special links between two classes. Generalization is represented by a triangular link as shown by the example in Figure 6.7.

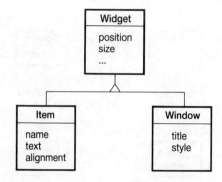

Figure 6.7   An example of generalization.

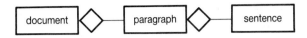

Figure 6.8 An example of aggregation.

Aggregation is also represented as a special form of association, indicated by a diamond at the composite end of the link. For example, in describing a document, we might wish to say that it is composed of paragraphs, which are in turn composed of sentences (Figure 6.8).

It will be appreciated that these characteristics of the object model mirror very directly the capabilities of Prolog++. Generalization corresponds directly to class inheritance; aggregation corresponds to the parts hierarchy. We will therefore not explain them further at this point.

Dynamic modelling

Dynamic modelling, the second technique in OMT, is used to represent the *events* in the system which change the *states* of the objects. The state of an object is represented by both its attribute values and the links by which it is connected to other objects by means of a *state diagram.*

Consider the situation in a graphical user interface when a mouse button is pressed within the area of a button. The immediate action is to 'arm' the button, typically by changing its colour. When the mouse button is released the 'callback' of the button is invoked. However the action can be cancelled by moving the pointer outside the area of the button and releasing the mouse button. There are thus four possible states for the button as shown in the state diagram, Figure 6.9.

Since this is a 'state' diagram, there are no extra boxes for the actions of the system. In the example in Figure 6.9 the actions are obvious. If we wish to record what the system does in response to the event it can be marked on the event arrow following the symbol '/'.

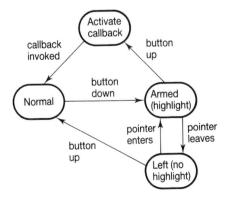

Figure 6.9 State diagram for a button.

In general there can be a state diagram for each individual class of objects in the system. These diagrams can be continuous, as above, or they can represent the whole life cycle of an object. Initial states are represented by solid circles and final states by bulls'-eyes. In addition, diagrams can be nested, avoiding the well-known limitations of finite state systems. Nesting is indicated by using the label 'do:' inside an activity, naming the diagram to which transfer is to be made.

Other features of the arcs on state diagrams include Boolean *conditions*, which are written within square brackets, and *attributes*, written within round brackets, which are data values conveyed by the event. The complete notation can be summarized as shown in Figure 6.10.

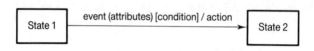

Figure 6.10   Features of arcs in a state diagram.

This type of state diagram abstracts very conveniently from the real life situation and recalls the entity state diagrams introduced by Jackson (1983). The steps do not correspond to any one particular program. There may be one to perform accessions, another for withdrawals, and so on. The diagram also does not represent the whole database corresponding to the library. It stands for an arbitrary item that is stored in the library. Different items will be in different states at different times.

Events are instantaneous. *States* correspond to the interval between two events received by an object. Usually changes can be considered to occur instantaneously in the events which are represented by the transition between states, but this is not always so. Some operations, called activities, may take time to complete. These must be represented by states.

The state diagrams we have shown correspond to simple finite state machines. It is perfectly possible to use nested diagrams which escape from this limitation. To do this, a state may name another state diagram.

Functional modelling

Functional modelling is the third and most detailed technique of OMT. It describes the computations within the system, using the technique of dataflow diagrams. These are still an abstraction of the program because they do not represent the control flow, but rather the functional dependencies of one part of the system upon another. They have gradually supplanted the earlier techniques of flowcharts and structure charts, which make far too many commitments about the actual logic of the program for effective use as design tools.

The functional aspect is primarily, though not exclusively, the declarative part of the computation. We have suggested in this book that the declarative representation of a program has many advantages in expressing the microfeatures of a program. It uses a mathematical notation, avoids dependence on state changes at the low level and facilitates debugging and proving a program correct. There is an easy mapping between dataflow diagrams and logic programs, which means that the transformation from dataflow diagrams to logic programs can be simplified.

As an example, a top-level representation of an automated teller machine (ATM) is shown in Figure 6.11. There are two actors in this process: the user and the bank account. The cash card is simply a data store, because it contains only passive information accessed by the system. By contrast the bank account is active. Not only does it supply the balance and limits but it also can pass special instructions to the teller machine, such as to retain the card. The main part of the program are the five processes shown in ellipses.

Ellipses in data flow diagrams represent *processes*; arcs represent the *dataflows*; boxes stand for *actors*; and parallel lines stand for *data stores* which are passive recipients and suppliers of data.

There is little in the way of *control flow* in this diagram. It is not the aim of the dataflow diagram to represent the level of decision at which control is important. A common mistake is try to represent all of the information that traditionally occurs in a flowchart. Where some parts of the chart are only activated conditionally dotted lines may be used to represent a Boolean 'token', which activates part of the graph.

Processes in the dataflow diagrams must be implemented eventually as operations on objects. There are various ways of expressing these operations that have been used in different design methodologies: decision

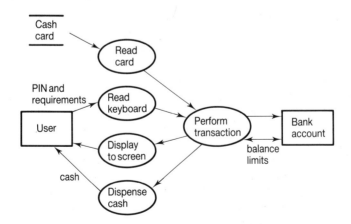

Figure 6.11 Dataflow diagram for an ATM machine.

tables, equations specifying output in terms of some input, axiomatic definitions (pre- and post-conditions), pseudocode or natural language. Given that logic programming has a strong history as a specification language, we will suggest that Prolog++ can be used for this, not simply using definite clauses, but also using negative information, or *constraints*.

There is an inevitable tension between rigour and clarity in producing the functional specification. It is not the intention of the design stage to produce a complete working model of the system, yet imprecision can lead to a situation where unanticipated difficulties are uncovered later, or what is implemented differs from what the designers had in mind.

There is no automatic solution to this problem. Much depends on the judgement of the designer. But where important details must be clarified early in the design process it is often very valuable to produce a prototype of part of the system which will enable these issues to be resolved with the client.

For example, one might be able to produce a single-user version of part of the system, knowing that the subsequent generalization to a multi-user environment is well understood and is relatively trouble free. This may be especially true in the object-oriented environment where individual components of the system are well modularized. However, if a critical problem is the performance of the overall system, then such a single-user prototype may be entirely irrelevant.

Most design environments therefore include a battery of techniques so that the designer can make an appropriate choice of tools for each particular situation.

6.3   The library example

Let us now consider the application of the Object Modelling Technique to the library example. What we wish to do is to show how the different techniques lead to a design for a suite of programs which is stable and flexible and to map out the basic code in such a way that a prototype of the system can be constructed and evaluated. Program design is an iterative process: when a design has been elucidated it is then possible to criticize and see what aspects of the original objectives can and can not be satisfied. It is common to find that customers change their mind in the light of the prototype – demanding either more or less than what was originally thought necessary. So it is desirable to reach this point as early as possible, because the later that changes are made in the specification the more expensive are the changes.

The OMT approach starts not with function, as we did when looking at the problem earlier in the chapter, but by clarifying the basic objects involved in the domain. One popular way to do this is to write down the nouns in the requirement description and then prune this list to eliminate spurious classes. Applying this to the problem statement earlier in the chapter generates the following words:

book	recording	index
item	video	access
limit	borrowing levels	borrowing limit
borrower	author	user
lending record	title	penalty
overdue notice	subject	catalogue
reservation	Boolean search	bibliographic entry
renewal	capability	indexing system
fine	fields	special collection
payment	multiple steps	

By no means all of these words name sensible classes. Some (author, title) are clearly *attributes* of other classes (book). Some (renewal) name *operations* rather than objects. Others (access, indexing system) are too vague to be useful, while others (partial query, catalogue) are irrelevant.

6.3.1 Object modelling

The most basic objects in the system are *books*, *borrowers*. We will initially model these objects as simply as possible: books have titles and authors; borrowers have a name and a limit in the books that they may borrow at any one time. These are represented as shown in Figure 6.12.

Though these start as simple objects, we mustn't forget that they represent a large part of the investment in the system: entering the original data, checking it for accuracy, backing it up, keeping it up to date. This is what much of the activity in a library system is about. In earlier design approaches these might be thought of as relatively static databases and thus would only be considered as data dictionary entries. Because they are fundamental, we model them as objects anyway, without waiting to see whether they are 'active' or 'passive'.

Other reasonable object classes that emerge from the list are: lending record, reservation, overdue notice, borrowing limit, fine. These are all related to transactions occurring within the library system. There is another group of items, index, search, step, relating to searching of the indexes. Although searches do not extend over a time period, their organization is one of the more complex parts of the system and will be considered in more detail later.

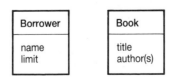

Figure 6.12   Basic objects in the libary system.

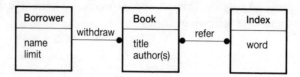

Figure 6.13 Associations in the library system.

A fundamental association between the two classes in the library system is a *withdraw* relation. A borrower can withdraw a number of books at one time, but each book may be withdrawn by only one borrower at a time. The relationship is thus many-to-one. The index is another basic association and has a many-to-many relationship with the book class: the book entry will normally contain many indexed words, and the word in the index will have many occurrences in book entries. The associations are represented in OMT as illustrated in Figure 6.13.

In programming terms it would of course be possible to represent the borrowing association as attributes of the individual objects, but this is not in general desirable. For one thing, only a fraction of the book stock is ever withdrawn at any one time. Thus to provide a status field for every book is wasteful. It is better simply to record the actual withdrawals. This is even more important for the borrower record which might need to reserve space for a large number of entries.

Most libraries make a clear distinction between relatively static lists and dynamic entries. Book and borrower names are regarded as static, withdrawal records are dynamic. Since the dynamic entries typically take only a fraction of the space of the static entries, this distinction also helps to make the system more robust: the dynamic items can be backed up more often, and the backup of relatively static items only performed at night or weekends.

The minimum attribute for the withdrawal might be the due date for the return of the book. This is represented by a link attribute attached to the association shown by Figure 6.14.

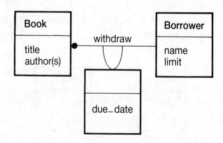

Figure 6.14 Link attributes of the book-borrower association.

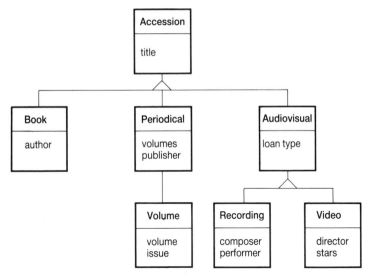

Figure 6.15   Refinement of the accession class.

The next step is to refine these categories. In the library example, both of the basic classes can easily be refined. It may be desirable to represent different classes of borrower, which have different privileges. Similarly, books are not the only type of object in the library: tapes and videos are mentioned in the problem statement and these often have very different borrowing rules from books: for example, the basic loan usually incurs a fee. Another example is periodicals, which are a special case of books, but have, in addition to a title, a volume and issue number, but they do not have an author. We may therefore make three classes – books, periodicals and audiovisuals – a refinement of a more general class, say *accession*, which only has a single attribute, *title* (though we will continue to use the central category of books in the description) (Figure 6.15).

Most libraries only make a single catalogue entry for periodicals and don't catalogue each individual issue – one of the reasons they are often reluctant to loan them. The use of an object-oriented methodology raises the possibility that these entries can be generated when necessary without permanent entries in the database.

Note that the functionality of the previous definition of a book, such as the *withdraw* link, can be automatically inherited by each of the two classes. It is not necessary to draw separate diagrams for each of these classes.

Another feature which can be refined in the original diagram is *withdrawal*. Reservations share many common features with withdrawal – they are both requests by borrowers to withdraw books, with only the result different. Renewals are also very similar. We therefore may make both of these a refinement of a more generic *request* (Figure 6.16).

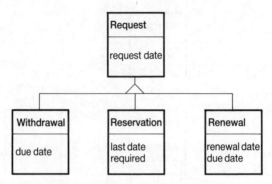

Figure 6.16   Refinement of the request class.

Another major component of the library system concerns the rules which apply to borrowers, including borrowing times, charges and fines. It is tempting to embed this information within other modules, but because these aspects tend to change from time to time this is a dangerous strategy. The rules need updating rules like every other object in the system and may change qualitatively by, for instance, the introduction of new categories of books or borrowers. However, for most purposes these can be considered as passive data stores which are accessed by the other components.

There is also a component centred around the production of reports, of which overdue notices are the most visible. The characteristic of reports is that they are periodic activities, which may be triggered by other events in the system (such as a book being overdue for a certain amount of time) or simply that they are required at regular intervals. The trigger may be from outside the system (when certain modules are run) or inside, by a clock, modelled as an object which initiates activities. At this point we simply note the possibilities, because how they are triggered needs to be decided at a later stage. The objects associated with the reports are primarily transitory, relating to the form and production of these reports.

Finally there is the component of the system devoted to searching. This is an important component which has many more common characteristics of Prolog programs: a central declarative core which can be specified very straightforwardly but which requires very different data structures for an efficient implementation, and a dynamic element which records the major steps of the program. This will be considered in more detail in a later section.

6.3.2   Dynamic modelling

Conventional techniques identify two primary objects that must be modelled dynamically: books (or accessions) and borrowers. Though their behaviour is obviously related, at the abstract level at which design occurs they are

Figure 6.17   State diagram for books.

usefully considered separately. Books can be withdrawn and returned; borrowers can reach their limits or be disallowed from borrowing for other reasons.

The basic state diagram for books is very simple (Figure 6.17). It consists of two states: *in library* and *on loan*, with two actions, *withdraw* and *return*. States are represented by rounded boxes, and actions by the box between them.

In fact, the entire life cycle of a book from accession to final discard may be represented by the state diagram shown in Figure 6.18.

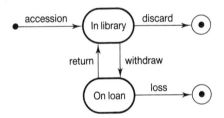

Figure 6.18   State diagram for the life of a book.

Similarly the progress of the user of the library can be traced from his or her initial registration, including this time three states: the normal state in which he or she can withdraw books, and two abnormal states in which only the return of books is allowed (Figure 6.19).

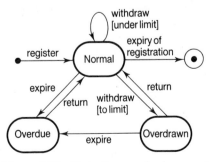

Figure 6.19   State diagram for borrower.

This captures the 'logic' of the borrower's situation, though the system may never represent the user's state explicitly. The state will probably be recomputed each time it is needed from the information stored in the borrower's record.

At a more detailed level of design it is possible to refine these models by considering, for instance, the sequence of actions that the librarian goes through when issuing or returning a book. We will examine this type of transaction later when considering the indexing system. But at this point we will turn to the third leg of the design methodology: functional modelling.

6.3.3   Functional modelling

As an example of the functional model we will look at the act of withdrawing a book. If we take a simple model in which any borrower is able to withdraw any book, the logic may be represented using a dataflow diagram as in Figure 6.20. We have taken the simple assumption here that the status and records of the borrower and books may be considered separately. This will be refined later.

There is a pleasing symmetry in this diagram, reflecting the two parts of the transaction: checking and updating the borrower and book records. The difference between this dataflow diagram and a flowchart is immediately apparent. The dataflow diagram only records the functional dependencies and ignores the many intricate control elements that will need to be considered at the programming level. For example, it doesn't care whether the book or borrower is validated first; it doesn't specify what happens when the borrower wishes to withdraw several books at once. In particular it doesn't specify in any detail what happens in the error conditions, which are indicated by the

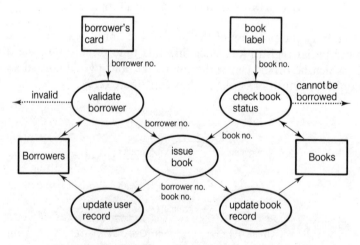

Figure 6.20   Dataflow diagram for book withdrawal.

dotted lines in Figure 6.20. At this level of analysis, it is usually desirable that error conditions are seen as exceptional.

The analysis demonstrates a classic possibility of conflict in the system: the system needs two resources to proceed: the borrower's permission and the availability of the book. In a distributed system with many checkout desks there is a possibility of error if the same borrower is active in more than one, or the same book is presented at two different checkouts. Normally neither of these possibilities can occur because each resource is unique. But in another context it may be necessary to take more careful precautions. This is one of the motivations for the concurrent treatment of objects that will be considered in Chapter 7. But for the moment we will assume that there is a single thread of control which prevents any errors.

There is an assumption in the dataflow diagram that we need to refine. We have assumed that books and borrowers are entirely separate and in effect the files recording details of books and borrowers contain all the details of the withdrawal of books from the library. In fact, this is unlikely to be the case.

For one thing, only a fraction of the book stock is ever withdrawn at any one time. To provide fields for every book recording its withdrawal status is wasteful. It is better simply to record the actual withdrawals. This is even more important for the borrower record which might need to reserve space for a large number of entries.

Most libraries make a clear distinction between relatively static lists and dynamic entries. Book and borrower names are regarded as static, withdrawal records are dynamic. Since the dynamic entries typically take only a fraction of the space of the static entries, this distinction also helps to make the system more robust: the dynamic items can be backed up more often, and the backup of static items only performed at night or weekends. In the dataflow diagrams there is a distinction between objects which are active – they can change as well as produce their own queries – and datastores which are passive.

Hence to check the book's status two steps are necessary: it is first necessary to check its status in the catalogue; then, assuming this is OK, one must ensure that it has not already been withdrawn. We have earlier modelled the association between borrowers and books as a many-to-one association. It is now necessary to consider how that is represented at a class level.

The simplest form is to consider just the instances of class withdraw as the dynamic entries (Figure 6.21). As an association entity, these have implicitly the identity of both book and borrower, as well as the attributes of the association such as the due date. However it then becomes a lengthy operation to decide whether a borrower is over the limit: first his or her entitlement must be computed, then all the books he or she currently has out must be checked and subtracted. It is worth having another instance called borrow which summarizes the current state of a borrower.

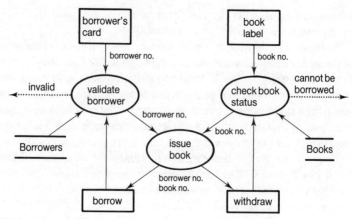

Figure 6.21   Refinement of the dataflow diagram for book withdrawal.

Both of these classes are *associations*, in OMT terminology, in that they carry the identifiers of both book and borrower.

We may similarly analyse the other main activities of the checkout system. The dataflow diagram for the return of a book (Figure 6.22) is slightly simpler than the withdrawal.

One of the differences between the OMT methodology and previous approaches which used the classic 'waterfall' approach (in which each stage should be completed before the next is started), is that one is not expected to proceed systematically from stage to stage without any backtracking. It is difficult to make a design without understanding the whole system, so

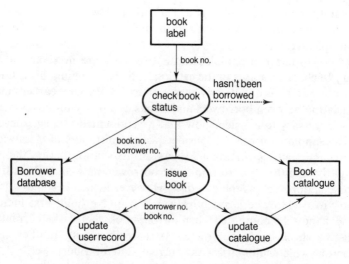

Figure 6.22   Dataflow diagram for the return of a book.

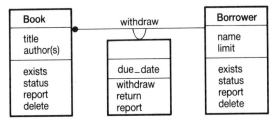

Figure 6.23   Association links with methods.

OMT promotes an iterative approach. We need to understand the operations required and provided by each object before we can write any more formal account of what they are doing. In this case, having drawn the state transition and dataflow diagrams, we need to return to the object model and fill in the third part of the object boxes which were left unfilled last time: the methods for each object.

We therefore need to model the association between books and borrowers, which we do by two classes, one based on the book and the other on the borrower, thus directly implementing the scheme outlined earlier. We can now fill in also the methods for these classes, as shown by Figure 6.23.

The purpose of methods withdraw and return are obvious. The status method is used to determine the current disposition of a book or borrower, and the report methods are used in the generation of reports.

6.3.4   Specification or prototype

One of the dreams of program developers was to be able to give a complete logical specification for a project in advance of writing the program. For this purpose complete specification languages, such as VDL and Z, have been developed and promoted. But it has always proved harder than anticipated and very few, if any, running systems have ever been developed in this way.

Consequently most systems use only small approximations to this ideal. Decision tables, equations, pseudocode and structured English are commonly used to express the specification in more or less rigorous terms.

The traditional 'waterfall' approach, in which analysis leads to design, which is finished before coding starts, leading to testing and finally integration, is equally suspect. It is too easy for a structure to become established early on which is not appropriate to the problem, and it is then nearly impossible to change it in the light of experience.

One popular alternative is to produce a prototype which can demonstrate the principles and be used for testing out key parts of the design. Prolog is widely regarded as a useful prototyping tool because of the combination of its logical basis and efficient implementation. Designs can be stated clearly and because it is a general purpose language it doesn't suddenly become more difficult to express a design, as is often the case with fourth-generation languages when they stray outside their intended domain. But it is less valuable if it cannot be used in the final product. Nobody wants to start again with a new formalism, but some of the features that make Prolog good as a prototyping tool, such as automatic space allocation and invertability, do not scale up well to large-scale information processing.

For instance, one may wish to use a proprietary database system to store the main part of the data, or use an existing windowing interface. Most Prolog systems provide the technical means for making these interfaces. But Prolog does not by itself suggest the best structure for breaking down a program into parts, which can be easily coded in different systems. One needs the type of modularity provided by objects to make it easy.

A viable strategy for doing this is as follows:

(1)   Develop a prototype in Prolog++ which expresses as simply and cleanly as possible the requirements of the system, breaking it down at an object level in the manner suggested by the Object Modelling Technique.

(2)   Analyse this prototype in terms of the scaling up that is required, any obvious inefficiencies and any special hardware or software requirements that cannot be provided within Prolog++.

(3)   Recode those modules indicated by the analysis, keeping as far as possible the same interfaces between the modules.

In this way it is possible to move smoothly from prototype to final implementation without losing the essential integrity of the prototype or the momentum generated by the first trials. This approach to design is known as exploratory programming.

This may suggest that Prolog++ has always to be the controlling element. This is not necessarily the case. The main driver of the program may be one of the critical components. Many commercial Prolog systems now incorporate the means of embedding Prolog code within applications expressed in different languages. Thus it is possible to make the appropriate choice at all levels.

The linkage between the objects will probably not use all the potential capabilities of Prolog++ such as complex unification and backtracking. These are capabilities that are of more use within an object. It is better to make calls between objects obey a simple call-and-answer discipline which can be mimicked in any algorithmic language. If success or failure needs to be signalled it is easy to use Boolean functions with other results passed by reference parameters.

As an example of a prototype let us consider some of the methods for the withdrawal operation. In order to make the association class concrete it is necessary to add to the list of attributes for the withdraw object values for the values of the association. Thus the heading for class withdraw is:

```
class withdraw.
attributes book, borrower, due_date.
```

In order to define the withdraw operation – which takes two arguments, the id of the book and the borrower – it is necessary to determine whether the status of book and borrower pemit the operation, and determine the loan period. This can be simply represented by the clause:

```
withdraw(Book, Borrower) = ok :-
    book@status(Book) = ok,
    borrower@status(Borrower) = ok,
    rules <- borrowPeriod(Book, Borrower, Date),
    create(Rec, [book = Book, borrower = Borrower, due_date = Date]).
```

Note that this returns a result: ok. There are several possibilities for error which may also be returned. We use a binary term which is easy for the user of this routine to handle: the first argument gives the item in error, the second the type of error.

```
withdraw(Book, Borrower) = status(book, Stat) :-
    book@status(Book) = Stat,
    Stat \== ok.
withdraw(Book, Borrower) = status(borrower, Stat) :-
    borrower@status(Borrower) = Stat,
    Stat \== ok.
```

But the real work is done within the book and borrower classes. Let us illustrate the status method in the book class:

```
status(Book) = withdrawn :-
    instance withdraw <- book(Book),
    !.
status(Book) = ok :-
    exists(Book),
    !.
status(Book) = unknown.
```

Here there are three exclusive cases. The use of the cut operator is quite valid here. It could be easily replaced by negated conditions on the other clauses, or conditional expressions, but is clearer as it stands. The first clause performs a search of all the instances of withdraw to see whether the book has been withdrawn.

Note that both of these are class methods; the one because it creates an instance of the class, the other because it is used partly to check whether there is a corresponding instance of the class.

The other methods could be similarly elaborated. There are no special algorithms or storage methods here, and it would not scale up to a realistically sized system. But it is perfectly adequate to be used as a basis for a prototype.

6.3.5 Searching the catalogue

So far the problems that we have been considering in this section are rather classical data processing problems. They concern the changes which occur in the state of the components of the library system which must be checked and recorded for subsequent use, but they are essentially simple transactions. There is no great depth in the computation which must be performed prior to these changes taking place. The complexity of analysis that takes place in a compiler or expert system is absent at this level. So we will look at the other common component of the interface: the process of searching for a book and coping with the successive stages of the search. This will provide a useful example for exploring the use of prototypes in program development.

This problem is rather more complex than the typical 'information retrieval' system, because there are several discrete 'clues' that the user can give: they might know the author, or be reasonably sure of the period in which it was written as well as part of the quotation. Titles often include only very common words, so it may be necessary to prune the search by differing means. People often remember a title incorrectly, substituting a word which sounds or means something similar, which leads to various search-widening possibilities. Thus the process may need to be iterative, with the user guiding the search towards the desired target. A number of Artificial Intelligence techniques may be used to aid this search, although in this chapter we will only consider the basic approach.

At the heart of the system is a 'Boolean search' facility, which the user need not be aware of at all, but is the key to any search technique in large free-text databases. This allows one to search for a combination of words using the operators 'and', 'or' and 'not'. To make a practical implementation of this one must first index all the words in the database, forming an 'inverted file' structure, and apply the operators to the inverted file.

The heuristic techniques we will demonstrate for controlling the search will be rudimentary, since the main aim is to show how a large database can be made available with reasonable efficiency. Also, this chapter will not cover the user interface since this topic is dealt with at length in the previous chapter.

This shows both the power and the limitations of the Boolean search technique. By casting the net wider we get irrelevant articles; by constraining it we may miss articles that are valuable. Within this paradigm the trade-off is inevitable. Yet there are other ways to improve the search using knowledge of the subject, and this is a likely reason why we might want to have such a facility available in a high-level language such as Prolog. New 'knowledge-based' searching techniques incorporate Boolean techniques though they also use semantic associations to improve the accuracy and recall.

Such a Boolean system is normally implemented as follows: first the text is scanned and each word recorded together with a reference number which indicates the item and position within the item. A sorted list of occurrences is compiled for each word, excluding common words such as 'the' and 'made' (the so-called 'stop list'). There might be of the order of 100 000 different words in this list, with an average of 20 to 30 entries. Some may have 1000 occurrences while maybe one-third of the total number appear only once. For example, in one free text database 'Martin' appears 238 times in 85 articles, whereas 'Luther' appears 110 times in 14 articles. These lists are stored along with the original text, or in some cases are used in conjunction with techniques to compress the original text.

To perform a search the Boolean function uses simple set operations on the lists:

and – intersect the lists – all items in both lists

or – combine the lists, eliminating duplicates

not – set difference – all items in the first, not in the second.

These are all binary functions, including negation, which is only used to reduce an already formed list, not to find the complement of a set of occurrences. In addition one needs a unary function to map word templates such as 'philosoph*' into the set of words it matches in the text. In this case '*' can match all the endings -e, -er, -ers, -ia, -iae, -ic, -ica, -ical, -ically, -icus, -ie, -ies, -ique, -ize, -izing, -izings, -os, -y.

A query can be formulated directly by a message sent to the object. For example, a query for Martin Luther which excludes references to Martin Luther King can be rendered as a Prolog++ term:

```
not(and('Martin', 'Luther'), 'King')
```

The result will be a list of the books that satisfy the query. In most such systems other forms of match are available which specify how close the words are, but for the purposes of illustration these refinements are not necessary.

How do we develop this idea into a workable reality?

There are two important components: one is to develop the appropriate algorithms and storage arrangements so that the searching can be done efficiently within the resource bounds available. The other is to make the system easily usable by the ordinary library user.

This second requirement is not trivial. The user interface in many library systems is so poor that it is impossible to make available the real power of searching. It is therefore crucial to be able to develop both of these aspects in parallel. One does not want to develop complex algorithms and then to discover that half of the code will never be used, or, even worse, some simple requirements cannot be handled.

This is the role of the prototype. One of the real strengths of languages such as Prolog++ is that they can be used for rapid prototyping. Often it is very simple to express the core of a problem so that it can be tried out on small examples without the need for a large amount of programming.

What this does *not* mean is that it is always necessary to use one system or language for prototyping and another for the 'real' implementation. Efficiency depends primarily on the algorithms used and only secondarily on the language. It is usually possible to identify the bottlenecks in a prototype implementation and by focusing on those parts achieve an acceptable level of performance without recoding the whole program. In this case it may be possible to use existing indexing routines in a package or database system or it may be desirable to recode them in a lower level language such as C. The advantage of this approach is that the higher level code is easier to maintain and adapt to changing circumstances.

The Boolean operators are not an easy idea for the casual user of a library system to grasp. So one might present a simplified picture (see Figure 6.24) to the user at first, which conceals the complexity.

The defaults for searching on different fields need to be carefully chosen so that they are usually the appropriate ones. For example, it is assumed the user is looking for a book: selecting *Video* as an alternative would change the fields that are displayed. Entering several words in a line will usually select any items which have those in any order, but in titles that may throw up too many possibilities and one may wish to be more exact. This is something that needs to be explored via a prototype.

The notion of a 'combination search' allows the user to perform a complex search in one operation, or gradually to refine the search by narrowing or broadening previous searches.

There is a particular linguistic problem associated with the operators: English does not have the same use as Boolean algebra. For example, if

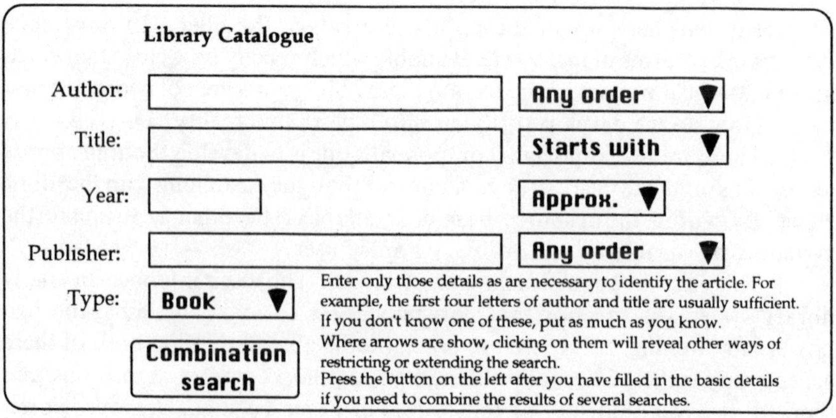

Library Catalogue

Author:	[ ]	**Any order** ▼
Title:	[ ]	**Starts with** ▼
Year:	[ ]	**Approx.** ▼
Publisher:	[ ]	**Any order** ▼
Type:	**Book** ▼	
	Combination search	

Enter only those details as are necessary to identify the article. For example, the first four letters of author and title are usually sufficient. If you don't know one of these, put as much as you know.
Where arrows are show, clicking on them will reveal other ways of restricting or extending the search.
Press the button on the left after you have filled in the basic details if you need to combine the results of several searches.

Figure 6.24   A simple initial screen for a book search.

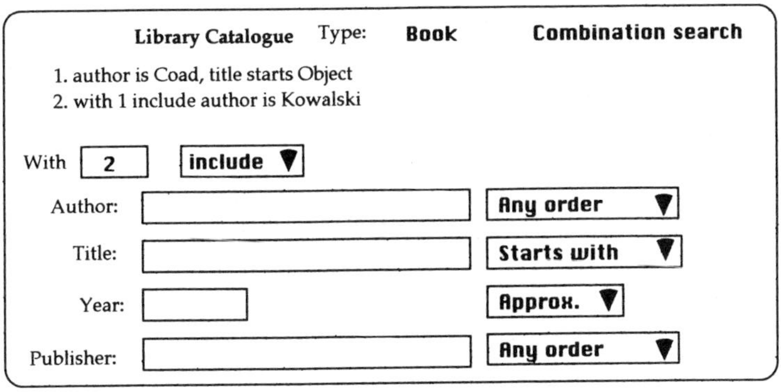

Figure 6.25 A more complex continuation screen.

someone says 'I'd like books by Coad and by Kowalski', it means something subtly different to 'I'd like books by Coad and Kowalski'. The first could be represented by:

or(includes(author, 'Coad'), includes(author, 'Kowalski'))

and the second

and(includes(author, 'Coad'), includes(author, 'Kowalski'))

The use of other operators, such as $+$ and $-$ have a similar problem. We will therefore suggest the use of the English verbs *select*, *include* and *exclude*, to stand for *and*, *or* and *not* respectively. In fact, complex and searches are also triggered by the use of several words in one field, or the use of several fields, and the user need not be overly concerned with this.

A suitable continuation screen for handling more complex queries might look as in Figure 6.25.

Here the numbers refer to queries that have already been formulated or executed. If they have been executed then details of the number found and a means of inspecting the results will also be needed. However it is not necessary at this level to clarify these details. What we need is a flexible way to combine different queries and display the partial results. It shows the need to be able to store and recall the query formulae and the results.

We can now consider the dynamics of the query process. By unifying the construction of large queries and the progressive refinement of the query profile we can simplify the way in which the query profiles are displayed, but there are still many separate pieces of information to display:

(1) A potentially long list of query profiles.
(2) The 'hit list' summary for a particular query. That is, the number of items found.

(3)   One-line summaries of the titles found by the queries which the user can browse through to pick out items of interest.

(4)   Full details of the item found, including any publication details, shelf position and current loan status.

How these are displayed on the screen will depend on the capacity of the screen, which may be anything from an 80×24 'glass teletype' to a full-page colour bit-mapped screen. The function of the prototype in this case is to assess the ease of use in the different configurations that are possible in order to know what are the potential benefits of more expensive hardware and software solutions and whether they are worth the corresponding costs.

The heart of the search may be expressed as a simple program, Program 6.1, which returns the key of a single record.

In Program 6.1, the first three clauses express the Boolean part of the search, whereas the third and fourth clauses make access to the database and to the results of previous searches, respectively. The program find in the object strings matches a list of words in the target. The access functions to the database and a couple of sample entries are shown below. In this way it is simple to limit the search to any particular field.

```
field(author, Key, Contents) :-
    ref(Key, Contents, _,_,_).
field(title, Key, Contents) :-
    ref(Key, _,Contents, _,_).
field(year, Key, Contents) :-
    ref(Key, _,_,Contents, _).
field(publisher, Key, Contents) :-
    ref(Key, _,_,_, Contents).
```

```
ref(2, 'Aït-Kaci, H.', 'Towards a meaning of LIFE', 1991, 'Journal of Logic
    Programming, vol 16, Nos 3&4. pp195–234').
ref(3, 'Atkinson, M., F. Bancillhon, D. DeWitt, K. Dittrich, D. Maier,
    S. Zdonick', 'The Object-Oriented Database System Manifesto. W. Kim,
    J. Nicolas, S.Nishio (Eds) Deductive and Object-oriented Databases',
    1990, North Holland).
```

Program 6.1   A specification of the search.

```
search(and(A,B), Key) :- search(A, Key), search(B, Key).
search(or(A, B), Key) :- search(A, Key) ; search(B, Key).
search(not(A,B), Key) :- search(A, Key), \+ search(B, Key).

search(includes(Field, A), Key) :-
    field(Field, Key, Contents),
    strings <–find(Contents, A,_).
search(item(N), Key) :-
    previousSearch(N, List),
    member(Key, List).
```

Thus if we posed the earlier query to this system we would get four different answers:

```
?-search(or(includes(author, 'Coad'), includes(author, 'Kowalski')), Key)
Key = 11;
Key = 12;
Key = 32;
Key = 33;
no
```

We could of course return these as a single solution using findall:

```
?-findall(Key, search(or(includes(author, 'Coad'), includes(author,
    'Kowalski')), Key), List).
List = [11,12,32,33], Key = _
```

but it is easy to see the inherent inefficiency of this program, even though it works. For each part of the search we have to scan every word in the relevant part of the database. There has to be a quicker way and of course there is. It is possible to preprocess the database and extract every word of significance so that we have a straightforward index to the database:

```
author('Coad', [11, 12]).
author('Kowalski', [32, 33]).
```

At this point, the three Boolean operations on the list simplify to set operations on ordered lists:

```
search(and(A,B), List) :-
    search(A, List1),
    search(B, List2),
    intersect(List1, List2, List).
search(or(A, B), Key) :-
    search(A, List1),
    search(B, List2),
    merge(List1, List2, List).
search(not(A,B), Key) :-
    search(A, List1),
    search(B, List2),
    differ(List1, List2, List).
```

We can now manipulate these lists instead of searching the whole database and the complexity of the search operation is reduced from the total number of words in the database to the number of occurrences of the particular words in which we are interested.

This gives a great boost in efficiency but it is still not adequate for coding a real system, because the lists of items might easily run into the

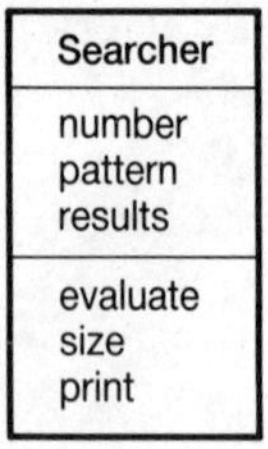

Searcher
number
pattern
results
evaluate
size
print

Figure 6.26   The search object.

thousands and be too long to manipulate efficiently with the simple techniques that we are assuming. The next stage therefore is to change the representation so that we encapsulate both the queries and the results of those queries within objects.

Our prototype gives us almost immediately the signature for such an object (Figure 6.26).

The attributes for the searcher object include the reference number by which the user refers to it, the search pattern and some means of internally referring to the results. We have included a method to evaluate the search, although the other two methods are more useful and will in general invoke the evaluate method implicitly. These get the size of the resultant set and print its contents in an appropriate way.

At this point there is no need for us to know the internal representation of the result list. Consequently we are free to change its representation and even the language in which the object is implemented. Because it is only accessed by those methods and they are enough for our purposes we can now postpone any further elaboration to the implementation stage, when one can choose the appropriate representation. This might use an existing indexing or database package or be specially designed.

6.3.6   Conclusions

Much of this chapter concentrates on more traditional 'software engineering' techniques than is normal for books dealing with Prolog. But we should not think that in this respect Prolog is any different from other computer languages. If it is to become part of the everyday armoury of tools employed by designers and programmers then it must be able to work alongside other tools. The use of the Object Modelling Technique with Prolog++ provides such a methodology.

The three stages of modelling provided by OMT do not map equally easily into the finished program. The object model works well in defining the overall structure of the program, but the dynamic model is essentially a design tool which is effectively thrown away when the program is built. Similarly the dataflow diagrams are primarily used in design, although they have use in explaining and documenting the design decisions. There has been plenty of research devoted to automating these processes, but it should be remembered that they are first and foremost techniques of human problem solving.

We have attempted to show how a prototyping methodology can be used in the development of a large system. By concentrating first on a program which is simple to implement it is possible to demonstrate very early in the development process a realistic model of the final product which can be used to clarify the actual design. The client is often unable to properly criticize a design without seeing such a working model.

It is important to encapsulate the components of that model so that the individual objects can be separately developed into full-scale programs. This is where the use of private representations is crucial. Instead of dealing directly with the represented object, it is accessed by means of a set of methods which perform the necessary tasks. One then has the freedom to implement each component using the most appropriate tools.

This chapter has not attempted to discuss the whole process of program design, which includes many topics including the mapping of software to hardware, and the management of datastores. For this the reader is referred to texts such as Rumbaugh *et al.* (1991), Booch (1991) and Coad and Yourdon (1991b).

SUMMARY

Program design uses a process of modelling to generate successive iterations in the design process:

- Object modelling defines the main classes, inheritance structures and relationships.
- Dynamic modelling charts the main state transitions of the system.
- Functional modelling describes the computations within the system.

This is demonstrated by means of a library loans system, incorporating a Boolean search system. The particular value of using Prolog++ is that it is possible to produce a series of prototypes which capture very cleanly the specification of the system and can be used to clarify the design at an early stage and as a foundation for the final implementation.

7
Objects – the way ahead

7.1 Introduction

In the previous chapter we painted a picture of the way in which objects and logic meet together in the context of program design. First, the objects within the domain are considered, with their relationships of inheritance, aggregation and association. A second layer consists of the dynamic behaviour over time in the interaction and evolution of these objects. The third, most detailed, aspect is the functional or declarative behaviour of the objects within themselves.

From the perspective of current programming languages on sequential 'von-Neumann' machines this represents the most practical approach to the construction of large programming systems today. Inheritance provides the reusability that is essential for the production and maintenance of large software systems. The logical component within the objects themselves presents a significant advance on the imperative constructs that form the basis of most object-oriented languages. But the dynamic interaction between independent processes is hard to capture within a logical framework.

In this chapter we want to look beyond what is routinely available today to see the direction in which things are moving. The concurrent execution of programs not only brings faster execution of programs but provides a declarative treatment of assignments. It provides some answers to the questions of process interaction. But we also want to look at object-oriented databases, which are a natural extension of the techniques which we have been exploring with Prolog++ but need extra support in certain areas. Finally we will look at some of the alternative approaches that have been used to combine logic and object-oriented programming.

Object-oriented programming has grown up from the practical world of computing without very much input from the world of theoretical computer science. It is only in the last five years that the theorists have approached it seriously and attempted to capture formally what makes it successful. But their efforts have indeed clarified many of these issues.

The combination of two of the most dynamic ideas on the computer scene is potentially explosive: it can either set free enormous creative energies or wreck carefully constructed paradigms. Already logic programming has transformed a traditional notation – formal logic – into a dynamic means of combining specification and execution. It breached what was seen in the 1970s as an impenetrable barrier between the declarative and the procedural. Yet the still static view of a logical theory is not enough to encompass the highly complex world in which we find ourselves. Logic programming has to find a way to relate to the irreducible complexity of changing situations.

The central layer of our OOLP sandwich – the dynamic behaviour of objects over time – is at this point rather conventional: we have not offered a radical alternative to the way in change is handled. Prolog++ uses the equivalent of the normal assignment statement to store the state of an object between calls to an object. We have argued that this is the correct engineering compromise with today's computers. What we need to do at the moment is to 'lift' the level at which change of state comes into operation. Declarative tools simplify the construction of traditional sequential computations: they become shorter, closer to the original explanations, easier to develop and maintain, without undue efficiency penalties.

One of the basic accompaniments of object-orientedness that we identified in the first chapter was the notion of concurrency. As we observed there, most object-oriented programming languages do not provide actual concurrency and nor does Prolog++. Instead, assignment is used effectively to simulate concurrency, though it obviously does not give all of the benefits and indeed is a liability when one attempts to design parallel computers.

Assignment is foreign to the declarative nature of logic programming, but with the sequential Prologs available today it is the only way to provide the impression of concurrency. However, for the last ten years there has been a growing interest in the use of Prolog-like languages for parallel computers. Because these are still something of a rarity in practice, this aspect has not yet reached the popular consciousness, though the speedups achieved are already attracting attention.

There are already a few products on the market catering to the parallel processor market. The most popular form is for what is called the 'shared memory multiprocessor', represented by products like the Sequent Symmetry and Alliant. These use a number of conventional microprocessors (such as the Intel 386 and i860) with a large common bank of memory, usually supervised by the Unix operating system. But there are also systems available for transputers, a group of micros specially designed for parallel computations and featuring very high speed data links. Recently, systems constructed from

Intel's i860 and Sun's Sparc microprocessors have provided performance exceeding that of the traditional Cray-style supercomputer.

So far it has not been possible to provide full implementations of Prolog for parallel computers, for reasons which will be explained below, and variant forms, usually known as 'concurrent Prologs' after one of the early systems (Shapiro, 1983). In fact there are a number of variants. Parlog (Clark and Gregory, 1986) was developed at Imperial College, London, Guarded Horn Clauses by ICOT in Japan and a version called Flat Concurrent Prolog at the Weissman Institute, Israel. Because these provide significant new capabilities for demonstrating object-oriented features that are not available in sequential Prolog, and there are already object-oriented languages available for them, we will concentrate on one of these in this chapter, known as 'Strand' (Foster and Taylor, 1989; Foster and Stevens, 1990), together with its object-oriented form, known as 'Step'. Syntactically, Strand is very close to the conventional form of Prolog used in this book, so it should not be too difficult to adjust.

7.2   Concurrency and Prolog

Most programming languages are inherently sequential, because of the nature of the assignment statement. If one has the two statements in Pascal:

```
x := x + 1 ; print(x)
```

then interchanging them will produce a different result:

```
print(x) ; x := x + 1
```

If one wants to run a Pascal program on a parallel computer, one needs to be careful to run statements which depend on each other in the correct order. This is a difficult problem, which substantially reduces the potential benefits of using parallel computation. It is either necessary to rewrite the program in another language designed for multiprocessors or accept substandard 'speedups', the usual measure of success in parallel computing. If one has a linear speedup, this means that doubling the number of processors will double the speed of the program. In practice, not only is the speedup considerably less (50% of linear is considered good) but there is a natural limit for any particular program. After, say, six processors, little or no further speedup is achievable. Since microprocessors are so cheap these days, it would be nice simply to be able to add more as the needs of your company expand. Unfortunately this is not possible with conventional programming languages.

Horn Clauses, the part of logic which provides the basis of Prolog, are not inherently sequential. There are two 'composition operators' in Horn Clauses comparable to the sequencing ';' of Pascal: one is the 'and' operator

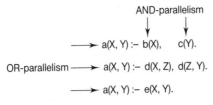

Figure 7.1   AND- and OR-parallelism.

that joins together subgoals in a clause. The other is the existence of alternative clauses for one predicate. These provide two potential forms of parallelism, normally known as 'AND-parallelism' and 'OR-parallelism'.

They may be illustrated by the set of Prolog clauses shown in Figure 7.1.

In the first clause, the two subgoals joined together by the 'and' operator, *b* and *c*, are independent of one another. Because there are no shared (or global) variables between the two goals, the results of one cannot affect the other. It is therefore perfectly permissible to execute the two in parallel. This is therefore called AND-parallelism.

Since the three clauses which define the predicate *a* are independent of each other, it is also possible to evaluate these in parallel. As they give rise to alternative solutions, this is called OR-parallelism.

Unfortunately, not every situation is so simple. Take the second clause, which illustrates a simple transitivity relationship. While it is possible to evaluate the two subgoals independently, the existence of the shared local variable Z means that the solutions to the two subgoals must be correlated. In fact, it is almost certainly pointless to do what many relational databases do in this situation: form two sets of solutions to the two subgoals and then take the intersection of the two. In almost all cases, solving one subgoal reduces the number of possible solutions to the other subgoal so much that it makes no sense to try and produce two different sets of solutions.

Consequently the standard approach is to label one instance of the variable as a 'producer' of a value and the other as the 'consumer'. Then both goals can be run in parallel until the point at which the consumer tries to instantiate the variable. At this point the consumer process will be suspended until the producer produces a binding. This allows some execution in parallel but without the confusion that arises from unconstrained parallelism. Several approaches have been tried for labelling the variables: either explicitly (as in Concurrent Prolog, Shapiro, 1983), by mode declarations on predicates (Parlog, Clark and Gregory, 1986) or by restrictions on the heads of clauses (Strand).

Neither are things straightforward for OR-parallelism. The most obvious difficulty doesn't occur in pure Horn Clauses but in Prolog: the cut operator. It isn't permissible to try a clause after a cut until the 'guard' before the cut is known to fail. This imposes a sequencing on the clauses which limits the potential parallelism, though alternative operators similar to the cut have been tried. In addition, compile-time indexing techniques are possible in many programs which can often select only one of the clauses to evaluate with little overhead, so that parallel execution brings no benefits.

OR-parallelism is quite easy to apply and for some well-known combinatorial problems, such as the eight queens puzzle, it produces quite respectable speedups. But in more realistic programming situations the results are less favourable. Also it can easily be *too* successful, with the program execution being fragmented between a large number of processes each with a very small task, giving rise to unacceptable overheads.

In fact, it is not the potential benefits of speed that have given rise to the most interest in parallel execution of Prolog-type programs, but another characteristic of executing them in parallel, in particular that known as the *process model*. When several goals with shared variables can be started in parallel, these can act as processes having private state with communication channels linking them. Very elegant models can be built from these.

7.2.1   The process model

To see how the process model works, let us first consider the difficulty in building processes with private state with the normal sequential definition of Prolog. A very simple model of an object is one which stores a single number and will accept three messages:

becomes(Val)	replaces the current value with this number
add(N)	adds N to the current value
value(X)	returns the current value

We will model these messages as Prolog terms (we could use Prolog++ but it doesn't change much). The only way to accumulate the messages in pure Prolog is to use extra parameters to store the 'before' and 'after' state, as follows:

```
process(becomes(V), _, v(V)).
process(add(N), v(V), v(X)) :-
    X is N+V.
process(value(X), v(X), v(X)).
```

We can now execute this by a sequence of procedure calls, such as:

```
?-      process(becomes(2), _, X1),
        process(add(3), X1, X2),
        process(add(-1), X2, X3),
        process(value(X), X3, X4).
X=4,    X1=v(2), X2=v(5), X3=v(4), X4=v(4).
```

Well it works and clearly we could store a much more interesting set of data in these terms: for instance a 'pairlist' of names and values or a tree-structured dictionary. But it is unsatisfactory for two reasons: first, the calling process has to do the hard work of storing the intermediate results. This means extra parameters passed around the calling procedures. But the second problem is that the contents of the 'state' variable are available to the caller, who can tamper with it or present an illegal term instead of the expected form. They show themselves also in the fact that there is no very good way to initialize the state at the beginning.

The way out of this dilemma is to make the process call itself each time and to pass the state information 'privately'. It can do this if the operations are passed as a list, instead of in separate procedure calls. We can modify the previous miniprocess as follows:

```
process(Message) :-
    process1(Message, x(0)).

process1([], _).
process1([becomes(V)|Ms], _) :-
    process1(Ms, v(V)).
process1([add(N)|Ms], v(V)) :-
    X is N+V
    process1(Ms, v(X)).
process1([value(X)|Ms], v(X)) :-
    process1(Ms, v(X)).
```

There are two extra clauses at the start of process1, one to start and one to finish the process. The work is done in the second private process process1. The procedure can be invoked with the same sequence:

```
?- process([becomes(2), add(3), add(-1), value(X)]).
X=4
```

This has solved the privacy and initialization problems nicely. The 'state' information of the process is entirely specified by the program and the only access is via the advertised messages. By means of unification these can pass information in both directions, as is shown by the value message. And the outer routine process provides the initialization to start the whole thing off.

But in a sequential language it is only of academic interest. All the messages must be passed at one time to make it work. To make it useful, each item on the list needs to be sent separately and the recursive calls to process1 need to delay until the item is sent.

Let us look therefore at a concurrent logic programming language, Strand, to see how it behaves.

7.2.2   Strand – a simple concurrent Prolog

The syntax of Strand is almost identical with that of Prolog, but there are a number of restrictions in the interpretation of clauses which enable it to function efficiently in a parallel environment.

(1)   If there are constants or terms in the head of the clause, the process will not choose that clause until these are bound. That is, there is no unification in the head of the clause, only a restricted form of pattern matching.

(2)   Each clause is assumed to have a 'guard', written as | in the body of the clause which separates the *preconditions* from the *body*. Only system-defined goals such as > may appear before the guard. Any other calls must appear after it in the body. If it does not appear it is assumed to occur before the first subgoal. No variable assignments can take place before the guard.

(3)   Only one clause will be chosen for each call, but it need not be the first. Any clause of which the parameters match the head and whose preconditions succeed may be chosen.

A rule of the form:

$$H :- G_1, G_2,..., G_m \mid B_1.$$

thus represents a process, with the body goal B_1 continuing its execution. If there are no goals in the body, the process terminates. If there are more than one, the process *forks*, and the subgoals continue in parallel.

Variables are assigned in the body of the clause using the assignment operator :=. This is implemented as a *write* operation to a remote machine, so it is important that it cannot be revoked. The converse operator – *read* the value of a variable – will cause execution of the clause to suspend.

Though these conditions may appear restrictive, many rules need little modification. For example, the process program above needs no alteration. If we consider a clause such as:

```
process1([add(N)|Ms], v(V)) :-
    X is N+V,
process1(Ms, v(X)).
```

then it will not be invoked until the list element [|] is bound, and a template add(N) appears. At this point the processor will commit to this clause. It could be that the value of N is not yet available. In this case the addition would suspend until it became available.

The main style difference between Prolog and Strand is when writing procedures that form tests. Failure of a call leads to a process terminating, so tests are written to return a result which can then be used as a test. For example, here is the classic member test. Note the guard in the third clause.

```
member(_, [], Res) :- Res := false.
member(X, [X|_], Res) :- Res := true.
member(X, [Y|Ys], Res) :-
    X =\= Y |
    member(X, Ys, Res).
```

Strand has been designed with a very efficient interface to conventional programming languages such as Fortran and C. Many scientific programs written in these languages do not run effectively on multiple processors. It is not that there are not substantial sections of code that could be run in parallel, but that for this to be done requires a flexible interface between subprograms. This interface must be able to synchronize the execution of different parts of the program and provide buffering of intermediate results so that one part of the program can 'run ahead' of another.

Strand provides an excellent 'harness' for this type of activity, for which reason it has become popular for use in parallelizing programs such as weather forecasting and genetic manipulations, which require large amounts of computation. In one sense this is already 'object-oriented' programming, but the addition of Step makes this paradigm even more useful.

7.2.3 Message passing

The most important object capability in a distributed system is how to send messages reliably from one process to another. Since we are dealing with a concurrent program whose parts may execute in an unpredictable order it is important that the messages reach the destination in the right order or they may not have the desired effect. Simply defining procedure calls whose effect depends on some mysterious 'side-effect' is not good enough. Lists form a communication channel between the processes down which the messages will be sent.

A simple example of a one-way process with these requirements is an input/output channel such as a printer. It would certainly be undesirable that because of some scheduling uncertainty, output messages sent from different parts of the program came out in the wrong order.

We will define this communication channel by means of a logical variable which is bound to a list of messages to be sent to the printer. For simplicity we assume these messages comprise the characters or terms to be output. The printer itself will be controlled by a single program whose sequence can be controlled by the constraints already outlined.

Printing can then be done by a number of assignment statements such as these:

```
print(Output),
...,
Output := ['The first sentence. ' | Out1],
...,
Out2 := ['The third sentence. ' | Out3],
...,
Out1 := ['The second sentence. ' | Out2],
...,
Out3 := [],
```

These statements may appear in different procedures in the program and may be executed in any order. The final statement 'finishes' the output. If we assume they were executed in the order shown, then the fact that the third sentence was output before the second sentence is entirely immaterial as the resulting list will be:

```
Output = ['The first sentence. ','The second sentence. ',
          'The third sentence. ' ]
```

To control the printer we must ensure that the printing of one item is finished before the next item is started. The conventional way of doing this in Strand is to use an extra 'synchronization' variable in the lower-level routines. This is tested by a built-in predicate called 'data' which suspends until its parameter is bound to something. The procedure is as follows:

```
print(In) :- print(In, []).
print([],_).
print([A|B],Sync) :- data(Sync) | write(A,S), print(B,S).
```

The semantics of Strand ensures the output is done correctly. When it is originally invoked, the parameter is unbound, so print/2 suspends and waits for it to be bound to a term. When the first sentence is presented it tests the Sync variable (which is bound to []) and starts executing both the write statement and the next print statement. The third sentence causes no immediate action, but when the second sentence is sent, both second and third sentences can be output. However the second will not start until the Sync variable has been bound by the first call to write. Similarly the third will not start until the second is finished. The nil list which terminates the output doesn't need to wait as it is doing no output, so it finishes immediately.

All the delays and synchronizations, even those at a lower level governing the behaviour of the printer, can be performed correctly by using similar techniques, and these are totally transparent to the program writer.

We have shown these actions in their most primitive form, but it is easy to 'abstract' them using the technique of difference lists. If we use a version of print/3 whose definition is simply:

```
print(Val, L1, L2) :- L1 := [Val|L2].
```

together with a program to end the printing process:

```
endPrint(L) :- L := [].
```

then the same program can be rewritten:

```
print(Output),
...,
print('The first sentence. ', Output, Out1),
...,
print('The third sentence. ', Out2, Out3),
...,
print('The second sentence. ', Out1, Out2),
...,
endPrint(Out3),
```

This is no easier for the user, but it hides the physical representation so that the implementer has the freedom to use different techniques when appropriate. We will later show how 'syntactic sugar' can make it appear more like a conventional procedure call.

It might appear that this technique restricts one to a single sender and receiver of messages, but in fact it is quite general. To demonstrate this let us assume that two different processes want to send messages to a third but that the order in which they send the messages is undetermined in time. Each of the senders can have their own message channel and the key problem is to merge the two into a single channel.

We can implement this using a predicate merge/3 of which the first two arguments are the input channels, and the last is the output channel. The code (ignoring termination) is simply the following:

```
merge([A|B], C, D) :- D := [A|E], merge(B,C,E).
merge(A, [B|C], D) :- D := [B|E], merge(A,C,E).
```

Which of the clauses is executed depends on which channel first has a message. If it is the first channel, the first clause will be selected, if it is the second, then the second. If both appear simultaneously, either might be chosen. The program is completely *nondeterministic*. For many formalisms this is a problem, but for a logic-based system it is quite normal. Although the AND-parallel logic languages have given up the ability to produce multiple solutions, they have not become deterministic. In fact, they may be less constrained in their results than a sequential Prolog system because they do not necessarily follow the top-to-bottom clause ordering that Prolog uses.

7.2.4   Objects as perpetual processes

The two capabilities outlined above – the ability to pass messages and to store information internally – provide us with the basic capabilities that are needed to define objects using a pure logic programming paradigm. Here is a definition of an object, taken from Shapiro and Takeuchi (1983):

> 'A (perpetual) object is a process that calls itself recursively and holds its internal state in unshared arguments.'

This definition is based on Hewitt's (1977) Actor model of parallel computation. This sees the world divided into opaque objects to which one can send messages and from which one can receive replies. The replies depend purely on the current internal state of the object, and there are a number of limitations on the way channels can be set up to ensure the semantics of the entire system.

This contrasts strongly with the logic programming paradigm in which everything is unchanging and open to inspection. Yet it is not entirely inconsistent. The evaluation of any recursive predicate involves a number of different internal states, yet this does not make the system nondeclarative. In building a large system it is inevitable that one treats the components as 'black boxes' which are not open to casual inspection and simply respond to external messages. So the actor model may have a role in establishing a more comprehensive framework for logic programming.

It may be recalled that in Chapter 2 it was pointed out that the use of side-effects including assignment and input/output were not really compatible with the logic programming philosophy. Yet to explore the full capabilities of object-oriented programming it was necessary to use assignment to store the internal state of an object. With concurrent logic programming systems we have found a declarative notion of 'state' which can take us into the next generation of computer systems in a way that the traditional assignment statement cannot.

7.2.5   Step

The problem with writing programs using messages and local storage is that the text becomes swamped with recursive clauses and lists of messages. It's rather like writing in assembler language once again! Yet one is writing the same type of code over and over again. These are standard clichés which can and should be automated.

Step is an object-oriented language written on top of, and compiled into, Strand in a similar manner to the compilation of Prolog++. It provides a level of 'syntactic sugar' which makes the message-passing cliché much more natural to use. There are some unnecessary differences between Prolog+ + and Step which may be eliminated in future versions, but these should not obscure the basic similarities.

A Step program has up to five sections: name of the class (the current version of Step does not use the word 'class' – only the name of the class is used; the word is added here for clarity), declarations, initialization, methods and Strand code. Each section is introduced by a keyword and the class is terminated by the keyword 'end'. Here is a very simple object which simply outputs the contents of each message received to the screen. It requires only the methods section:

```
class output.
methods
    message(−1, Reply) =>
        Reply := stop.
    message(Num, Reply) =>
        Num =\= −1 |
        Reply := continue,
        display(Num).
    last => true.
end.
```

The words methods and end are keywords which delimit the different sections of the object. Within the methods section, the message appears on the left of the symbol =>. On the right is the Strand code executed when the message is received (=> is thus equivalent to :- in Prolog++). **Last** is a special message which terminates the object stream. The Strand code corresponding to this program is also very simple, though rather longer, and shows the principle by which the compilation is performed:

```
output([message(−1,Reply)|M] :-
    Reply := stop,
    output(M).
output([message(Num, Reply)|M]) :-
    Num =\= −1 |
    Reply := continue,
    display(Num),
    output(M).
output([last|M]) :-
    M := [].
```

Each message, except for last message, corresponds to a clause of a recursive procedure and the messages are patterns to be matched in the head of the clause. Because of the way patterns are matched in Strand, an object will normally suspend immediately it has been called and await for an input message to arrive on its input stream.

An object in Step has (by default) a single input stream, which converts to a single argument, by which it receives its messages. To send messages to another object requires an output channel, or list, called ostream. In this case the stream is local to the object and is therefore declared as invisible, by a keyword which appears before the declaration.

To *initialize* the object one simply calls it as a normal predicate, with the stream as argument. To *send a message* to the object one uses the functor ':', which is analogous to '<–' in Prolog++. Thus to initialize the output object from within Step and send it several messages one could write the following code:

```
class user.
invisible Out ostream.
methods.
    doit =>
        output(Out),
        ...,
        Out: message(first),
        ...,
        Out: message(second),
        ...
```

The stream name Out is a variable which names the stream by which messages are to be sent to the output object. Unlike Prolog++, Step uses names which are akin to normal variables to name the streams by which messages are sent to objects. However their scope is *not* a single clause but the whole object. Hence it is necessary to declare the stream in the head of the object.

Step imposes some ordering on the program. If there are several calls to an output stream then they are placed in that order on the stream. So one can rely on the code above to display the messages in the right order, even if the actions are completed in a different order.

An object is not limited to a single input stream. It can have several input streams and several output streams. The messages in the methods section must then be tagged with the appropriate stream. As an example, let us recode the nondeterministic merge presented earlier as a Step program. This time we include a proper termination clause:

```
class merge.
In1 stream. In2 stream. Out ostream.
methods
    In1: X => Out : X.
    In2: X => Out : X.
    In1: last, In2: last => true.
end.
```

To code termination properly we have required that the last message appears on *both* streams, by using a conjunction in the message head. If the last message only appears on one stream it will not be enough for the method to be chosen.

In summary, streams in Step may be either input or output, and may be visible, in which case they are included in the calling sequence which initiates the object, or invisible, in which case they are initiated from within the object.

7.2.6   State variables in Step

Step supports the notion of state variables which are very similar to the slots of Prolog++. Unlike streams these are scalar values which persist from one message to another, but can be changed internally by an operator called **becomes** (since the more obvious := has already been used by Strand).

We will demonstrate this with a simple object called 'count'. This receives four messages, set(X), inc, dec and val(X). The parameter X is assumed to be bound to an integer, which the inc and dec messages increment and decrement respectively.

```
count.
invisible Value state.
methods
    set(X)      => Value becomes X.
    inc         => Value becomes Value + 1.
    dec         => Value becomes Value - 1.
    val(X)      => X := Value.
end.
```

The becomes operator can take an arithmetic expression on its right hand side in the same way as the := operator in Prolog++. But there is one significant difference. The new value set by the becomes operator is only accessible with the next message received by the object. The 'assignment' is actually a replacement in what in Chapter 2 was called an *accumulator*.

Because it has only the default input stream visible it is set up with only a single parameter, but the recursive clause has more parameters. Thus the clauses for the count may be given as follows:

```
count(Messages) :- count(Messages, _).

count([set(X)|M], Value) :-
    V is X,
    count(M, V).
count([inc|M], Value) :-
    V is Value + 1,
    count(M, V).
count([dec|M], Value) :-
    V is Value - 1,
    count(M, V).
count([val(X)|M], Value) :-
    X := Value,
    count(M, Value).
```

The translation for this object is very similar to the predicate assign which was introduced earlier, with one exception. No initial value is given to the internal value stored inside the object, whose initial value is undefined and does not have the check on accessing an undefined value that was suggested earlier.

There are several possible ways of correcting this situation. One is to allow the object to initialize its own state variable, which it can do with the addition of an extra **initialize** section, written as a piece of arbitrary Strand code after the variable declarations.

```
count.
invisible Value state.
initialize Value becomes 0.
methods ...
```

The initialization code is thus equivalent to:

```
count(Messages) :- count(Messages, 0).
```

An alternative approach is to make the state variable visible rather than invisible. In this case the initial call which sets up the object can set the value.

The header then becomes:

```
count
Value state.
methods ...
```

and the call to start the object might be:

```
count(Messages, 0)
```

Although this allows the user of the object to initialize the state variable, it does not compromise the encapsulation, because the only way to change the state variable subsequently is by means of messages sent to the object.

To complete the picture, a fourth type of state variable is possible, an output state variable, with designation **ostate**. This is a variable which is not used very often but is usually used as a flag or final state of an object and can be unified at any point during the execution of the object.

7.2.7 The eight queens example

In Chapter 4, we showed how the eight queens problem could be programmed using object-oriented techniques and used it as a paradigm example of using assignment in a Prolog++ program. We will now show how this problem is solved in a declarative manner using Step.

Each queen has an input and output channel (represented as the top line of arrows in the diagram below) by which it accepts an instruction from the queen to its right and passes on other instructions to the queen on its left.

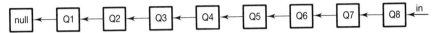

As before, each queen can accept three messages from the queen on the right: first, next and canAttack. On receiving a first message it tells the queen on its left to find its *first* acceptable solution, then tries to find a row which is acceptable to the queens on the left. It does this by sending them a series of canAttack messages, specifying the row and column which it is trying. To this it gets a response of either 'yes' or 'no'. If it finds a suitable position it succeeds itself. If not it sents a next message to the queen on its left. This causes that queen to search for its next acceptable position and it may in turn send next messages to its left.

Each queen has three variables: the Column is visible, as it is set up by the initialization; the Row it is currently attempting is an invisible, local variable; the Neighbour is an invisible output stream. Immediately after the variable information in the header comes the initialization code which initializes the Row and sets up the channel to the next queen:

```
object queen.
Column state. invisible Row state.
invisible Neighbour ostream..
    Row becomes 1,
    Next is Row − 1,
    next Queen(Next).
```

When we look at the methods, two things are immediately obvious. First, most of the methods must now return an explicit result, in this case *yes* or *no*, rather than succeeding or failing as in the Prolog code. Second, only the routines which can be called from outside the object are given in the methods section. The others are recorded as normal Step in the code section.

```
methods.

first =>
    Neighbour : first,
    Row becomes 1,
    testOrAdvance.

canAttack(R, C, Res) => Row == R | Res := yes
canAttack(R, C, Res) => Row =\= R |
    D1 is Row − R − Column + C,
    D2 is Row − R + Column − C,
    checkDiag(D1, D2, R, C, Res).
```

```
next (Res) => advance, Res := yes.

print(X) =>
    Neighbour : print(Y),
    X = [' Row ',Row, ' Column ',Column | Y]).

code.

nextQueen(0) :- nullQueen(Neighbour).
nextQueen(N) :- N>0 | queen(Neighbour).

checkDiag(0,_,_,_,Res) :- Res := yes.
checkDiag(_,0,_,_,Res) :- Res := yes.
checkDiag(A,B,R,C,Res) :- A=\=0, B=\=0 |
    Neighbour : canAttack(R,C,Res).

testOrAdvance :-
    Neighbour : canAttack(Row, Column, Res)
    attack(Res).

attack(no).
attack(yes) :- advance.

advance :- Row == 8 |
    Neighbour : next(Res),
    row becomes 0,
    attack(Res).
advance :- Row < 8 |
    Row becomes Row+1,
    testOrAdvance.

end.
```

The definition of the null queen is very simple: it doesn't need any internal state: all it has to do is to produce appropriate responses to all the messages, either succeeding or failing.

```
nullQueen.

first => true.

next(Res) => Res := no.

canAttack(_, _, Res) => Res :- no.

print => true.

end.
```

7.2.8   Inheritance in the Actors model

There is one omission from Step from our list of characteristics of object-oriented languages. Step provides encapsulation and concurrency but no inheritance. An earlier language from the author of Step – Polka, based on the Parlog dialect – did provide inheritance based on the earlier suggestions of Shapiro and Takeuchi, but it was omitted from Step. The reasons for this are interesting.

The type of inheritance that follows naturally from the Actors model supposes that all the ancestors of an object from which it inherits properties are themselves fully fledged objects. This is normally called *delegation*. This can be easily modelled within the concurrent LP languages: each object has separate private channels back to the ancestor through which it passes back the information. This can also cope with multiple inheritance using several channels, though the internal mechanisms become somewhat cumbersome.

One problem is that when we create an *instance* of an object, it is also necessary to create fresh instances of all its ancestors. So instead of creating one object, we may need to create half a dozen separate objects, each of which has the normal object overhead. The situation is illustrated in Figure 7.2, which shows a typical hierarchy with the addition of the objects created by an instance of one class.

Part of the reason that Actors was designed this way was that in addition to changing state variables, the aim of the designers was that the *program* of an actor should be equally malleable. The use of self-modifying code was a popular technique in the early days of computing when memory was a severe limitation, but the practice is the antithesis of declarative programming and is frowned upon by most programming professionals. Similar effects can be acheived by creating new objects, which is also part of the Actors philosophy.

But there is another perhaps more important difficulty with inheritance in this model which has to do with dynamic binding and the self variable. To be able to provide this facility with the explicit channel system that is used in concurrent Prologs, an inheritance path would need to have two channels, one to pass the message up, and another to pass self messages back down again. But when they reach the original object, there is a deadlock. It is currently awaiting a response to its original message and to do that it

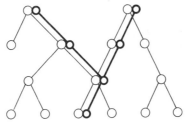

Figure 7.2   Small part of a hierarchy with added instances.

must defer the consideration of other incoming messages. But this message
is itself an incoming message.

Consequently the type of inheritance that can be provided in this
manner is a rather poor copy of the system provided in a Smalltalk-like
system. Delegation and inheritance are increasingly seen as alternative
approaches. Formally both can be used to simulate the other, but it is not
clear that delegation should be used in the same way. It is better for the
object explicitly to delegate behaviour to the other object. Thus providing
an automatic inheritance method is not justified.

7.2.9   The process model – an appraisal

Having presented the current work in concurrent models of logic
programming and their integration of the object-oriented paradigm it is now
time to appraise what has and has not been achieved.

It is clearly important that a class of object-oriented programs has
been shown to have a well-founded semantic model. By demonstrating how
pure logic programs can cooperate by sending messages to each other,
working in a concurrent environment, a significant step has been made
towards the understanding of concurrent processes. It also demonstrates a
pure approach to encapsulation.

The concurrent approach puts some constraints on the way in which
objects can communicate: it is necessary to set up explicit communication
channels between objects and use those channels for all communications.
This makes programs somewhat more difficult to write and it may be the
reason why this approach has not yet been applied to very large systems.

Within the object, programs in languages like Step end up looking
very similar to Prolog++ programs, modulo the differences in programming
style required by the concurrent language. They use a similar type of
assignment statement to store the state from call to call, but this is simply
a syntactic convenience; underneath the program is using the standard Prolog
form of accumulators.

Can we therefore consider that the use of the database to record state
in Prolog++ is simply an implementation optimization? We could refer to
the process implementation as a justification and use an equivalent method
in the implementation.

In certain cases the answer is yes. But things are not quite so easy
when we consider issues such as backtracking. Logically a change of state
should be reversed when the program backtracks. But programs are very
often executed for their effect; the programmer does not want the changes
to be undone.

The primary justification of logical and functional approaches to
computer science is to be able better to understand and analyse the programs
that are being written. It is only in as far as they manage this that these
methods really help. The real vindication would come therefore from the

ability to reason about programs written in this way. Is the program with all its accumulators and recursive calls really easier to understand?

The relatively slow takeup of this style of coding in the programming community might suggest that it does not meet a perceived need. On the other hand, parallel and distributed computers are far from common yet and it may be that these techniques have not yet reached the point of liftoff.

7.3   Persistence and object-oriented databases

A considerable conceptual simplification in the design of programming languages has been achieved by the idea of persistence (see Atkinson *et al.*, 1983). In essence the ideas are as follows.

Traditional programming languages deriving from the Algol tradition have two ways of storing information: in data structures (arrays, records, and so on) and in files. The data structures in a program are typically discarded at the end of execution and any information that persists must be transferred to a file. In many cases file structures are much less expressive than data structures and it is much harder to record certain types of relationships, for example a circular structure or a dag (directed acyclic graph). If one simply 'freezes' the data structures at the end of execution and picks them up next time, then all the problems of file structures, and even databases, disappear.

Some elegant implementations have proved that the idea is feasible. But as will be immediately evident, the main problem with this notion is practical: it is not easy to draw a line between transient objects which need to be thrown away after use and the persistent objects which will be useful later. The danger is that one accumulates a vast mass of uninteresting data, or, alternatively, that a large amount of information is carefully stored in permanent storage only to be thrown away later by some means of garbage collection.

In Prolog there is a clear dividing line between data structures which are part of a computation and items which are asserted in the (dynamic) database. In the early days of Prolog's popularity, many novice programmers saw that there was an equivalent of the assignment statement in the assert/retract pair of predicates and simply replicated the style of programming common in Fortran or BASIC; only to discover their programs ran immensely inefficiently.

To take a trivial example, the simplest algorithm to reverse a list in Prolog has order N^2 in the length of the list:

```
nrev([], []).
nrev([A|As], Bs) :-
    nrev(As, Cs),
    append(Cs, [A], Bs).
```

In order to get over the appending of ever-lengthening lists, the programmer hits on the idea of storing the partial list so far constructed and puting the next element at the front of it. Using Prolog++ she eagerly encodes it as:

```
attribute list = [].
arev([], As) :-
    As = @list.
arev([A|B], C) :-
    list := [A|@list],
    rev(B, C).
```

She is puzzled to find her program hardly speeds up at all. It is not until she realizes that she needs to use a subsidiary procedure with an extra parameter that the penny finally drops:

```
rev(A, B) :- rev(A, [], B).
```

```
rev([], As, As).
rev([A|As], Bs, Cs) :-
    rev(As, [A|Bs], Cs)
```

If the new programmer persists with Prolog, she learns a whole new style of 'declarative programming' in which temporary results are passed around as extra parameters to procedures (or *accumulators*) and only the more permanent data was asserted in the database. She then finds her programs speed up often by an order of magnitude! Indeed with a good compiler, suitable programs are competitive with or beat programs written in conventional languages such as C.

Changes to an object in Prolog++ are coded as changes in the Prolog database. Object variables are not intended simply as local variables in a procedural language as in the second example above. They are designed to record state changes, even if it is relatively transient, such as the position of a window on a screen.

Given this coding, the dividing line which has proved problematic in persistent approaches has been drawn rather neatly. The persistence of the Prolog database is an implementation issue which is relatively straightforward. The main reason for this is that a Prolog term is primarily symbolic. Any machine dependent parts, such as addresses and complex data structures, have an immediate syntactic representation which does not change by being placed in backing store. The main exception to this is an unbound variable. When this is asserted into the database it is 'objectified' by changing the representation of any variables that occur in the term.

Suppose we consider a pair of terms in an expression such as

```
sister(ann, X), mother(X, jan)
```

then in a computation these two are linked by the variable X, which has not yet been evaluated. If these were (independently) asserted into the database, then the link between the two variables is broken.

    sister(ann, X1).
    mother(X2, jan).

Each variable can be subsequently assigned a different value. We are, of course, free to assert this as a single term, in which case the variable will still be shared between the two terms, although any *other* links it has will be broken.

Thus an 'objectified' variable has been given, in logical terms, a universal qualification. If we want to express an existential quantifier in a Prolog system, then it is necessary to use a unique value as a 'Skolem' constant. In an object-oriented system this will normally be an object identifier.

In Chapter 3 it was shown how the notion of *object identity* was applied to the instances of an object. A unique term is used to name an object and this is of purely internal interest. It is not connected in any essential way with the external *name* of the object or with any other object.

There are two problems that arise from this term. One is that this name must be maintained across several invocations of the program and the same name should not be used for two different objects. This is primarily an implementation issue which has a number of possible solutions. In the present implementation this is guaranteed by the system if the *save* and *load* primitives are used. In using a large object-oriented database this would not be adequate as it is undesirable to load all the instances simultaneously into primary memory. Hence in this case the responsibility is left to the user to guarantee uniqueness. The main problem in extending this scheme is in dealing with a number of independently created databases.

The other problem is to do with the way the definition of an object can change. Over time it is quite normal to extend the definition of an object and this creates few problems because any old programs relating to the objects will not know about any new attributes we have introduced. But it may be desirable to discard existing attributes: at this point any program that assumes these will stop working as before. We might do both at once, and change the use of an existing attribute.

These problems are familiar in database systems, but they need to be considered again in the presence of inheritance. For example, if an attribute is deleted in a class inherited by other classes, then it may be necessary to modify all inheriting classes. Prolog++ follows the example of Orion (Kim *et al.*, 1990) in not modifying affected instances when the schema of an object is changed, but interpreting the instances in the light of the new definition. The question of schema evolution in the context of object-oriented databases is considered in some detail by Kesim (1993).

There is live interest in the database community over the mix of deductive and object-oriented databases (see Kim *et al.*, 1990) and Prolog appears to be becoming a language of choice for exploring these issues within this framework (see Embury *et al.*, 1992). But there are substantially different views about what a database formalism should provide. For example, most database systems provide an ad-hoc query language and it is disastrous if this allows extremely expensive or nonterminating computations. However it is vital to keep open this possibility in the language used for database programming. The database tradition has been to concentrate on formalisms which are complete and trouble free, whereas much of the impetus towards object-oriented databases has come from the ability to program tight code which will make a multimedia database accessible efficiently.

But object-oriented databases lack an adequate data model and the problems of handling object identity have led some critics (for example Ullman, 1991) to suggest that there can be no proper foundation. One of his criticisms is concerned precisely with the identification of every dynamic term in a logic program with an object, which thus removes any declarative base for the system.

7.4   Other OOLP systems

A number of other OOLP systems apart from Prolog++ are already being distributed and we describe some of these below. There is also a large number of experimental systems that have been used locally or have been the subject of dissertations which are not included here. A recent bibliography (Davison, 1992) lists nearly 200 references.

When reviewing these systems one needs to realize that there are three very different traditions which have given rise to object-oriented systems. The first, derived from Simula and Smalltalk, has already been discussed fully in this book. The second derives from the 'frame' notion in Artificial Intelligence (AI) (Minsky, 1975; Schank and Abelson, 1977). Since much of the development of Prolog has been conducted in AI circles, it is not surprising that this should be well represented in the object systems built in Prolog. The third tradition is the Actors paradigm developed by Hewitt.

Frame systems (exemplified by Lap) concentrate on record structures with 'slots' into which values can be plugged. Unlike other object systems they are not considered as a syntactic building block for writing programs, but as a dynamic data structure which is simply created and manipulated like any other data structure. Thus in its purest form the object system simply consists of a set of procedures which are called from Prolog to manipulate the objects, which are named by Prolog atoms and exist with their values in a database which is only accessible via these procedures.

Because of the system of operator declarations available in most forms of Prolog it is easy to provide 'syntactic sugar' so that operations such as assignment can be performed using the familiar infix operator :=, but apart from this there is little attention to providing any syntactic support. This means that there is also little or no *encapsulation* possible in these systems. Any procedure which knows the name of an object has as much access to its internals as any other.

Instead of methods which are associated with a class, the slots in a frame can have *procedural attachments*. These are usually structured as side-effects which happen before and after assignment and other operations on the slots. These therefore serve many of the same functions as the encapsulation available in other object-oriented languages: of checking, for instance, that an assignment is reasonable in the current context. In Prolog terms these attachments are simply extra conditions that are executed before and after the actual operation. If a *before* attachment fails, then the operation will not be performed.

This approach to protecting the objects has adherents because it is arguably a more flexible strategy than the encapsulation approach. If you don't like the attachments provided by someone else then it is easy to get in and change them to what is needed. However this policy leads to precisely the kind of unpredictability that advances in software engineering are trying to prevent. Different parts of a large program might 'fiddle' with shared objects in different ways, so that any coherence will rapidly break down.

The seminal work on combining Prolog with object-oriented programming (Zaniolo, 1984) derived much more closely from work in AI on 'isa' hierarchies. This represented parameterized objects with methods lists, expressed directly using Prolog operators. An example is from geometric shapes:

```
reg_poly(N,L) with
    [(perimeter(P) :- P is N*L),
        what_is_it(a_reg_polygon)].
```

Inheritance can be expressed as a specialization of the object:

```
square(L) isa reg_poly(4,L).
```

and a query is expressed using the : operator:

```
?-square(6):perimeter(X).
X = 24
```

Ancestors are produced in the order in which they are declared, thus leading to a type of 'nearest-first' search. Inheritance is overriding, with the first method found being used. *Self* communication is not supported and nor is there any consideration of mutable objects.

One approach that does address the issue of mutable objects is Conery's (1988) paper on logical objects. This is an ingenious extension of the Prolog notation to include an extra literal on each side of the Horn Clause. That on the left hand side references an existing object. On occurrence on the right hand side it is immediately suspended until it can be unified with another occurrence on the left. A definition of a 'push' operation on a stack (the object) can be represented as follows:

$$push(X) \land stack(S) <- integer(X) \land stack([X|S]).$$

Here the connectives are logical ands, to distinguish them from the clausal notation for logic, in which a comma on the left hand side stands for a disjunction (but on the right for conjunction). This specifies only a single stack: to get the effect of multiple instances of an object one might generate a unique parameter for each object.

This approach was implemented either by a meta-interpreter or compilation into Prolog clauses using the database and more recently using a parallel version of Prolog. But it has not been extended to handle other object features such as inheritance or encapsulation.

Other appoaches to mutable objects have laid more emphasis on logics other than first order. One approach (Chen and Warren, 1988) uses intentional logic. This views logical variables essentially as functions of time so that one considers the entire history of an object. A second approach uses linear logic. Another (Sergot and Kesim, 1991) uses the event calculus. Another uses category theory based on temporal logic (Fiadeiro and Maibaum, 1992).

So far, these theoretical approaches have not made any practical contribution to the programming of objects, so we will turn to the systems that have received some use around the world.

7.4.1   Lap

Lap is an object-oriented system system from the French company ELSA. It was conceived by Philippe Roussel, who was part of the original team at Marseille who wrote the first Prolog system in the early 1970s. It has a very comprehensive set of object-oriented features and is distinguished by the dynamic approach it takes to object creation. Unlike Prolog++ there are no textual object entities, only procedure calls to Lap procedures to create and manipulate objects. Once this has been done, messages can be passed between objects in the standard way and the value of slots can be queried and changed.

There are two basic kinds of object in the Lap system, **models** and **instances**. Models correspond to classes in most object-oriented languages in that they express the inheritance and other structure of a number of similar objects, and each instance is based on a model. Every object is characterized by a set of **slots**, which are names to which values can be assigned for an instance of that object.

For example,

```
?- new_model(vehicle, []),
      new_model(truck, [parents: = vehicle]).
```

Two classes are now created: truck inherits properties from vehicle.

```
?- new_slot(fuel_level, [], vehicle, []),
      new_slot(total_weight, [], truck, []).
```

This sets up attributes for the models which have previously been created, without any default values (the extra parameters).

```
?-new_method(add_fuel, [], truck,
      [body: = with(TRUCK, [QTY], []) activate
          (TRUCK..fuel_level = FLEVEL,
          NEW_LEVEL is FLEVEL + QTY,
          TRUCK..fuel_level : = NEW_LEVEL)]).
?- new_instance(truck1, truck, [total_weight: = 22000]).
```

These two calls set up methods for a class and an instance of the class. We will not explain this in detail – hopefully the calls above give the flavour of the implementation. The utility of the procedures provided is undoubted. It is possible to set up complex objects, including multiple inheritance, multiple value slots, and semantic links between objects. By specifying a purely procedural link between the logical and object domains, freedom is left to the implementer to optimize the representation of the objects in many ways.

Lap has an extensive library of graphical facilities, including facilities for displaying objects graphically. In addition, later versions of Lap have a somewhat more friendly syntax.

But it would certainly appear that the main intention of the designers was to provide specific capabilities for dynamic behaviour within Prolog including simulation and graphical displays. Lap is based on the AI-derived Frame model and thus has no capabilities for encapsulation or for the declarative description of objects.

7.4.2 Emicat

Emicat was originally designed by Dessault Electronic for the French Atomic Agency, but is distributed by Delphia as part of the Delphia Prolog system, available on Unix systems and mainframes.

7.4.3 Esp and Mandala

Extended Self-contained Prolog (Esp) was probably the first fully functioning OOLP system. Developed at the ICOT, the Institute for New Generation Computer Technology in Japan, it was designed for use on the Personal Sequential Inference machine (PSI) under the SIMPOS system. However a variant called CESP (Common ESP) is now available that runs on most Unix systems.

Esp includes class definitions which define attributes (or slots) and methods and the possibility of local predicates. In Esp the object instance is represented as the first parameter of a predicate, which is anomalous if there is no significant 'state' in the object. Inheritance is defined by 'before', local and 'after' components, which allows maximum flexibility but is somewhat inefficient, as no shortcuts are possible. Before and after 'demons' are also supported, which can prevent the execution of a method.

Though it supports some concurrent activities, Esp is basically a sequential language. Mandala (Furukawa *et al.*, 1984; Ohki *et al.*, 1988) is designed for parallel machines and uses the language KL1 (Knowledge Language 1) which is based on the concurrent logic programming language GHC (Guarded Horn Clauses). KL1 (and hence Mandala) is therefore more in the style of Step and Parlog + +, though it derives partly from the work on Vulcan (Kahn *et al.*, 1986). It is based on the process model of concurrent objects modelled by recursive procedures, supporting inheritance and 'part of' hierarchies, instance variables and methods.

7.4.4 L&O (Logic and Objects)

This system is described in McCabe (1992) and is based on a concept called 'class templates'. These are classes which are parameterized when they are called enabling a declarative approach to generic descriptions of objects. For example, a set of trains having speed S, colour Cl and country Co are described by:

```
train(S, Cl, Co) :{
    colour(Cl).
    speed(S).
    country(Co).
    journey_time(Distance, T) :-
        T is Distance/S.
    }
```

Variables in the class label are available in any of the clauses described in the body of the class. One may then make a query by using both an instantiated form of the term naming the object, and the predicate described. For example,

```
?-train(120,green,britain):journey_time(200,X)
```

At this point the class parameters may be considered simply as another way of passing parameters to the enclosed predicate, but these parameters may also be shared internally, giving a rather more natural programming style.

Inheritance is supported by both inclusive inheritance, which is written bird <= animal. and by overriding inheritance, in which only predicates not defined locally may be inherited, written bird « animal.

L&O's approach to a changing object is to have an object return a new label with changed parameters. It subscribes to the value theory of identity: an object is defined by the value of its attributes; hence any two objects of the same class having the same attributes at some point in their evolution cannot be distinguished. Though this does not tally with the normal object-oriented concept of identity, it is of course always possible to give each object a unique identifier to distinguish it.

7.4.5 Life

Life is a multifaceted language (the name stands for Logic, Inheritance, Functions, Equations) developed by Hassan Aït-Kaci, whose aim is to integrate logic, functional, object and constraint methodologies. The most characteristic feature of Life is the ψ-term, which consists of a set of attribute value pairs, which may be nested to any depth. For example,

```
X: person(name => id(first => string, last => S:string),
     spouse => person(name => id(last => S),
        spouse => X)).
```

The attributes such as name and spouse apply to the type person. Their values appear after the symbol ⇒. Prolog-type variables can also be used to express facts, such as the shared last name S of the spouse and the fact that a person's spouse's spouse, X, is the person themself (a circular term). These ψ-terms can be unified in a similar fashion to those in unification grammars (see Pereira and Shieber, 1987). If two similar-named terms have different attributes then the terms will unify, but any shared attributes must unify themselves.

```
a(b => c, d => e)     unifies with
a(d => e(f => g))     to give
   a(b => c, d => e(f => g))
```

As this indicates, any atomic symbol in Life is actually an object which can have attributes. The attributes can be used as tagged parameters to a procedure if desired. Any ψ-term can denote a functional application if its root symbol is defined as a function.

Inheritance is based on a lattice of types specified with the operator <|. For example,

```
student <| person.
```

The inheritance algorithm allows unification of terms, including the unification of greatest lower bounds. For example, given, in addition,

staff <| person. workstudy <| staff.

then a student object could unify with a staff object, provided their arguments unify.

Assignment is supported in Life, including assignment to terms, though no semantics is as yet forthcoming, though this issue is addressed by Zaniolo (1990). Encapsulation is not supported. For such a wide-ranging language this is no great fault, as it is clearly necessary to establish the small-scale viability of such an approach before making provision for the large scale.

Life is also a constraint language. In Prolog, certain operations are invalid. For example, if one encounters the statement: X is Y*Z and the values of Y and Z are not currently instantiated to numbers, then Prolog will produce a run-time error. A constraint language would rather record the fact that the only values that can be assigned to X, Y and Z are those that satisfy X=Y*Z and continue. Life has this constraint property. Under-specified operations will be delayed until they can be completed. Though this inevitably makes the evaluation process more complex, it can also lead to huge performance increases, given the right constraint satisfaction algorithms. This is currently one of the most active and promising areas of logic programming development.

A language like Life is clearly at the edges of the definition of object-oriented programming languages, but it deserves consideration. In logic programming, the (Herbrand) universe is composed of flat and featureless symbols. Objects have both structure and behaviour and their formal status is currently in question. Experiments such as Life may resolve these questions.

7.5   Where next?

Logic programming and object-oriented programming are two very different approaches to programming. But it is not difficult to put together a language which uses both. As the previous section has shown, there is no shortage of candidates. What is much more difficult is to show how the two paradigms fit together. That is what much of this book has been trying to achieve.

One approach is to take what fits easily and discard the rest. Coming from the logic programming paradigm, one can easily add inheritance and avoid the complications of changing objects. Approaching it from the object side one can implement simple rule bases and ignore the use of Prolog for anything procedural or algorithmic. Both of these approaches have been tried.

A more pragmatic approach is to consider the use of objects for window interfaces and similar components and build a set of dynamic primitives which support the type of operations needed to build these objects. This is seen in the use of frame-like systems. What is provided is a set of slots combined with inheritance. There is no real attempt here to use the modularity aspects of objects to build a large system.

These approaches are less than satisfactory. They consider approaches to programming as simply a set of techniques from which one draws the best mix: all tactics but no strategy. They ignore the fact that both approaches have identifiable weaknesses. For logic programming, the weakness is its difficulty in scaling up to large systems. It provides a very direct method of representing the knowledge about a particular domain and provides a solid foundation on which to build bigger systems. But it works best on the small scale and is no better than imperative techniques when considering reusability.

For object-oriented programming it is as if the lessons of the last 15 years had not been learned. The difficulties of developing, debugging and maintaining object-oriented code are no less than any other procedural language at the basic level. It is only when a sufficient amount of code has been accumulated that the additional benefits of reusability become significant. It doesn't have many of the advantages of symbolic code, such as the source language tools and clear semantic theory. Indeed there are still discussions and disagreements about what actually object-oriented programming is.

One of the ongoing debates in the object-oriented world is over 'hybrid' and 'pure' object-oriented languages. This might be between the merits of Objective-C and C++, or Object Pascal compared with Smalltalk or Eiffel. One thing that is obvious to the observer is that the pure languages have often repeated the mistakes of the earlier high-level languages, either at the level of language design or compiler implementation. There do seem to be distinct levels involved and a strong argument for hybrid products, at least until the issues have beeen clarified at the different levels.

One issue that clearly has *not* been settled for object-oriented logic programming languages is how to handle change. In this book we have handled it in a very pragmatic fashion and have not investigated the work currently going on in research laboratories about 'logics of change' such as some intensional and modal approaches. The reason is that whatever the results that have been achieved, they are not yet at the point at which they can be applied to practical systems. Indeed they may never reach this stage. Hence they don't yet benefit the programmer, except in the area of concurrent programs, where they do show significant benefits.

Prolog++ is an evolving language, and its implementation – written in Prolog and compiling dynamically into Prolog – means that it can react quickly both to user requirements and to advances in methodology. Though it is impossible to predict, future versions will probably show increased support for graphical user interfaces and object-oriented databases as well as more debugging tools geared specifically to Prolog++. It will probably also spread to other platforms on workstations and mainframes. There is considerable interest in extending the ISO Prolog Standard in an object-oriented direction, and this would affect its appearance also.

APPENDIX A
Prolog++ syntax and methods

The syntax is presented top-down using a modified form of BNF which is close to the conventions for DCGs, the normal Prolog grammar formalism. The only unusual feature is the use of parameterized productions such as sequence(p) which are defined using variables. These are given at the start.

Nonterminal symbols are single words starting with a lower case letter. Terminal symbols are enclosed in quotes. Variables start with upper case.

The following symbols may be read as:

→	produces
|	or
.	ends the production
%	comment to the end of the line

Parameterized productions are:

[X]	→	X | .	% optional
{ X }	→	X { X }| .	% repeated 0 or more times
sequence(X)	→	X | ',' sequence(X) .	% values separated by commas

The following symbols are not defined, and follow the standard Prolog definition: atom, name (=atom), variable, integer, number, prolog_term (that is, any Prolog simple or compound term).

% Class definitions

class_definition	→	class_begin sentences class_end.
class_begin	→	'class' name '.'.
class_end	→	'end' name '.'.

279

sentences	→	sentence '.' sentences	
	|	sentence '.' .	
sentence	→	declaration	
	|	definition.	

% Declarations

declaration	→	category sequence(name)	% class belongs to
			% category
	|	inherits sequence(name)	% inherits from classes
	|	part sequence(part_specification)	
	|	[visible] [object] attribute sequence(initializer)	
			% defaults are private and
			% instance
	|	[visible] sequence(method).	% default is public

category	→	'category' | 'categories'.

inherits	→	'inherit' | 'inherits'.

part	→	'part' | 'parts'.

attribute	→	'attribute' | 'attributes'.

visible	→	'public' | 'private'.

object	→	'instance' | 'class'.

part_specification	→	name ['*' term].	% term gives number

method	→	name '/' integer	% methods
	|	name '//' integer.	% functions

initializer	→	name	
	|	name '=' term	
	|	name 'is' term	% equivalent to = +(term)
	|	name 'inherited'.	

% Definitions

definition	→	procedure_head [':-' statements]
	|	function_head [':-' statements] .

procedure_head	→	message_handler
	|	constraint_handler
	|	error_handler
	|	event_handler.

message_handler   →   name ['(' sequence(prolog_term)')'].

function_head   →   message_handler 'is' expression
                   | message_handler '=' term.

constraint_handler →   'invalid' '(' name, prolog_term')'.   % attribute, value

error_handler   →   'when_error' '(' prolog_term, prolog_term ')'.
                                                              % error, message

event_handler   →   'when_assigned' '(' name, prolog_term, prolog_term')'
                                                       % attribute, before, after
                   | 'when_created'
                   | 'when_deleted'.

% Statements

statements   →   statement
                   | statements ',' statements   % ambiguity handled by
                   | statements ';' statements   % operator declarations
                   | statements '−>' statements
                   | 'forall' statement 'do' statement
                   | 'while' statement 'do' statement
                   | 'repeat' statement 'until' statement
                   | '\+' statement
                   | 'not' statement
                   | variable   % instantiated at run-time
                   | set '(' prolog_term ',' statement ',' variable ')'
                   | term '' statement.

statement   →   send_message
                   | attribute_assignment
                   | control
                   | '(' statements ')'.

set   →   'setof' | 'bagof' | 'findall'.

send_message   →   [receivers '<−'] messages.

receivers   →   term | '(', sequence(term) ')'.

messages   →   message | '(', sequence(message) ')'.

message   →   name ['(' sequence(term) ')'] | variable.

assignment   →   term noisy_assign expression
                   | term quiet_assign expression.

noisy_assign	→	':=' | '+=' | '−=' | '*=' | '/='.	% invokes when_assign
quiet_assign	→	':==' | '+==' | '−=' | '*==' | '/=='.	% doesn't
control	→	'!' | 'true' | 'fail' | 'repeat'.	% same as Prolog

% Expressions

expression	→	term.	
term	→	variable	
	|	+ term	% evaluate as arithmetic
			% expression
	|	'&' prolog_term	% take as literal
	|	'all' term	% all instantiations of term
	|	term 'suchthat' statement	% class such that some
			% statement holds
	|	[term] '@' term	% functional message
	|	'self'	
	|	'super'	
	|	isa_link	
	|	partof_link	
	|	term binary_op term	
	|	unary_op term	
	|	'(' term ';' term ')'	% alternate terms
	|	'[' [argument [list_tail]]']'	% also can be open
	|	atom	
	|	number	
	|	name '(' sequence(term) ')'.	
list_tail	→	',' term list_tail	
	|	',' term	
	|	'|' term.	
isa_link	→	'category' [term]	% all classes in category
			% named
	|	'super_class' [term]	% the super class of a class
	|	'sub_class' [term]	% subclass of a class
	|	'ancestor_class' [term]	% ancestor of a class
	|	'descendant_class' [term]	% descendant of a class
	|	'instance' [term]	% an instance of a class
	|	'class' [term] .	% instance's class name
partof_link	→	'composite' [term]	% root of current part
	|	'super_part' [term]	% immediate instance
			% above

	'sub_part' [term]	% any instance directly
		% below
	[term] '#' number	% a specific subpart

binary_op   →   '+' | '−' | '*' | '/' | '//'
            | '/\' | '\/' | '≫' | '≪'.

unary_op   →   '−'.

A.1   Prolog++ operator declarations

```
% class declarations
op(1010, fx, [category, categories, inherit, inherits, part, parts,
     attribute, attributes, method, methods])
op(1010, xfx, [attribute, attributes, method, methods])

% visibility
op(990, fx, [public, private, inherited])
op(980, xf, [inherited])

% execution control
op(970, fx, [forall, while, repeat])
op(960, xfx, [do, until] )

% procedural messages
op(950, xfx, ( <− ))

% assignment operators
op(700, xfx, [ :=, +=, −=, *=, /= ])
op(700, xfx, [ :==, +==, −==, *==, /== ])

% context switching
op(650, fy, [ &, + ])

% all instances of a term
op(600, fy, all)
op(600, xfx, suchthat)

% is-a links
op(100, fy, [category, class, instance, super_class, sub_class,
     ancestor, descendant])

% part-of links
op(100, yfx, # )

% mnemonic instance name
op(50, fx, $)
```

% attribute lookup
op(50, fy, @)
op(50, yfx, @)

A.2   Prolog++ basic methods

compile(C,SL)	create a new class with name C and definition list of sentences SL
create(N)	create a new instance of this class, with name N
create(N,AL)	create a new instance and perform the assignments in the list AL
create(N,AL,ID)	create a new instance with mnemonic name ID and assignments AL
delete	delete this instance
delete_all	delete all instances of this class
dump(File)	dump all instances of this class into File
dump(File,CL)	dump all instances of classes in list CL into File
duplicate(N)	create a new instance N of this class with the same attributes as current object
isa_class	checks whether this is a class (not an instance)
isa_instance	checks whether this is an instance (not a class)
kill	remove the definition of a class
load(F)	read class definitions from file F
optimize	optimize the definition of this class
reset	deletes all attributes and dynamic facts for this object
reset(A)	remove current value of attribute A
restore(File)	restore instances from named file into which they were previously dumped
save(F)	write the definition of this class into file F

APPENDIX B
German verb example

B.1 The main verb class

class verb.

attribute roots, auxiliary.
% verb <— conjugate(voice, tense, person, mood, list of words)
% verb = (the infinitive)
% voice = active, passive
% tense = present, past, perfect, future, pluperfect, futurePerfect
% person = s1, s2, s3, p1, p2, p3
% mood = indicative, subjunctive
% words = a list of all the resultant words
% e.g. machen <— conjugate(active, present, s3, indicative, [hat, gemacht])

```
conjugate(active, present, P, M, [V]) :-
    present(P, M, V).
conjugate(active, past, P, M, [V]) :-
    past(P, M, V).
conjugate(active, perfect, P, M, [A, V]) :-
    on (S, @auxiliary),
    S <— present(P, M, A),
    pastParticiple(V).
conjugate(active, pluperfect, P, M, [A, V]) :-
    on (S, @auxiliary),
    S <— past(P, M, A),
    pastParticiple(V).
conjugate(active, future, P, M, [A, V]) :-
    werden <—present(P, M, A),
    infinitive(V).
```

```
conjugate(active, futurePerfect, P, M, [A, V, S]) :-
    werden <- present(P, M, A),
    pastParticiple(V),
    on (S, @auxiliary).

conjugate(passive, present, P, M, [A, V]) :-
    werden <- present(P, M, A),
    pastParticiple(V).
conjugate(passive, past, P, M, [A, V]) :-
    werden <- past(P, M, A),
    pastParticiple(V).
conjugate(passive, perfect, P, M, [A, V, worden]) :-
    sein <- present(P, M, A),
    pastParticiple(V).
conjugate(passive, pluperfect, P, M, [A, V, worden]) :-
    sein <- past(P, M, A),
    pastParticiple(V).
conjugate(passive, future, P, M, [A, V, werden]) :-
    werden <- present(P, M, A),
    pastParticiple(V).
conjugate(passive, futurePerfect, P, M, [A, V, worden, sein]) :-
    werden <- past(P, M, A),
    pastParticiple(V).

root(R) :-
    @roots = [R|_].

end verb.
```

B.2   Verb endings

class endings.

```
presentEnding(P, indicative, E) :-
    person(P,[e, st, t, en, t, en], E).
presentEnding(P, subjunctive, E) :-
    person(P,[e, est, e, en, t, en], E).

pastEnding(P, indicative, E) :-
    person(P,[te, test, te, ten, tet, ten], E).
pastEnding(P, subjunctive, E) :-
    person(P,[te, test, te, ten, tet, ten], E).

%person picks out the appropriate item from a list
person(s1,[P|_], P).
```

```
person(s2, [_,P|_], P).
person(s3, [_,_,P|_], P).
person(p1, [_,_,_,P|_], P).
person(p2, [_,_,_,_,P|_], P).
person(p3, [_,_,_,_,_,P], P).


%join = concat, but if stem ends in d or t, or some others, may add e
%   (concat is built-in in MacProlog)
join(Stem, e, Word) :-
    concat(S, el, Stem), !,
    concat(S, le, Word).
join(Stem, Ending, Word) :-
    name(Stem, S),
    checkEnd(S, Ending, End),
    name(End, E),
    append(S, E, W),
    name(Word, W).


checkEnd(Stem, T, ET) :-       %add an e to the ending if justified
    hardEnd(T, ET),
    append(_, [K,M], Stem),
    hard([K,M]), !.
checkEnd(Stem, st, t) :-
    append(_, [S], Stem),
    isS([S]), !.
checkEnd(Stem, en, n) :-
    append(_, "el", Stem), !.
checkEnd(Stem, en, n) :-
    append(_, "er", Stem), !.
checkEnd(_, T, T).


hard("dn").     %dn
hard("hn").     %hn
hard("kn").     %kn
hard("tm").     %tm
hard([_|C]) :- C="d".     %_d
hard([_|C]) :- C="t".     %_t


hardEnd(st, est).
hardEnd(t, et).
hardEnd(te, ete).
hardEnd(test, etest).
hardEnd(ten, eten).
hardEnd(tet, etet).


isS("β").
isS("s").


end endings.
```

B.3   Types of verbs

class weak.

inherits verb, endings.
attribute infinitive, auxiliary.

when created :-
    writeseqnl([self, infinitive, @infinitive, auxiliary, @auxiliary]).

present(P, M, V) :-
    root(R),
    presentEnding(P, M, E) :-
    join(R, E, V).
past(P, M, V) :-
    root(R),
    pastEnding(P, M, E),
    join(R, E, V).

pastParticiple(P) :-
    root(R),
    concat(ge, R, Stem),
    join(Stem, t, P).

end weak.

class strong.

inherits verb, endings.
attribute infinitive, roots, auxiliary.

when created :-
    writeseqnl([self, infinitive, @infinitive, roots, @roots, auxiliary,
        @auxiliary]).

present(P, indicative, W) :-
    person(P, [e, st, t, en, t, en], End),
    join(@presentStem(P), End, W).
present(P, subjunctive, W) :-
    person(P, [e, est, e, en, et, en], End),
    join(@root, End, W).

past(P, indicative, W) :-
    person(P, [", st, ", en, t, en], End),
    join(@pastStem, End, W).
past(P, subjunctive, W) :-
    psubEnd(P, End),
    join(@subjStem, End, W).

```
pastParticiple(P) :-
    @roots = [_,_,_,_, P|_].

presentStem(P, Pres) :-
    (P=s2 ; P=s3), !,      %2nd & 3rd person sing. are different
    @roots = [_, Pres|_].
presentStem(_, Pres) :-
    @roots = [Pres|_].

pastStem(R) :-
    @roots = [_,_,R|_].

subjStem(R) :-
    @roots = [_,_,_,R|_].

psubEnd(P, End) :-
    person(P, [e, st, e, en, t, en], End),
psubEnd(s2, est).          %extra possibilities for 2nd person
psubEnd(p2, et).

end strong.


class modal.

inherits verb, endings.
attribute infinitive, roots.

present(P, indicative, W) :-
    singleEnding(P, E), !,
    @roots = [_, Pres|_].
    concat(Pres, E, W).
present(P, indicative, W) :-
    plural(P), !,
    root(R),
    join(R, E, W).
present(P, subjunctive, V) :-
    root(R),
    presentEnding(P, subjunctive, E),
    join(R, E, V).
past(P, M, V) :-
    root(R),
    pastEnding(P, M, E),
    join(R, E, V).

pastParticiple(P) :-
    @roots = [_,_,_,_, P|_].

singleEnding(s1, ").
singleEnding(s2, st).
singleEnding(s3, ").
```

```
plural(p1).
plural(p2).
plural(p3).

end modal.
```

%the auxiliary verbs are spelled out partly for efficiency,
%partly to demonstrate an alternative approach

class haben.

inherits verb, endings.

```
infinitive(haben).
auxiliary(haben).
pastParticipate(gehabt).

present(P, indicative, W) :-
    person(P, [habe, hast, hat, haben, habt, haben], W).
present(P, subjunctive, W) :-
    person(P, [habe, habest, habe, haben, habet, haben], W).

past(P, indicative, W) :-
    person(P, [hatte, hattest, hatte, hatten, hattet, hatten], W).
past(P, subjunctive, W) :-
    person(P, ['hätte', 'hättest', 'hätte', 'hätten', 'hättet', 'hätten'], W).

end haben.
```

class sein.

inherits verb, endings.

```
infinitive(sein).
auxiliary(sein).
pastParticiple(gewesen).

present(P, indicative, W) :-
    person(P, [bin, bist, ist, sind, seid, sind], W).
present(P, subjunctive, W) :-
    person(P, [sei, seist, sei, seien, seiet, seien], W).
past(P, indicative, W) :-
    person(P, [war, warst, war, waren, wart, waren], W).
past(P, subjunctive, W) :-
    person(P, ['wäre', 'wärst', 'wäre', 'wären', 'wäret', 'wären'], W).

end sein.
```

class werden.

inherits verb, endings

infinitive(werden).
auxiliary(sein).
pastParticiple(geworden).

present(P, indicative, W) :-
    person(P, [werde, wirst, wird, werden, werdet, werden], W).
present(P, subjunctive, W) :-
    person(P, [werde, werdest, werde, werden, werdet, werden], W).

past(P, indicative, W) :-
    person(P, [wurde, wurdest, wurde, wurden, wurdet, wurden], W).
past(P, subjunctive, W) :-
    person(P, ['würde', 'würdest', 'würde', 'würden', 'würdet', 'würden'], W).

end werden.

B.4   Verb dispatcher

class dispatch.

%The conjugate method drives the whole program. It finds the appropriate
%class and creates an instance of it, and forms the root forms once only

conjugate(Verb, Voice, Tense, Person, Mood, String) :-
    getInstance(Verb, Instance),
    Instance <— conjugate(Voice, Tense, Person, Mood, String).

getInstance(haben, haben) :- !.
getInstance(sein, sein) :- !.
getInstance(werden, werden) :- !.
getInstance(Verb, Instance) :-   %have we already created it?
    instance descendant_class verb = Instance,
    Instance <—infinitive(Verb),
    !.
getInstance(Verb, Instance) :-   %no, so make one now
    verbType(Verb, Type, Roots),
    root(Verb, R),
    aux(Verb, Aux),
    Type <— create(Instance, [infinitive = Verb, auxiliary=Aux,
        roots=[R|Roots]]).

verbType(V, strong, [Pres, Past, PastS, PP]) :-
    strongVerb(V, Pres, Past, PastS, PP), !.
verbType(V, strong, Roots) :-
    strongVerbType(V, N), !,
    makeRoots(V, N, Roots).

```prolog
verbType(V, irregular, [Pres, Past, PastS, PP]) :-
    irregularVerb(V, Pres, Past, PastS, PP), !.
verbType(V, modal, [Pres, Past, PastS, PP]) :-
    modalVerb(V, Pres, Past, PastS, PP), !.
verbType(V, weak, []) :-
    root(V, R).

root(X, R) :-
    name(X, String),
    (append(Root, "en", String), ! ; append(Root, "n", String)),
    name(R, Root).

makeRoots(Verb, Num, [Pres, Past, Subj, PP]) :-
    strVowel(Num, V, PresV, PastV, SubjV, PPV),
    root(Verb, Root),
    changeVowel(Root, PresV, Pres),
    changeVowel(Root, PastV, Past),
    changeVowel(Root, SubjV, Subj),
    changeVowel(Root, PPV, PP).

formPP(Verb, N, P) :-
    strVowel(N,_,_,_,_,V),
    changeVowel(Verb, V, Part),
    concat(ge, Part, P).

%vowels for regular classes of strong verbs
%strVowel(group, inf, present, past, pastSubj, pp)
strVowel(1, a, 'ä', ie, ie, a).
strVowel(2, a, 'ä', u, 'ü', a).
strVowel(3, e, i, a, a, o).
strVowel(4, ei, ei, ie, ie, ie).
strVowel(5, i, i, a, 'ä', u).
strVowel(6, ie, ie, o, 'ö', o).
strVowel(7, e, e, o, ö, o).
strVowel(8, e, ie, a, 'ä', e).
strVowel(9, e, i, a, 'ü', o).
strVowel(10, ei, ei, i, i, i).

changeVowel(Inf, Vowel, Stem) :-        %by changing first vowel group
    name(Inf, A),
    name(Vowel, V),
    replaceVowel(A, V, S),
    name(Stem, S).

replaceVowel([L|Ls], New, Stem) :-       %as strings of characters
    vowel([L]), !,
    stripVowel(Ls, L1),
    append(New, L1, Stem).
replaceVowel([L|Ls], New, [L|Ss]) :-
    replaceVowel(Ls, New, Ss).
```

```
stripVowel([L|Ls], Ls) :-
    vowel([L]), !.
stripVowel(L, L).

vowel("a"). vowel("e"). vowel("i").      %a,e,i enough here
    %A verb can take either sein or haben

aux(Verb, [sein]) :-
    seinVerb(Verb), !.
aux(Verb, [sein, haben]) :-
    seinOrHabenVerb(Verb), !.
aux(Verb, [haben]).

end dispatch.
```

B.5   The windowing interface

class verbWindow.

```
inherits window.
part tryButton, cancelButton, personGroup, tenseGroup, voiceGroup,
    moodGroup, editBox, listBox.
attribute position = (78, 72), size = (356,198), title = 'Please select the
    right option'.

when_created :-
    editBox # 1 <- setValues([position = (10,130), size = (322,16)]),
    listBox # 1 <- setValues([position = (170,50), size = (124,68),
        text = [bringen, fallen, finden, gehen, haben, helfen,
        kennen, machen, 'müssen', reden, rufen, schreiben, sein,
        tragen, wechseln, werden], selected = [finden]]).
try :-
    personGroup # 1 <- on(Person),
    tenseGroup # 1 <- on(Tense),
    voiceGroup # 1 <- on(Voice),
    moodGroup # 1 <- on(Mood),
    listBox # 1 <- on(Inf),
    conjugate(Voice, Verb, Tense, Person, Mood, String),
    editBox # 1 <- set(text, String).

end verbWindow.
```

class tryButton.

```
inherits button.
attributes position = (60,160), size = (60,20), text = 'Try'.
activate :-
    super_part <- try.
end tryButton.
```

class cancelButton.

inherits button.
attributes position = (230,160), size = (60,20), text = 'Try'.
activate :-
    super_part <− close.
end cancelButton.

class personGroup.

inherits radioGroup.
parts radioButton∗6.
attributes position = (5,5), size = (45,120), height = 16,
    texts = [ich, du, er, wir, ihr, sie], on = er.
end personGroup.

class tenseGroup.

inherits radioGroup.
parts radioButton∗6.
attributes position = (50,5), size = (120,120), height = 16,
    texts = ['Present', 'Past', 'Future', 'Perfect', off,
    'Pluperfect', 'Future Perfect'], on = 'Present'.
end tenseGroup.

class voiceGroup.

inherits radioGroup.
parts radioButton∗2.
attributes position = (170,5), size = (70,120), height = 16,
    texts = ['Active', 'Passive'], on = 'Active'.
end voiceGroup.

class moodGroup.

inherits radioGroup.
parts radioButton∗2.
attributes position = (240,5), size = (100,120), height = 16,
    texts = ['Indicative', 'Subjunctive'], on = 'Indicative'.
end moodGroup.

B.6   Some representative verb tables

%strongVerb(infinitive, present, past, pastsubj, pastParticiple)
%only root is given for tenses
strongVerb(befehlen, befiehl, befahl, 'befähl', befohlen).
strongVerb(beginnen, beginn, begann, 'begänn', begonnen).
strongVerb('beißen', 'beiß', 'biß', biss, gebissen).

strongVerb(bitten, bittet, bat, 'bät', gebeten).
strongVerb(empfehlen, empfiehl, empfahl, 'empfähl', empfohlen).
strongVerb(essen, 'ißt', 'aß', 'äß', gegessen).
strongVerb(fallen, 'fäll', fiel, fiel, gefallen).
strongVerb(fangen, 'fäng', fing, fing, gefangen).
strongVerb(fechten, fich, focht, 'föcht', gefochten).
strongVerb(fressen, 'friß', 'fraß', 'fräß', gefressen).

%Strong verbs with some regularity

strongVerbType(blasen, 1).
strongVerbType(halten, 1).
strongVerbType(raten, 1).
strongVerbType(schlafen, 1).
strongVerbType(fahren, 2).
strongVerbType(graben, 2).
strongVerbType(laden, 2).
strongVerbType(schlagen, 2).
strongVerbType(tragen, 2).
strongVerbType(wachsen, 2).
strongVerbType(waschen, 2).
strongVerbType(bersten, 3).
strongVerbType(brechen, 3).
strongVerbType(gelten, 3).
strongVerbType(helfen, 3).
strongVerbType(treten, 3).
strongVerbType(sprechen, 3).
strongVerbType(bleiben, 4).
strongVerbType('heißen', 4).
strongVerbType(leihen, 4).
strongVerbType(meiden, 4).
strongVerbType(reiben, 4).
strongVerbType(scheiden, 4).
strongVerbType(scheinen, 4).
strongVerbType(schreiben, 4).
strongVerbType(schreien, 4).
strongVerbType(schweigen, 4).
strongVerbType(treiben, 4).
strongVerbType(weisen, 4).
strongVerbType(zeihen, 4).
strongVerbType(dringen, 5).

strongVerbType(finden, 5).
strongVerbType(klingen, 5).
strongVerbType(schwinden, 5).
strongVerbType(springen, 5).
strongVerbType(singen, 5).
strongVerbType(sinken, 5).
strongVerbType(trinken, 5).
strongVerbType(winden, 5).
strongVerbType(zwingen, 5).
strongVerbType(biegen, 6).
strongVerbType(bieten, 6).
strongVerbType(fliegen, 6).
strongVerbType(fliehen, 6).
strongVerbType('fließen', 6).
strongVerbType(kriechen, 6).
strongVerbType(riechen, 6).
strongVerbType(schieben, 6).
strongVerbType(wiegen, 6).
strongVerbType(heben, 7).
strongVerbType(pflegen, 7).
strongVerbType(melken, 7).
strongVerbType(lesen, 8).
strongVerbType(stehlen, 8).
strongVerbType(sehen, 8).
strongVerbType(sterben, 9).
strongVerbType(werben, 9).
strongVerbType(werfen, 9).
strongVerbType(gleichen, 10).
strongVerbType(reiten, 10).
strongVerbType(schleichen, 10).
strongVerbType(gewinnen, 11).

modalVerb('dürfen', darf, durf, 'dürf', gedurft).
modalVerb('können', kann, konn, 'könn', gekonnt).
modalVerb('mögen', mag, moch, 'möch', gemocht).
modalVerb('müssen', 'muß', 'muß', 'müß', 'gemußt').
modalVerb(sollen, soll, soll, soll, gesollt).
modalVerb(wissen, 'weiß', 'wuß', 'wüß', 'gewußt').
modalVerb(wollen, will, woll, woll, gewollt).

seinVerb(bleiben).
seinVerb(fallen).
seinVerb('fließen').
seinVerb(gehen).
seinVerb(gelingen).
seinVerb(geschehen).
seinVerb(gleiten).
seinVerb(kommen).
seinVerb(kriechen).
seinVerb(laufen).
seinVerb('löschen').
seinVerb('mißlingen').
seinVerb(rennen).
seinVerb(schleichen).
seinVerb(schmelzen).
seinVerb(schrecken).
seinVerb(schreiten).
seinVerb(schwinden).
seinVerb(sein).
seinVerb(sinken).
seinVerb(springen).
seinVerb(steigen).
seinVerb(sterben).
seinVerb(wachsen).
seinVerb(weichen).
seinVerb(werden).

seinOrHabenVerb(biegen).
seinOrHabenVerb(brechen).
seinOrHabenVerb(dringen).
seinOrHabenVerb(fahrenfliegen).
seinOrHabenVerb(fliehen).
seinOrHabenVerb(liegen).
seinOrHabenVerb('reißen').
seinOrHabenVerb(reiten).
seinOrHabenVerb(schneiden).
seinOrHabenVerb('schießen').
seinOrHabenVerb(schwimmen).
seinOrHabenVerb(sizten).
seinOrHabenVerb(stehen).
seinOrHabenVerb('stoßen').
seinOrHabenVerb(streichen).
seinOrHabenVerb(treiben).
seinOrHabenVerb(treten).
seinOrHabenVerb(verderben).
seinOrHabenVerb(ziehen).

APPENDIX C
The eight queens problem

Below are the Prolog and Prolog++ versions of the eight queens problem introduced in Chapter 4.

C.1 Prolog version

To make comparison easier, here is the same algorithm as that used in the chapter, generalized to N queens, coded in Prolog and using backtracking.

```
queens(N,Rows) :-
    makeList(1,N,Cols),
    place(Cols, [], [], N, Rows).

place([], _, _, _, []).
place([C|(Cols], Col, Row, N, [R|(Rows]) :-
    getRow(R,N),
    \+ canAttack(Col, Row, C, R),
    place(Cols, [C|Col], [R|Row], N, Rows).

canAttack(_, [Row|_], _,Row) :- !.
canAttack([Col|(Cols], [Row|Rows], C, R) :-
    CD is Col−C,
    (R is Row+CD ; R is Row−CD), !.
canAttack([_|Cols], [_|Rows], C, R) :-
    canAttack(Cols, Rows, C, R).

getRow(X,N) :- upto(1,8,X).

upto(N,U,N) :- N =< U.
upto(L,U,X) :- L < U, N is L+1, upto(N,U,X).
```

```
makeList(L,U,[L|List]) :-
    L = <U, N is L+1, makeList(N,U,List).
makeList(L,U,[]) :- L>U.

writeSolution ([] , []) .
writeSolution([C|Cols], [R|Rows]) :-
    writeseqnl(['Row ',R,'Column ', C]),
    writeSolution(Cols,Rows).
```

C.2   Prolog++ version

```
class queen.
attribute row, column, neighbour.
class attribute max.
```

```
% call to initiate N linked objects, returning last one
initial(N, LastQueen) :-
    nullQueen <- create(Null),
    initial(1, N, Null, LastQueen),
    max := N.
```

```
initial(N, Max, Neighbour, Last) :-
    N > Max -> Last=Neighbour
    ; create(Queen, [column = N, neighbour = Neighbour]),
    initial(+ N+1, Max, Queen, Last).
```

```
first :-
    @neighbour <- first,
    row := 1,
    testOrAdvance.
```

```
testOrAdvance :-
    @neighbour <- canAttack(@row, @column) -> next
    ; true.
```

```
canAttack(R, C) :-
    (@row = R
    ; R is row + column - C
    ; R is row - column + C
    ; @neighbour <- canAttack(R, C)
    ), !.
```

```
next :-
    @row = 8 ->
        @neighbour <- next,
        row := 1,
        testOrAdvance
    ;   row += 1,
        testOrAdvance.
```

```
print :-
    @neighbour <- print,
    writeseqnl(['Row ',@row, 'Column ',@column]).

when_assigned(row, Old, New) :-
    writeseqnl(['Col ',@column,from,Old,to,New]).

end queen.

class nullQueen.

first.

next :- fail.

canAttack(_, _) :- fail.

print.

end nullQueen.
```

Bibliography

Aït-Kaci H. (1991). Towards a meaning of LIFE. *J. of Logic Programming*, **16**, (3, 4), 195–234

Aït-Kaci H. and Nasr R. (1986). LOGIN: A logic programming language with built-in inheritance. *J. of Logic Programming*, **3**, 185–215

Apple (1990). *Hypercard Reference*. Apple Computer Inc., Cupertino, CA

Atkinson M. P., Bailey P. J., Chisholm K. J., Cockshott P. W. and Morrison R. (1983). An approach to persistent programming. *Computer Journal*, **26**(4)

Atkinson M., Bancillhon F., DeWitt D., Dittrich K., Maier D. and Zdonick S. (1990). The object-oriented database system manifesto. In *Deductive and Object-oriented Databases* (Kim W., Nicolas J. and Nishio S., eds.), New York: North Holland

Berlage T. (1991). *OSF/Motif^{TM}: Concepts and Programming*. Wokingham: Addison-Wesley

Booch G. (1991). *Object Oriented Design with Applications*. California: Benjamin/Cummings

Borland, International (1991). *Turbo Vision for C++ User's Guide*

Bowen K. and Moss C. D. S. (1992). *International Conference on Practical Application of Prolog*. Dorking, UK: Applied Workstations Ltd

Budd T. (1991). *An Introduction to Object-oriented Programming*. Reading, Mass.: Addison-Wesley

Cardelli L. (1988). A semantics of multiple inheritance. *Information and Computation*, **26** (2/3), 138–64

Chen P. P. (1976). The entity relationship model – towards a unified view of data. *ACM Trans. on Database Systems*, **1**(1) (March), 9–36

Chen W. and Warren D. S. (1988). Objects as intensions. *Proc. 5th International Conference and Seminar on Logic Programming*, MIT Press

Clark K. L. and Gregory S. (1986). PARLOG: Parallel programming in logic. *ACM Trans on Programming Languages and Systems*, **8**(1), 1–49

Coad P. and Yourdon E. (1991a). *Object-Oriented Analysis* 2nd edn. Englewood Cliffs, New Jersey: Prentice-Hall

Coad P. and Yourdon E. (1991b). *Object-Oriented Design.* Yourdon Press, New Jersey: Prentice-Hall

Colmerauer A. (1987). Opening the Prolog-III universe. *Byte*, **12**(9), August

Conery J. S. (1988). Logical objects. *Proc. 5th International Conference and Seminar on Logic Programming*, MIT Press

Cox B. J. (1986). *Object Oriented Programming. An Evolutionary Approach.* Reading, Mass.: Addison-Wesley

Davison A. (1987). Polka: a Parlog object oriented language. In *Parallel and Distributed Object Oriented Programming Workshop*, University of London & British Computer Society, October

Davison A. (1990). *STEP: An Object Oriented Strand.* UK: Strand Software Technologies, Markyate, AL3 8JP

Davison A. (1992). A survey of ligic programming-based object oriented languages. In *Object-Based Concurrency* (Wegner P., Yonezawa A. and Agha G., eds.) Reading, Mass.: Addison-Wesley

Dincbas M., van Hentenryck P., Simonis H., Aggoun A., Graf T. and Berthier F. (1988). The constraint logic programming language CHIP. *Proc. Int. Conf. on Fifth Generation Computer Systems*, Japan: Tokyo, 693–702

Embury S., Jiao Z. and Gray P. M. D. (1992). Using Prolog to provide access to metadata in an object-oriented database. *Proc. Int. Conf. on Practical Application of Prolog*, London

Fiadeiro J. and Maibaum T. (1990). *Towards Object Calculi.* Tech. Rept., London: Dept. of Computing, Imperial College

Fiadeiro J. and Maibaum T. (1992). Temporal theories as modularisation units for concurrent system specification. *Formal Aspects of Computing*, **4**, 239–72

Foster I. and Stevens, R. (1990). *Strand: New Concepts in Parallel Programming.* Englewood Cliffs, New Jersey: Prentice-Hall

Foster I. and Taylor S. (1989). Strand: a practical parallel programming tool. In *Proc. North American Conference on Logic Programming*, MIT Press

Furukawa K., Takeuchi A., Kunifuji S., Yasukawa H., Ohki M. and Ueda K. (1984). Mandala, a logic based knowledge programming system. In *Proc. FGCS '84*, Tokyo: ICOT 613–22

Harel D. (1987). Statecharts: a visual formalism for complex systems. *Science of Computer Programing*, **8**, 231–74

Hewitt C. (1977). Viewing control structures as patterns of passing messages. *Artificial Intelligence*, **8**(3), 323–64

ISO (1993). *Draft Standard for the Programming Language Prolog.* ISO/IEC CD 13211-1: 1993 (E)

Jackson M. A. (1983). *System Development.* Englewood Cliffs, New Jersey: Prentice-Hall

Kahn K., Tribble E. D., Miller M. S. and Bobrow D. G. (1986). Objects in concurrent logic programming languages. In *OOPSLA '86 Proc. ACM*, 242–57

Kay A. C. (1977). Microelectronics and the personal computer. *Scientific American* 231–44

Kesim F. N. (1993). Temporal objects in deductive databases. *PhD Thesis*, London: Dept. of Computing, Imperial College

Kim W., Nicholas J-M. and Nishio S. eds. (1990). *Deductive and Object-Oriented Databases*. New York: North Holland

Kowalski R. A. (1979). *Logic for Problem Solving*. New York: North Holland

Kowalski R. A. and Sergot M. (1986). A logic-based calculus of events. *New Generation Computing*, **4**(1), 67–95

Licklider T. R. (1989). Ten years of rows and columns. *Byte*, December, 324–31

McCabe F. G. (1988). Logic and objects. *PhD Thesis*, Dept. of Computing, Imperial College, University of London: Available as Tech. Report 86/9, Dept. of Computing

McCabe F. G. (1992). *Logic and Objects*. Englewood Cliffs, New Jersey: Prentice-Hall

Meyer B. (1988). *Object-oriented Software Construction*. Englewood Cliffs, New Jersey: Prentice-Hall

Minsky, M. (1975). A framework for representing knowledge. In *The Psychology of Computer Vision* (Winston P., ed.), New York: McGraw-Hill, 211–77

Ohki M., Takeuchi A. and Furukawa K. (1988). An object-oriented programming language based on the parallel logic programming language KL1. In *Proc. FGCS '88*, 895–909, Tokyo: ICOT

Pereira F. C. N. and Shieber S. M. (1987). Prolog and natural-language analysis. CSLI Lecture Notes 10, Chicago, III: University of Chicago Press

Reiter R. (1980). A logic for default reasoning. *Artificial Intelligence*, **13**(1), 81–132

Rumbaugh J., Blaha M., Premerlani W., Eddy F. and Lorensen W. (1991). *Object-oriented Modeling and Design*. Englewood Cliffs, New Jersey: Prentice-Hall

Schank R. C. and Abelson R. P. (1977). *Scripts, Plans, Goals and Understanding*. Hillsdale, New Jersey: Lawrence Erlbaum

Schmucker K. J. (1986). *Object-Oriented Programming for the Macintosh*. New Jersey: Hayden Book Co.

Selman B. and Levesque H. J. (1991). The tractability of path-based inheritance. In *Inheritance Hierarchies in Knowledge Representation and Programming Languages*. (Lenzerini M., Nardi D. and Simi M., eds.) John Wiley & Sons Ltd, 83–95

Sergot M. (1982). A query-the-user facility for logic programming. *Research Report DOC 82/18*, London University: Dept. of Computing, Imperial College

Sergot M. and Kesim F. N. (1991). *On the Dynamics of Objects in a Logic Programming Framework*. London University: Dept. of Computing, Imperial College

Shapiro E. Y. (1983). A subset of concurrent Prolog and its interpreter. *ICOT Technical Report, TR-003/172*, Japan: Tokyo

Shapiro E. Y. and Takeuchi A. (1983). Object oriented programming in concurrent Prolog. *New Generation Computing*, 1, 25–48

Snyder A. (1986). Encapsulation and inheritance in object-oriented programming languages. In *OOPSLA '86 Proc. ACM*, 38–45

Touretsky D. S. (1986). *The Mathematics of Inheritance Systems.* CA: Morgan Kaufmann and London: Pitman. Was *Report CMU-CS-84-136*, Dept. Computer Science, Carnegie Mellon University, Pittsburgh, PA

Ullman J. D. (1991). A Comparison of Deductive and Object-Oriented Database Systems. *DOODB91*. Berlin: Springer-Verlag

Voda P. J. (1988). Types of Trilogy. *Proc. 5th International Conference and Seminar on Logic Programming*, MIT Press

Wegner P. (1987). Dimensions of object-based language design. In *OOPSLA '87 Proc. ACM*

Zaniolo C. (1984). Object-oriented programming in Prolog. In *Proc. International Symposium on Logic Programming*, Atlantic City, IEEE

Zaniolo C. (1990). Object Identity and Inheritance in Deductive Databases. In *Deductive and Object-oriented Databases* (Kim W., Nicolas J. and Nishio S., eds.), New York: North Holland

Index